REDEMPTION

How Ronald Reagan
Nearly Ruined My Life

REDEMPTION

How Ronald Reagan
Nearly Ruined My Life

by

Barbara McVeigh

Dedicated to women lost to HIStory.
and honorable men who support them.

For my family, and the children around the world, with love.
And gratitude for life—thank you, Mom and Dad.

Published
First Edition: September 2016
Second Edition: July 2017

Redemption
How Ronald Reagan Nearly Ruined My Life

Copyright © Barbara McVeigh 2016, 2017.

No part of this book may be reproduced, copied, or used in any form or manner whatsoever without written permission, except in the case of brief quotations in reviews and critical articles.

Front Cover: Design by N. Mann; Photo by Peter Buettner
Book & E-book Design: Velin@Perseus-Design.com
Edited by Siobhan Gallagher

ISBN 978-0-9989111-1-3

FOREWORD

Do what you love.
Follow your passion.
Listen to your heart.

How many times do we hear this advice? To have the courage to follow our own dreams, our own path, and feel passion, trusting our inner compass and turning our sails to steer our own course instead of letting ourselves be driven by the prevailing winds? And instead, how many times do we hesitate, perhaps afraid to follow such advice, to follow our dreams? To listen to Robert Frost and take the road less traveled? How often are we told to ignore that voice and, instead, conform?

When my path first intersected with Barbara's, it was professional, through word of mouth. She was looking for someone to edit the second edition of this book, one she had previously self-published, and I edit books. It was a job in a long line of jobs, albeit admittedly my passion, a passion that, like Barbara, I would uncover, one that I was late coming to, a passion where, in order to explore it, I had to make radical changes, going against popular opinion, and almost completely reinvent myself. What I didn't expect was to discover how, despite the differences in details, our paths resembled each other's, and how we each craved nothing more than the pleasures of a truly simplified, low-stress lifestyle.

Much has been said and written about the collective conscience, or consciousness, with its origin being that it is a common set of beliefs, ideas and attitudes that bind people together and guide their actions—a shared ideology. Mary Kelsey, who earned her PhD in sociology from the University of California, Berkeley, and now lectures there, has described this phenomenon among social groups, notably mothers, who, once aware of the attitudes and ideas they share, act in solidarity with each other, as a community, and share their knowledge and resources rather than possessively guard them. This was something that Barbara was struck by, when her misgivings about how her children—how American children in general—were being taught in school led her to interact and engage with like-minded mothers who were banding together to home school their children.

When I read of her alarm upon viewing the insinuation and takeover of technology in the classroom, and how it discourages discourse and interaction, social skills that were part and parcel of our education, coupled with her struggles to separate her son from his addiction to videogames and the violence of his reaction, I understood her fear and uncertainty as to how to tackle it. It is all too new to find a playbook for it.

Tristan Harris is one individual who has come forward to shine light on how companies like Google encourage app developers to create apps that stimulate the brain's addiction center. When Charlie Rose interviewed him on *60 Minutes,* Rose admitted to being distracted during the interview itself, his fingers twitching to check his smartphone every ten minutes or so to stay "up to date."

Have we been brainwashed into thinking that if we're not on top of things the very minute they happen, somehow the world will end? As a child of the sixties, I grew up in a house with a single landline, before the days of even cassette tape answering machines, and we were taught in school that it was courteous to let a phone ring up to 16 times when telephoning someone in order to give them sufficient time to answer. Now we're expected to answer in three rings or fewer. It is demanded of us.

In the nineties, top executives carried pagers but if they were in places where pagers didn't work, it was accepted, and you rolled with it. Now, no one can ever truly escape being hunted down by a demanding boss or client, or an employee. I confess I watched this growing development with increasing discomfort, how our growing dependence on technology and the strain of being tuned in, connected, 24/7, left us no quiet time for peaceful reflection or to focus on the bigger picture. Silence is underrated.

By 2006, I knew something had to change for me. What, I didn't know. Unsure, I purged myself of my anchors: quit my job, sold my house, sold or donated virtually all of my belongings, and set off with my two little dogs to France, to a five-month housesit, hoping to spend a year abroad to clear my head. One year became three, as I bounced around Europe, before visiting the U.S. to see whether I wanted to return for good. I was excited by the prospect of reuniting with family and friends. I wasn't even out of the airport terminal when I knew in my heart I no longer would be happy there, that I did not want to return to that all too familiar frenetic, tech-dominated, money-driven lifestyle. So I returned to Europe and within a few months decided to settle in France, where I bought a tiny country house on a tiny slice of land, and happily settled into a place where neighbors drop in to chat or share the bounty of their vegetable gardens, do their shopping at the various outdoor markets where they buy dairy, produce, meat, and sometimes wine from the producers themselves, and where they reach for your hand instead of a cellphone.

France is hardly without its economic challenges, but I found that what is often expensive in the U.S., like housing and property taxes, costs less and prices remain fixed, with no bubbles. Conversely, consumables that are unbelievably cheap in the U.S. are far more expensive in France. (When I arrived in 2006, gas was €1.50/liter, about $8/gallon back then, and it has also barely fluctuated.) People are generally able to live near their jobs so transportation costs are low, and it gives them more time to spend with family. Healthcare costs are rigidly controlled by the government and remain affordable, particularly by U.S. standards, and France's national healthcare system is ranked the best in the world according to the World Health Organization. (That said, they still need to resolve their labor challenges.)

Mine is a lifestyle that's not for everyone, but I prefer an environment where seeing someone walk by, staring at their phone, is an oddity, not a norm. So many of us live lives bombarded by beeps and chimes that demand our immediate attention, and a continual stream of information washes over us too quickly to absorb. Critical thinking has given way to parroting sound bites (often contradictory ones), and we avoid interaction that doesn't mirror our opinions, as it's easier to hold fast to an ideology if we don't allow anything to poke holes in it. We find greater comfort in remaining within our cocoons, our bubbles, even burying our heads in the sand at times, and do whatever we can to protect that cocoon, despite its growing fragility, and its inevitable decay.

Barbara's book details how she burst out of that bubble. It was a rebirth that was unquestionably painful at times. It has also proved, ultimately, rewarding. Living modestly is by no means the same as living a small life. Barbara urges each of us to focus less on ourselves and more on the greater good. Doing this has been shown to increase a feeling of wellbeing and gives us the satisfaction of feeling a part of something greater than ourselves. And what could be greater, more important, than saving our planet? If each of us would make even a small contribution to reducing our carbon footprint, to live efficiently versus wastefully, to conserve water, conserve energy, how can it not make a difference?

As Barbara points out, fully 80 percent of the oxygen we breathe, that we take for granted every second of every day, is furnished by our oceans. Within those oceans, along with increasing acidification that destroys our ecosystems are more and more manmade "garbage" islands, where plastic waste circulates, and washes up onto previously pristine beaches in stunning quantities each and every day. An estimated nine tons of plastic is dumped into our oceans yearly, and inhabitants of all six of the world's habitable continents contribute. This is the butterfly effect. Is it really that much harder for us to perhaps hold onto a plastic container in order to toss it into a recycling bin instead of the trash, or worse, the ground? It takes that collective conscience to want to contribute to the greater good. There are many, just like Barbara, who are doing so much to save the planet. Now it's our turn to help them. And by doing so we help ourselves.

We must either turn our sails into the wind to chart our own course or let the wind take us where it will, including into dangerous waters.

The choice is ours.

Siobhan Gallagher, editor

INTRODUCTION

"America is facing a crisis," President Jimmy Carter announced, in a televised speech, "Crisis of Confidence," in 1979. The United States was in an energy crisis and a recession. There was fear about jobs and prospects for the future. Carter spoke about the loss of American values—of spirituality and how self-indulgence and consumption were damaging our freedom and integrity as a democracy. "Human identity is no longer defined by what one does, but by what one owns," he said. Carter had solar panels installed at the White House and 17,000 wind turbines in the state of California, as his energy department burgeoned with sustainable energy ideas and policies in order to ensure economic safety. He proclaimed it was the "moral equivalent of war" to battle against the use of fossil fuels in favor of alternative, more sustainable sources of energy, but pointed out that it was a good form of war, focused not on destruction but construction.

Carter was highly criticized for this speech and accused of failing to lead as a responsible president, instead choosing to pass the blame on to the American people. Carter warned the public that the upcoming Republican presidential candidate, Ronald Reagan, was a dangerous right-wing radical.

In 1980, Ronald Reagan was elected the fortieth president of the United States and won the election in a landslide, receiving the highest number of electoral votes ever won by a non-incumbent presidential candidate. He would put our country back together, claimed his supporters, who were fed up with long lines at fuel pumps and concerned for jobs, their security, and the future.

Reagan immediately shut down Carter's energy initiatives and, in time, had the solar panels removed from the White House and halted California's 17,000 wind turbines in his efforts to create policies and appoint cabinet members in support of the oil business. Reagan was backed by OPEC and had a strong relationship with Pope John Paul II. This election marked the beginning of what was termed "The Reagan Revolution," and signified a conservative realignment in national politics, officially marking the end of the sixties revolution, according to historians.

Now, thirty-eight years later, when we look back at this pivotal time in history, we can see precisely what "putting our country back together" meant, as we face yet another energy crisis. Today, the stakes are even higher. Not only are powerful political leaders like Richard Cheney and propaganda media mogul Rupert Murdoch exhibiting gross conflicts of interest by running billion-dollar global oil businesses but humanity's survival is also at risk because of the global ecological disaster we face, all of which can be directly linked to the Reagan Revolution. Reagan's decisions and policies have driven not only our nation but arguably the entire world into a crisis of acidifying oceans and potentially devastating climate change.

What is even more disturbing is that we had full knowledge of climate change in the 1970s, and the dangers it represents. Denis Hayes, on page 17 of his 1977 book *Rays of Hope: The Transition to a Post-Petroleum World*, wrote, "Carbon dioxide (CO_2), a by-product of all fossil fuel combustion, poses a greater problem … In late 1976, the Scientific Committee on Problems of the Environment, a leading independent group of international environmental experts, reported that it considered atmospheric CO_2 to be the world's foremost environmental problem."

Many people today are dedicating their lives to sustainable clean energy solutions and working to ensure our coasts remain protected for the next generations. Organizations are developing models for us to become individually responsible for the carbon we create based on our lifestyle choices. Educators are coming together on a national level to question our public education models and ask why children can identify more corporate logos than botanicals in their front yards. Individuals like world-renowned, eighty-two-year-old Dr. Sylvia Earle have seen firsthand the devastation that is playing out across our oceans, and she is leading the work with world leaders in an effort to create "Hope Spots"—locations and movements critical to improving and protecting the health of our planet's seas. She believes that if each of us were to witness what she has, she would not be viewed as an environmental radical, saying, "The consequences of our actions today will be directly related to our planet's functioning for the next 10,000 years."

The message of Carter's 1979 "Crisis of Confidence" speech needs to be heard loud and clear by everyone on the planet. We, the people, need to shoulder full responsibility and blame for not having listened then. We, the people, must forgive ourselves and assign no blame to others, because we must see that it's we, the people, who must generate the necessary change—not our politicians, and not our business leaders. We have been manipulated and dominated, but now we have the power, the vision, to see the truth.

What can we, the people, do?

We can listen to our elders, who know the guts it takes to face and overcome adversity and fear. One such living hero is the great Harry Belafonte, who sang songs and moved culture, uniting racial divides. "We need our artists," he says. "We need those who can weave a good story, and inspire people to be better than they think they can be."

Can we, the people, reimagine ourselves and create a new world before it's too late?

Although we can't change the past, we can come to a better understanding of who we are today, and what we stand for, by looking at that pivotal time in history when we foolishly listened to our fears instead of the visionary words of President Jimmy Carter. Our fears have led to broken educational systems, business agendas that dominate our identity, the way we think, and what has served to disconnect and disempower us as citizens of our country as well as the world. Jimmy Carter said, after solar panels on the White House were installed at his directive: "A generation from now, this solar heater can either be a curiosity, a museum piece, an example of a road not taken, or it can be a small part of one of the greatest and most exciting adventures ever undertaken by the American people, harnessing the power of the sun to enrich our lives as we move away from our crippling dependence on foreign oil."

Now is the time for "we, the people," to take the helm of our ship of a nation into new waters on a mission to reshape the American Dream, what we value, and shine that light on humanity, in the spirit of our Statue of Liberty, to become humbled, compassionate, and free. There are no excuses.

I believe our country can become a great power again, but not through warfare, and certainly not by force. I see a different story than that of our past. As we face acidifying oceans, climate change, and fear and anger in our culture, I believe the American people can unite on an unprecedented level. I think back to what the more than eleven thousand of our nation's air traffic controllers did in 1981, taking a stand for what they believed was honest and fair, knowing they risked everything in order to stand for truth. They proved to us that by standing their ground, like my own father did, you find gold, a deep shine in your integrity that outweighs everything else in life. Reagan called those union members federal criminals. But today, after thirty-five years of oil wars, oil spills, emerging terror groups, ocean acidification and climate change, and the political and business domination that grew out of the Reagan Administration, those union members can stand tall, knowing they took great personal risk to stand up for what they believed in, in the face of a president whom history has shown to be arguably one of the worst leaders in the history of the United States and inspire us, a new generation, a new global order, to strive for peace and justice.

Ronald Reagan, the "hero" of the Republican party, should be considered a federal criminal, if not a global criminal, and his proper place in history be established, as we come to understand the power of storytelling, domination, and manipulation designed to feed our fears and satisfy our short-term desires.

I grew up in Fremont, California, where the Ohlone people lived for three thousand years. We can listen to and learn from their ways and begin a new story for the world.

Introduction

"Sharing was a fundamental precept in the Ohlone philosophy. After a hunt, meat was distributed to friends, extended family members, and those members in the community who were in need. The hunter rarely kept any of the fruits of his hunt for himself, and women often gave their finest baskets of flour to another woman. They did not place value on the acquisition of physical wealth, but rather the esteem and friendship brought about by generosity. Living in moderation went hand in hand with the concept of sharing. It demonstrated that you were not greedy in accumulating wealth."

- Heather Hemingway, "From Peace to Present: A Look at the Ohlone Indians"*

Can we take a bow, with humility, today and learn to respect and nurture the sacredness of life? It's time to dream big and live humbly as we tack and set a new course, as a nation and as an entire planet.

Be kind, generous, and serve one another instead of your own self-interest. Doing so makes you a rebel in our world today. We need rebels. We need our rebels.

Be a rebel.

---

* This essay excerpt appears on the Monterey County Historical Association's website, part of a class assignment in SBSC 326, "History of the Monterey Bay Area, 10,000 B.C. to Steinbeck," California State University Monterey Bay, 1996, completed by Heather Hemingway, http://www.mchsmuseum.com/ohlonepeace.html.

Listen into the dreaming. Know who you are and where you come from and listen to the natural world.

- Elisabeth Sunday, photographer
"The Listening,"
(Western Pacific, Micronesia)

PROLOGUE

The time had come for my final voyage. I recognized long shadows extending, hot air cooling. A new season. A new life. The wind was shifting.

There had been storms, pirates, and danger, along with otherworldly moments of beauty and freedom. Like ancient mariners, I discovered new people, ideas, and landscapes invisible to me before. There was strange sea life too, quizzically disrespected and abused by a people who needed it most. I witnessed souls return from the living dead.

Tragically, my ship veered off course. Full of despair, I screamed, but I had no voice. My lover, my sailing mate, had been voyaging alongside me. With anger and frustration, he kept yelling, telling me what was wrong, and not what was right. I tried to take the helm when he wouldn't, and tack in a new direction. This made him angrier. The boat was sinking. "Let's jump ship!" I screamed. "Save ourselves! Don't forget our dreams!" He never heard me. Instead he listened to a goddess who, while naked in my bed, whispered sweet things, and they disappeared into the mist, bound for Greece.

Shipwrecked and alone, I had one last duty to perform and an offering to give. A man, a dream seeker, with powerful eyes arrived, along with sea captains and a deep sea diver. They showed me the power to penetrate the surface to where deep truths lie, revealing a new ocean and a whole universe.

Then came the Land of the Spirits.

Beyond the horizon, and surrounded by celestial bodies, it's that place where we all end up. There was my late great-uncle, a sailor, holding the compass of my voyage. He knew I missed our lazy afternoons, sitting together at his kitchen table, talking about life, love, and politics. He had stood up for me once, telling my sailing mate to make an honest woman of me when he saw a lack of respect. Yes, sometimes he'd complain about long-haired hippies saving the world. He hated people helping him. He could be unkind. But I always saw right through his words. He was a man of passion, high integrity, and pure love.

Blackness descended and I fell into an abyss. Exhausted and numb, I yearned to rest for eternity, when a swirl of energy took hold of me. A child angel came to my side and shared a sweet lullaby, played on a treasured white guitar. The soft notes lured me to my childhood dreams, back to when a blue sea star spoke to me, before a powerful leader wounded my family and others, and left us all for dead. The music took me deep into myself, where I heard my own heart and felt its rhythmic beat return. Then, like an electric blast, the music lit the torch of my soul, awakening me full score, and parted the dark passage back to the Land of Life.

With Magic, an old wooden boat, my late great-uncle's spirit gave me the helm, along with my voice. He told me to scream wildly and explore the deepest oceans. "Never let anyone stop you. Demand respect, and ally with the courageous, acknowledging those with humility." He pointed to the map of my dreams, from which I would navigate by the stars for the rest of my life.

The strangest thing about this voyage is that I never left my home on the San Francisco Bay.

Prologue

"Magic Bear #65" *Of Wind, Fog and Sail: Sailing on San Francisco Bay,* by Diane Beeston

THE END

November 13, 2014

I thought I could be a big person. I hadn't expected guts to contort. But they do, as I sit at the crowded fundraising luncheon for Pachemama Alliance, supporting Indigenous rights. Above me, a film projects the slashing and burning of the Amazon rainforest. Chinese oil companies are setting up shop. There is talk about the end of American democracy, the fall of capitalism.

Then I see him across the room.

Blood courses like fire through my veins.

He is well dressed and smiling, with his arm around her. They are both laughing, sharing a private joke, and looking at each other. He pulls out his checkbook when the donation call comes. I watch in disbelief.

He's donating? The same man who got angry when I slipped $20 to neighborhood kids for Girl Scout cookies?

The oxygen has left the room. Twenty-two years.

I had set out to do a good thing. A good thing for a whole big group of people. Maybe even the world. It seemed I was always trying to do a good thing for people, but it didn't seem to be helping me much.

Or was it?

"Excuse me," I say to my table host. "My husband is here with his girlfriend. I have to go." She looks at me with wide eyes. "I am so sorry," she says.

In a dream state I walk out of the auditorium along the San Francisco Bay to my parked car. The sky and water look cold steel grey, reflecting my heart. The Bay is empty of sailing boats too, those drifting white spirits where I had found sanctuary with my great-uncle, Robert Keleher, a sailor and my best friend. Or, perhaps more accurately, he had found me.

"Barbie, he never showed you respect," my uncle says in my ear, his words blowing across my cheek like the wind.

"I know."

We often talk. This despite the fact that he died twelve years ago.

When I start the car, my rage ignites along with it. How could he? We're still married! My mother's artwork still hangs on the walls of our house, along with most of my possessions. My great-uncle's chest sits at the foot of the bed, my beloved Chinese wooden chest that had once belonged to Madge, the love of his life.

That's where I'll go.

I drive.

I will not cry. Not yet.

Memories unravel faster than coiled line on a sailboat dropping anchor. I can feel spikes in my belly: child births, gardening, travels, sailing, dreams… And, of course, arguments. I try to make sense of how all this has come to be. This wasn't supposed to happen.

Or was it?

I cross the Golden Gate Bridge and look out to the Pacific Ocean I love so much.

"Ricci, I have to do this," I had told him just two months earlier, when we'd gone to dinner. "It's like I am supposed to do this." I had never produced a film before, but I had started producing a documentary film about the ocean. I had created this project, got the funding, pulled the team together with the help of a friend, a film director, and it was taking on a life of its own, with big international names trying to make right of the world. I was riding a runaway horse and holding on for dear life. "I can't walk away from it," I said.

I moved out of the house, cashed out my retirement savings, and borrowed money from my parents. I knew the move was hard on the kids, especially my son, who had become physically violent with me after Ricci's father died earlier in the year, and we couldn't agree on how to manage him. But I needed this project. I was exhaling everything I believed about life, the environment, and education and stuffing it all into this little twenty-minute film. I didn't like the way the world was going and I seized my first opportunity to have a say in it. And there was something more.

I could feel this entire project working through my soul, like I was connecting to something bigger than myself.

Ricci ordered an iced tea and fixed his gaze on the floor.

"Ricci, it's not like I'm leaving for another man. I'm trying to do good things in the world. I've got kids coming into this world. People talk about melting polar ice caps, acidifying oceans, but they worry more about getting kids to soccer practice."

"You'll find someone else," he insisted. He was convinced of it.

"Ricci, I'm not looking for someone else. I have to put my heart and soul into this project. I'm looking to create a voice so I can scream to the world to wake up!"

We'd been directionless for so long, our debt growing deeper and the roof and sides of our house growing rot. The marble floor needed weekly polishing, cobwebs multiplied by the hour in high ceilings, and new dirt trails paved the white carpet every week. I couldn't be burdened facing those needs each day as well as packing school lunches and planning play dates on top of this. We had no money for sitters, or family around to help. I needed absolute focus for this project. And, most importantly, I needed positive encouragement.

I smiled at Ricci. He didn't smile back.

"Look, even if I had a long list of guys, you'd still be at the top of the list." I kissed him. "Besides, the paperwork is all there."

"I'll get the house in shape," he promised, pleading. "I've got a job now. And I'll help with the children."

I knew he wanted to help, and I knew how crazy my actions seemed. My gut was whispering to me that it was right, even if my logical brain screamed differently.

We held hands as we walked out of the restaurant and hugged before getting into our individual cars. He was heading back to the house, with the kids and our pets. I was heading instead for my tiny new apartment in a town twenty minutes away, to work on the project.

I press more firmly on the gas pedal as I cross the Golden Gate Bridge. I look down to Sausalito, with its boats and docks, where so much of our married and family life had been spent.

Ricci texts me from the fundraiser. "Where are you? You said you wanted to meet her."

Yes, I had said that. Had I lied, thinking I was a bigger person than I was? I hadn't counted on crashing. Just a week before I had sat cross-legged on my apartment floor, talking with him on the phone. That was when he told me he had started a new relationship.

"It's like it's meant to be, Barbara. She's amazing. Like she was part of a past life of mine," he said.

I was struck dumb. I didn't know what to say to him. Maybe his mother had been right after all, that I was being selfish with what I was doing. I did move out, after all. We had taken off our wedding rings. I needed to breathe after ten years of so much craziness, running a nonprofit sailing organization and managing a house beyond our means. But I loved him.

I looked out to the tall redwoods outside my window, seeking comfort, the phone still pressed to my ear. A hawk stood atop one, a murder of crows trying to knock it down. I knew how it must feel.

"Barbara, you taught me how to be loving and kind. Now I can take that to a higher level, with her."

Was that supposed to make me feel good? Did he think that was a compliment?

"I've learned that we help each other reach higher levels," he said.

He was serious. Where did he come up with that idea? I had to think through this one. What if?

I took a deep breath, knowing I had a deadline and a group of people expecting a delivery that day. I was barely keeping it together. I had no evidence to believe the twenty-minute film would be anything, except the nagging hunch in my belly that insisted I needed to finish it, no matter what.

I stood up and walked outside, my eyes on the hawk, and listened to the squawking crows. They were getting louder.

"Ricci, do me a favor and keep it away from the kids." We hadn't told our twelve-year-old daughter or eight-year-old son anything about us yet.

"I'm sorry. It's too late."
The hawk spread its wings and flew from the tree.
All I could do was watch.

I drive faster, getting further from him as I draw closer to our home of fifteen years. My mind is spinning faster, along with my beating heart. How could he?

I knew the nonprofit sailing organization had thrust the final dagger into our relationship two years before, when I sat on the docks with the founder, Jane, a retired sea captain. I chose to listen to my dead uncle and keep the organization alive instead of listening to my living husband and let it go. Then I had to fight for our family honor. But did I really have to lose my family in the process?

Then there was this: over the last months I had witnessed Ricci become spiritual. He purchased a whole collection of Buddha statues, a deal he'd found on Craigslist, and lined the bedroom with them. When we hugged, he wanted us to hug "heart to heart," my left shoulder to his. He'd started ending his emails with "Blessings." Was he going crazy?

He had changed so much. But I can't think about it. Not yet.

And who am I to question sanity when, months before, I went to visit my old writing mentor, Bryna Stevens, in San Francisco, and heard her piano music coming from the blue sky just minutes before I learned she had been found naked and dead in her apartment? Trees had screamed at me, urging me to run for my life from a man who surely would have murdered me one full moon night. And a dead mother goat told me it was time to leave my marriage.

Logic was flying out the window. Fuck him. Twenty-two years together. A lousy two months apart.

I arrive at the house, our home of fifteen years, enraged. It is still my house after all. My name is on it. My furniture. My children. I know where the spare key is hidden. My son had shown me just days before, adding, "Dad said not to show you. He says you can't be trusted."

I enter the house and walk through the rooms just feeling, nothing more. It looks the same, yet smells different. Incense? That's new. Dishes are on the counter. That's normal. My daughter's bed is unmade. Legos litter my son's bedroom floor. Also normal.

I enter our bedroom. An unfamiliar pink laptop. Unfamiliar ruffled bedding covers the bed I had bought, schlepped home, and set up all by myself. His girlfriend's clothes are hanging in the closet, alongside my wedding dress.

My uncle's chest—my beloved chest—is at the foot of the bed.

That's it, I thought.

I rip art off the walls. My painting of the Chinese Buddha in the temple. My mother's sunflowers, in the bathroom. My daughter's stick figures of her and her little brother holding hands. I collect my treasures, including my most prized possession, my Uncle Bob's silver platter from the St. Francis Yacht Club, engraved with *Magic Bear 1963*, First Place. That very trophy that had started our sailing adventure had brought me to this place in time.

By the entranceway, I remove my coveted full-body portrait of a nude black woman crossing her arms, holding herself. I study the figure for a moment. She isn't hugging herself. She's protecting herself.

How had I not seen that before?

It is time to leave, to get my daughter from school. For the final time I stand in the living room while the light shines down through the high windows, illuminating floating thick dust particles and spiderwebs in every corner.

I close my eyes, fill my lungs, and ask myself, "Why did you leave this home, Barbara? Think hard. You are making one of the most important decisions in your life."

I hear the answer.

"He never respected you, Barbie."

The dust around me thickens, and settles on the furniture. I listen to the quiet as voices linger about me. Years full of memories.

"Goodbye," I finally say to a life I had but didn't have. I close the door, closing a chapter in my life. I stash the secret key back in its hiding place and drive away, remembering the day long ago we had driven our rented tiny U-Haul truck there, to that big house his parents had given Ricci in order "to give us a head start in life." We had all our possessions and thought-out plans, still redolent with our dreams to explore the world and be free.

What happened?

I pull up outside my daughter's school. I wipe my eyes and straighten myself in the rearview mirror before she climbs into the car. I see pain in her face. "Hi, sweetheart." I study her.

"Hi." She looks away.

"Are you okay?"

She looks back at me. "Mom, I'm learning to smile and pretend I'm happy."

My fractured heart falls into pieces.

"You met her, didn't you?" I say.

"I'm not supposed to talk about it. Oh, 'Do you want this? Or that?' And 'I have a present for you,'" Lucy mimics, sarcastically.

All I want to do is tell her how selfish and disrespectful her father is being, but I have to be strong for my daughter. How dare a woman walk into a family so fast, without giving space to children, or giving us time to heal? Where was respect? Where was sisterhood?

Who was this woman?

"It's going to be okay, sweetheart. I promise," I say, still unsure of it myself. "We'll get your brother later this afternoon." I press the gas pedal and head to my little apartment, wondering what disaster has just begun.

Little do I know I am headed toward redemption, at the highest level possible.

The 1980s

Thirty-three years earlier...

May 1981

I can't believe I'm actually with the smart kids this semester. I never thought I'd be accepted by the Junior California Scholarship Association. Some of my teachers were probably surprised since I was always put in the dumb classes in elementary school. But I lucked out with grades this semester, in junior high. We even got to go to Disneyland for a weekend field trip, just the smart kids. But first we toured Santa Barbara University. It was AMAZING! We visited the dorms where college students decorated rooms like they wanted, and there was the beach and ocean right by the school.

I love the ocean.

The teachers took us to the oceanography department. I saw a blue sea star sitting all alone in a tank. It looked so lonely and sad—it was as if I could feel what it was thinking and feeling. Professors talked about oceans around the world and all I could do was look at that lonely sea star and wish I could do something for it.

Mom and Dad have always taken me to the beach to play. Grandpa McVeigh used to fish off the pier in Santa Cruz. He's even pictured on the front cover of a Stagnaro Brothers old-fashioned brochure, holding a big lingcod. I wish we lived by the beach. Maybe I will, one day.

I usually go to the runoff ditch down the street, here in Fremont, where I play with the pollywogs. I jump the wire fence that says "Do Not Enter" and scramble down below the street level before anyone can see me. Some pollywogs have little legs and others don't. Frogs jump around, and I'll carry a few of them home in my bucket and play with them. One time I found a big frog, larger than my fist. I thought about kissing him and wondered if he'd turn into a prince and take me to his castle. I used to play in the meadows too, and find ladybugs, but the fields are all concrete parking lots or shopping malls now.

I've decided to be an oceanographer when I grow up. One more year of junior high left, plus four years of high school, and then graduation, in 1986. I'll study oceanography at Santa Barbara University, scuba dive, write, travel and take pictures of the beautiful world.

I've got it all figured out.

August 1981

President Ronald Reagan fired my father and Mom is crying. Reagan stood at a podium with the American flag waving behind him and the whole world watching, including our neighbors, friends, and my teachers. Reagan gave the union of professional air traffic controllers forty-eight hours to get back to work or become federal criminals and be fired from their jobs.

"Nope, not going back to work," Dad said, sitting in his armchair.

Last night we went to the union hall and everyone was there, families, the controllers, the media, and the union leaders. People had picket signs and were wearing blue union shirts emblazoned with "PATCO." Someone gave me a little button to wear showing a proud mouse next to an American Eagle it had just knocked out.

"Don't worry," the union leader, Domenic Torchia, said. He gave a big speech and everyone clapped in support. Over 13,000 air traffic controllers across the country are striking, good family guys mostly. Many even served in the military. "We are standing for truth and justice."

Everyone is still confident that Reagan will make a backroom deal with union leaders. Reagan made promises to controllers and so they voted him in. But I guess you're not supposed to strike against the government. Dominic said there were no other choices.

"Not going back," Dad said, from his armchair. "They'll give me my job back."

The media were sticking microphones in faces and writing stories, reporting the controllers were demanding more money.

"Nope, it's not about the money," Dad declared. "It's about safety and keeping your word." Dad had once come home late at night and sat in his armchair, in the dark, for hours. His equipment had failed at work and he had to recall from memory the position of every single airplane on his screen until the equipment got going again.

Mom looked scared.

"Mac, we'll lose everything!" The FBI had arrested some strikers and put them in jail.

Last night I laid awake in the dark and wondered if the FBI would come to take Dad. Maybe they'd take the whole family. Dad said if any black coats come to the door I should go to my room and shut the door. Imagine. What if they took the whole family?

"Mom, can I go to my guitar lesson?" We were running late. I liked my guitar lessons, although I'm never good at practicing. I'm learning classical style, with lots of pieces from the Renaissance. I can play "Greensleeves," and I'm always humming it because I play it over and over again. It's really the only piece I can play well.

I like sitting quietly with my guitar teacher, Joseph Blea, in the small room surrounded by music sheets and posters of musicians. Joseph is calm and nice. One time, after coming back from a family trip to the Grand Canyon, I had really bad chapped lips from sticking my head out of the car window, feeling the hot dry wind of the desert. Instead of teaching me music that day, he walked me to a store and bought me Blistex, a medication to soothe and heal my lips. Funny, the things you remember.

"We're running late, Mom." I said. I was ready to go, with my Takamine guitar in hand.

"Honey, we have some big things going on. I can't take you right now." People were calling us, asking all sorts of questions, and Mom was worried sick. I could tell.

Everybody says Reagan is the good guy, the good president who will put the country back together again. So why is my dad the bad guy?

Maybe my dad doesn't care about me and supporting our family. Even Grandpa says the most important thing is taking care of your family. My brother and sister, Jim and Chris, were old enough to already move out of the house and it's just me left, with Mom and Dad. Mom seems so scared. Dad has begun to drink. Neighbors are mad at us too. Patty's father yelled at Dad on the front lawn, in front of neighbors and all. He said the flight for his family vacation to Hawaii might be delayed, or even canceled, and he's not happy about that. They waited for years to make their family trip to Hawaii.

September 1981

"There's going to be a terrible airline crash," Dad said. Not just Dad. All the controllers are saying that.

Sure enough, Reagan fired the striking controllers, all 11,500 of them, and replaced them with temporary workers who don't have the same kind of skills. But there haven't been any airplane crashes, so people say Reagan knows what he's talking about and that's why we should listen to him. So, if Reagan is the good guy and knows what he's talking about, that definitely makes Dad the bad guy who doesn't know anything. Even Grandpa says so. He's so mad at Dad for making Mom worry and cry.

I hide from Patty at school. I can't face her. I feel like everyone is looking at me, the kid from the bad family.

My history teacher, Mr. Howard, and his wife, another teacher, were really concerned about me and how my family was raising me, so they brought me to their house to teach me housecleaning skills and learn about wages and work ethics and things like that, because they say my dad doesn't have a good work ethic. They're watching out for me, and it feels nice. Mrs. Howard gave me a big feather duster and took the time and care to show me how to dust.

"You start from the top shelf and you always work your way down. That way, you can use gravity to your advantage."

That made good sense, and I was getting the hang of it until Mom came over. Oh, she was mad. I've never seen Mom so mad, not even at Dad. Mr. and Mrs. Howard looked at my mother like she wasn't appreciative of what they were doing for me. I stood, watching the both of them go at it, and sling words back and forth. I didn't know who to listen to. I mean, here are my schoolteachers taking extra time after school for me. They must care about me, right? Maybe Mom is dumb. I mean, my teachers should know best, right? She should listen to them.

Yesterday, Mom said we might lose our house. I've already lost my guitar lessons and maybe there won't be money for college. Dad drinks a lot of wine and sits in the same armchair, claiming he's going to get his job back.

How did I end up with a bad dad and a dumb mom? I will never be like them. I can't wait till I'm grown up. I'll get out of here. I'll show them what it means to be educated, work hard, and live a good life.

June 1982

The good news was that Jim was coming home, here to Fremont. I miss my brother, my big brother, but he left to join the Navy and now it looks like he's found a wife from the South. He'll never come back to live here now. These last years I've listened to the stereo and music he left me, including a cassette tape, *The Best of Bread*. My favorite song "If" is like a lullaby, or a love song. I like to close my eyes and hum along. Then I push rewind and replay it over and over again. I'm surprised the tape hasn't broken.

The words soothe me in some strange way. I imagine, as the song says, how the stars would each extinguish when the world was done, and how I might fly away, holding my brother's hand. But he's not here. He's not around to protect me the way he used to.

Mom and Dad are always fighting. Dad is drinking more and more.

When Jim brought his fiancée to visit, Mom and Dad didn't fight. It was nice to see Jim, but it wasn't the same. He didn't really talk to me much. He mostly spent time with Mom and Dad and they talked wedding plans.

When I came home from school, they had left, without saying goodbye. The stereo was gone too, leaving just a rim of thick dust around it. Now I can't listen to music. Mom is back to crying. Dad is drinking again.

Jim is becoming an air traffic controller, like Dad was. Mom said Jim and his fiancée made an agreement that Jim will never strike against the government and be a criminal. He'll support his family and be a good family man. Family comes first. I wish my father was a good family man. I guess my brother loves his fiancée more than he does me. I feel so alone. I miss listening to my favorite song.

You're all that's left me too.

April 1984

I got a job! Not only a job, but a DREAM job! I can't believe I got it. I'm working at The Record Factory. It's an independent music shop and I get to sell Bay Area concert tickets too! All day we get to listen to Madonna, Steve Winwood, Culture Clash, Thompson Twins, and all the great music.

What's really cool is I'm learning about world music and musicians I haven't heard before. Music from Africa, Brazil, and Europe. They are like treasures, especially in this forgotten no man's land of Fremont. Bands like Let's Active, Eek-a-Mouse, Peter Case, The Smithereens, Stan Getz, Harry Belafonte, jazz artists and more—I LOVE JAZZ! Al Jarreau, Stan Getz, Cesária Évora, Juan Martín, João Gilberto, Caetano Veloso.

Most of these musicians are imports and independent labels. The more obscure, the more fun it is to discover new music and sounds. Randy says it's real music from real artists, not what the marketing companies push, with artists who just want fame and money. When the store manager isn't around, that's the music we play on the turntable. I only show the special customers those albums, the ones who look like they can appreciate what's real.

Then the concert tickets! Who would ever put a sixteen-year-old kid in charge of selling tickets to Culture Club and Duran Duran and think we're not corrupt? Well, good for us, because we are corrupt and we're a team. I'm getting front row tickets. Last week I even touched George Michael's foot when I reached onstage before I passed out and got crunched by the crowd behind me. Next week, I have front row tickets to New Order! More than that, I'm learning about all the underground clubs in San Francisco and the Bay Area. Mom doesn't like the way I'm dressing, but what does she know? At least she doesn't know about how drunk we get before the shows. Gina always throws up. But she can still drive her car. It amazes me.

I have a new boyfriend too. He's very sophisticated and has an English accent, not like a Fremont guy. Mom doesn't like him, but she doesn't know anything. We needed to go to the grocery store and Mom said to Robert, "If you dress like that, I won't be seen with you." He was wearing black lipstick and his black leather skirt, just like fashion you can find in London. I told mom she just didn't understand fashion.

Well, guess what she did! She went into her bedroom and came back out wearing dad's overcoat, cowboy hat, and boots.

"Mom, what are you wearing!" I shrieked. She looked crazy.

"If he dresses like that to the store, then this is what I'm wearing."

"You can't wear that to the store!"

My God! My friends might be at the store. What would they think of me?

Robert was laughing and was excited to go with her. He thought she was being cool. I got so mad at him. No way, José, would I let my mom do that. I'd be the laughingstock at the entire school if word got out! I'd die first. Robert later changed into pants and took off his lipstick.

He's teaching me about sex too. It's easier in skirts. Of course, if Mom and Dad found out, they'd totally freak out on me. Mom thinks I should stay a virgin until I'm married. Pilar's mom says have sex before you get married so you know whether you want to get married. Then there's Dad, who tells me you can use aspirin for birth control. Put an aspirin between your knees and squeeze them together. I don't know who to listen to, so I don't listen to anyone. I do what I want to do.

Dad is drinking more. He still says he'll get his job back. For now, he's trying to get his contractor's license and start a new business. Mom doesn't like it. She's says it's unreliable work, and he's always forgetting to invoice his customers. They still argue and Mom still cries. She found a job too, and so they're never home. I'm okay with that. I just sit around and watch MTV after school anyway. Mom doesn't like my grades, but school is so stupid. We just do what we're told and it makes no sense. Though, in English class recently, my teacher studied me over his glasses, like I did something wrong. He read one of my essays about the plastic plants that decorate Burger King's interior and gave me an A. I was a little shocked too. I like my photography class and working in the dark room, but my teacher spends more time with the popular girls, so I'm on my own and I don't really know what I'm doing. School is all a waste of time.

May 1985

I had a party at the house when Mom and Dad were gone. I got two kegs, a bunch of wine coolers and had almost the whole school over. That is until the police arrived. Mom came home early and saw what was going on. She caught Tamara and Joe in the bedroom—their bedroom—and I was throwing up in the toilet. I guess I'm on restriction now, whatever that means.

Dad didn't say a word until the next day.

"Barbie, come in here and sit in the chair. We want to talk to you." He tried to use his "big dad" voice, but what do I care? He's not a dad to me.

He put a bottle of wine in the middle of the living room. "Face it. Is this what you want in your life? Is this what and how you want to be?" He said it directly and clearly.

I looked at the jug of wine sitting there in the middle of the living room, like it was looking at me. I didn't answer him.

The next day I emptied his wine bottles down the sink and he yelled at me.

I just got my ears pierced for the fifth time. People at school say I've changed. Fuck everyone.

June 1986

You wouldn't believe what happened today at work. Record Factory just got bought out by this corporate music store called The Warehouse. They are forcing us to wear ugly blue polo shirts with the company name—YUCK! We can't wear our own clothes. Not only that but we had to remove any albums that are not on the top billboard lists. Only the popular music stays, that sells for big money. MONEY! All the good music—the imports and independent albums—were pulled.

Randy and I were looking at each other over the albums as we sifted through stacks, both feeling bad about it but not knowing what else to do. I mean, not Eek-a-Mouse? That's one of my favorite bands! Peter Case! NO! Let's Active also? They make the best music! People just don't understand their music. I felt bad doing it. I mean, unless the album is on the Billboard List and makes a lot of money, we can't have it at the store. Who says it's good music? It doesn't seem right, but they tell us that's what business is all about and just do our job if we want a job. I do want a job, but it doesn't seem right. It's just plain mean. Maybe I'll quit the job soon.

Randy and Eric got some acid and asked if I want to try it. Maybe I will. Last week, late at night, we hiked up the hills into Niles Canyon where people say the hitchhiking White Witch comes out at night and where the Zodiac Killer lives. We did find some zodiac signs, graffiti on concrete slabs, leading to the inside of a train tunnel. Then we felt the vibrations of the track and realized a train was coming. There wasn't time to get out, so we all squeezed together on the side of the wall, in a little cavity. The speeding train zoomed past, inches away, and we gripped each other tightly, screaming our heads off, which was muted by the loud, raging train. We were scared to death that one of us would get sucked out as it passed. We survived it. Then we danced on the tracks, feeling the swirling, crazy wild wind the train left behind.

Dad still sits in his armchair with big dreams to get his job back.

"Dad, you left your job." I remind him.

"I stood for what I believed in, Barbie."

For what, I wonder. My dad is crazy and in total denial. Delusional.

I have to get out of the house. I hate school. I hate living here. One more year and I'll be out of school. Then what do I do? There is no money. All my friends are going off to college. I guess I'll just go to a local junior college.

But I really want to travel and see the world.

I lie on my waterbed, sometimes smoking a clove cigarette when Mom and Dad are away, and just stare at my posters of Rome and Greece. One day I'll get there.

Mom is working at a job she hates to keep a house with a groomed lawn stuck in between a bunch of stores selling shit. Cars drive paved roads to paved parking lots to stores selling shit. I'm sick of it. Sick of it all.

Last week I cut school. I'm getting pretty good at forging parent letters now. I packed the car with friends and we headed to the Santa Cruz beach for the day. I love the beach. The ocean makes me feel free.

Other days I'll cut school and climb a tree that sits on the edge of a cliff up in the hills. My dog Gizmo climbs it with me. Together, we'll sit there all afternoon and look out across the valley. I like listening to the wind. Gizmo likes it too. I can tell by the way he looks. I think about the Ohlone People who once lived in this area and how beautiful life must have been, with wild bears and mountain lions.

I think of the women sitting by a fire together and weaving baskets while children run around naked and barefoot, all laughing together. Maybe a young Ohlone girl sat in this very tree long ago. I'll bet they didn't have to do all these stupid things that we have to do. They were free, weren't they? I once read the hunters gave the most prized meat to those most in need. The women gave the beautiful baskets away, not keeping things for themselves. It earned them honor and respect and everyone took care of each other. I like that idea. I don't feel anyone is taking care of me.

Gizmo stands like a white mountain lion the way he looks out to the valley, even if he is a little runt of a dog. It's just a matter of what you feel that makes the difference, I think, as a gust of wind swirls around us, blowing his fur and my long hair.

You wouldn't believe what I saw yesterday. Remember how, when I was little, I used to jump over the wire fence to the runoff ditch that's down the street, even though it said "Do Not Enter"? There I'd find so many pollywogs and baby frogs. The ditch has been covered with concrete. CONCRETE! Who would do such a thing? All the pollywogs and frogs are gone, killed. Doesn't seem right. It's so mean. The one genuinely wild place in this hole-in-the-world called Fremont.

I hate this town. One day I'll write, scuba dive, and travel the world. I'm going to do it all. But first, I have to escape Fremont.

August 1986

Just when you think it's bad, it gets worse. I was throwing the ball in the front yard when it bounced off the curb and into the street. Gizmo chased it and a car came around the corner and hit him. He yelped so loudly. He came running toward me but I could see something was wrong. I picked him up into my arms, he whined, looked straight in my eyes, and went limp. I screamed for Mom and Dad, but it was too late. Gizmo died in my arms.

I have to get out of here. I hate it here. All my friends have left for college. I'm still working at the dead-end music shop, putting price tags on cassette tapes I don't even like. I'm going to a local junior college that I don't like and I have to come home to a mess. Sometimes I think I'm escaping and go dancing where everyone is high. I want to get an education and live a good life. I want to get out of here. But last night I was pretty sure I'd never get out of here alive.

Bill asked me to watch his apartment while he was in Hawaii. We go out a lot but I'm not interested in him as a boyfriend. He knows I love the guitar and takes me to shows. We saw The Romeros, The Royal Family of the Guitar, not long ago, a Spanish father with three sons who play beautifully. Sometimes Bill gives me as much cocaine as I want, and he buys alcohol for me and my friends too. He doesn't ask me for anything. I think he just likes having me around because I'm young.

While he was away, though, I brought my boyfriend to his apartment just to hang out. When we arrived, Bill was there sitting on the sofa with a gun. He had been smoking pot and doing cocaine. His eyes were glazed over. He wasn't supposed to be back for another week. I was afraid, so afraid. I was sure he was going to shoot us. I talked calmly and we were able to leave.

I have to leave this town. Mom and Dad are broke and still fighting. Mom is still crying and so scared about finances and losing the house.

Pilar, my best friend, has moved to Santa Rosa and goes to the junior college there. Maybe I can get an apartment with her and start school. I have to leave. I hate this town. I have a bad family. I need to get out alive.

Please, let me get out alive.

The 1990s

October 1990

How do I start? So much has changed in the past four years. I did get out of Fremont alive, and I will never go back. Fremont is a hole in the universe. I'm living in San Francisco now, and going to school. It's not Santa Barbara University, but I'm getting an education. And I'm writing.

After four junior colleges, Ohlone, Chabot, Santa Rosa, and San Francisco City College, I'm a bona fide student at San Francisco State University. Mom got an evening bookkeeping job and was able to help me a little bit with tuition. I got a job at a law firm with an attorney, J. Michael Kelly, who had worked in the Carter administration, if you can believe that. After school, I take the hour-long train ride to work downtown at the Maritime Building, and along the way I do my homework, or stare out the window, daydreaming.

Mike has a large black-and-white photograph of himself sitting at an oval table with President Carter and others. Mike had worked for Carter's Energy Department. I sometimes look at it when Mike is out of the office, like it's looking at me. But I try not to think about politics. I'm too busy trying to earn a living, get through school, and live my dreams. I'm not leaning on Mom and Dad anymore. I'm almost completely independent, even if I'm barely surviving, financially. I'll eat Top Ramen every night if I have to. My shoes have holes in the bottom, but nobody can see them. I make sure I keep my feet flat on the floor wherever I am.

A few years back I got my first credit card. I bought a plane ticket and a Eurail Pass and went backpacking in Europe, and made it to Rome and Greece. I sat for hours inside the Roman Colosseum imagining the brutality people had watched, all in the name of entertainment. In Greece, I stayed in the seaside town of Parga where, in the year 1803, fifty mothers grabbed their children and threw themselves off cliffs, preferring mass suicide to living under a pasha's rule, to either be enslaved or killed by his army. I couldn't shake the feeling of desperation and how cruel we humans can be.

I fell in love with history and art, feeling how tragic and deep it can go. Why did I not learn these stories in school? I met people—travelers—who have inspired me to travel more. Now I love my literature classes, reading Chaucer, Wordsworth, Blake, and Shakespeare. I'm finally seeing the world and getting a real education. And I'm writing. WRITING! Nobody told me there is such an immense real world out here! Why was I stuck in school at the end of the BART line for so long, forced to do such stupid things and being sent off to Disneyland? It was all about information and making the school look good, with rah-rah football games, putting saccharine-sweet smiles on children, and being judged by grades that mean nothing in real life.

Best of all—I LIVE BY THE BEACH! A dream, just blocks away, by Ocean Beach, in San Francisco, even if the thick fog settles here. I sometimes do my homework while sitting in the sand dunes listening to the nearby surf. I live with Joe, which makes for cheaper rent. His stepdad is paying for him to go to school. His mom is a really good cook and we go to their house sometimes and she shares recipes with me. He's lucky that his family understands how important education is. I stopped doing any drugs after the scare with Joe one day. We had to take him to the hospital after a bad reaction to cocaine. I thought he was going to die and the nurse looked at me, asking what had happened. If he had died, I would have been the one to blame.

I realized then how stupid and dangerous drugs are and how lucky I was to have survived all those years. It was like the drugs numbed me to all the pain I was feeling. I was so stupid. I don't touch any drugs anymore. I don't dance or listen to music anymore either. I'm completely focused on school and work. I have to finish school, and then I'm going to travel, write, and live my dreams.

I often hang out with Joe's friend Rick. He's an international relations major and we talk about where the world is going. It's not pretty. Corporations are telling us how to live. Big money is getting pushed around. I don't like it.

I've been reading a lot by the intellectual and author Noam Chomsky and the way we use language and learn language. I love my literature classes—even if I'm not very smart, I'm getting through it. I will not be uneducated, like my parents. Mom still tells me how Dad isn't doing much, but he did get his contractor's license and has some business, except now the garage is completely filled with junk and he still forgets to bill his clients. She's angry that she can't help me more through school, and wishes she could. She knows I wanted Santa Barbara University. I remind her too, as often as I can.

My boss is good to me. He's like a father to me, a father I didn't have. I do my homework on the train from school to the downtown law firm. I don't like downtown. Everyone is in a rush and I feel everyone is mean to one another. But this is how educated people work and live, I suppose, so you have to learn to survive. The job is getting me through school. I have to remember that.

I'll get out one day.

I get this strange dream sometimes that the world will see me. I ask myself what do I have to offer the world? I don't know but sometimes I get this feeling that I will know. I want to go to Cairo, Florence, Paris, Moscow, and Berlin, and everywhere in between too. The world seems just out of my reach to grab it all. What am I to become? Self-serving for my own benefit? No, I have the capabilities of more, but what? I don't know but I will know one day.

I'm going to do it all and be free, writing, taking pictures, and traveling, sharing the beauty of the world.

I've got it all figured out.

I like sitting in the dunes and watching the waves. I come here often, to San Francisco's Ocean Beach, to think and to feel. I wonder all the time if I'm on the right track. School and work keep me so busy. It's hard to stop and let my mind wander to ask the big questions.

I asked myself today: *Am I an atheist?* I wonder if I am. As I wrote those words I felt as if a curse was to strike me down, and I prepared for a recurrence of the Great Earthquake. I didn't happen. Still, I wonder what I do believe in. The concept engulfs me all the time. What is good? What is evil? I'm reading *The Decameron,* by Bocaccio, and it's all about the mockery of the church in Italy and its corruption. I've never believed in organized religion. It's never been my thing. Even when I was little I thought it strange that a Native American couldn't enter heaven if he didn't believe in the Christian god. Hell must be a busy place, with thousands of years without a Christian god. Has there ever been a Blessed Virgin? A saint? A prophet? I mean, I'd rather think about life sitting by a tree or a river, or right here by the ocean. Aren't those the holy places instead of a constructed building that requires insurance papers, mortgages, and house cleaners? It just doesn't make sense to me, but what else is there?

I think about these things a lot.

June 1991

It's been an amazing trip so far, even if we are filthy dirty and our backpacks are heavy. Joe and I are traveling in Mexico together (my idea!) and we've been swimming in Agua Azul, a sky-blue river that snakes through the green rainforest of Southern Mexico, and we visited Chiapas, the southern Mexican highlands. The Mayan people are beautiful.

I sit in the plaza and simply watch women carry loads of wood up and down the cobblestone streets. I watch how they laugh and how their eyes reflect an ancient, quiet wisdom. It's amazing that I never learned about the Mayan civilization. I've climbed beautiful temples that are thousands of years old that stand erect, close to my own country. These traditional people are still living the way they have for centuries and they seem content, don't they? Why didn't my school ever teach us about the living ancient cultures? It's funny. School seemed to be all about cheerleaders, football games, and detention if we were late or talked in class. School was fake, with artificial rules, teaching us how to earn a living in the modern world. The natural world and ancient cultures are filled with color and the most interesting, beautiful people, music, art, and ideas.

I've been writing too. I could stay here forever.

Yesterday, though, I realized Joe and I won't last. We were sitting on a crowded bus, entering the mountains of Chiapas, when we made a stop and a young pregnant woman got on board and stood next to me. Her belly was huge. I told Joe to scoot over so she could share the seat with us. He complained that she probably had lice. I couldn't believe he had said that. So I ordered him to move over, and she sat down next to me. I observed her rough hands and the gorgeous colored ribbons twisted in her long black hair. She was wearing traditional clothing and the colors of blues, reds, and yellows made animals and symbols on her dress. She was so elegant, almost pure in that good way, and I could feel her calm, gentle spirit. She smelled earthy, a bit like smoke from a campfire. I imagined her childhood life, running barefoot through the mountains of the highlands of Mexico, a life so different from mine, where there was no nature except a runoff ditch and green manicured lawns. I wondered if she sat in trees, like I used to. I think she was thinking about me too.

When the bus came to a stop, she stood up and gave me the broadest smile I had ever seen, with bright white teeth against her dark skin and ribboned long black hair. "Gracias."

I watched her as she stepped off the bus and stood outside with other women, all in traditional dress. She pointed at me and her friends smiled at me and giggled.

"God, finally I can stretch out." Joe said. "I can't stand this bus ride. How much longer till we reach the town? I need a shower."

I knew right then and there I needed to return to Mexico.

By myself.

April 1992

Joe has moved out. I don't know how I'll pay for my San Francisco apartment and school, but I have just one more year of school and then I'm free. My boss is so cool, but I do work hard. He's giving me six weeks off this summer, and I plan to do a trip to Mexico and Guatemala all by myself. I can't wait. Mom will come with me for one week. She says she's scared I'll be kidnapped or something. She's never been out of the country before.

Again, I don't know how I'll get through this next year financially. But I'm going to do it. I'm almost done with school.

Last month I got a birthday card from my Great-Uncle Bob. I really don't know him other than from the stories I'd hear from my family that he was old and cranky and hard to be around. Mom says he used to be really good-looking, a fun uncle who loved listening to jazz and big band music. After his wife died, he withdrew from everybody, she said.

But for as long as I can remember, he's always remembered my birthday with a handwritten note and a $20 bill, so I decided to drive by his house to say hi, and I brought him chocolate chip cookies. When he answered the door, he acted really mad and upset that I drove so far just to say hello.

"Well, why the hell did you do that?" he said to me at the door. But I saw a little smile behind those words, even if he was playing mean. He invited me into his house, a beautiful Victorian house that he keeps up all by himself, with a sitting lounge and a dining room with a beautiful table and a glass cabinet filled with polished crystal and tableware perfectly lined up. His kitchen is old-fashioned—a little yellow table and chairs, everything just so. I see Grandma's homemade crocheted hot pads dangling next to the stove.

"Well, Barbie, have you had lunch?" he said, as if he were forced to ask. I hadn't, so he made a couple of tuna fish sandwiches and we sat down and talked about school and family. That seemed to give him a small smile, even if he tried to hide it. Then he paused, as if thinking about something.

"Have you ever had a highball?" he asked. This time the tone was a little different, more inviting, I guess you could say.

I watched him make the drink with such care. He placed two glasses on the counter, side by side, and carefully poured the whiskey and ginger ale, adding ice and stirring and rattling the ice against the glass. I could see his mind was somewhere else as he stirred.

We drank together and continued talking. He told me my dad was a bad man for hurting Mom and my family, doing what he had done. It's hard having a bad father. I saw his newspaper open to the financial pages. Pen marks and notes covered the stock lists. He saw me looking.

"Reagan put this country back together. He saved the country, got us back on track economically, making this country great again, Barbie."

Photos of his two brothers—my grandfather and my other great-uncle, Don—were on the wall. They had served during World War II. Uncle Don had been lost at sea for over a month after the Japanese bombed his Navy ship. He was found, skin and bones, but alive. My grandfather voluntarily enlisted, leaving his wife and his two kids for three years.

Then Uncle Bob started talking again.

"This guy came to the door yesterday, a long-haired hippie, asking me to sign some 'Save the World' petition. I told him to cut his hair and tuck in his goddamn shirt, to go get a real job."

I couldn't believe my ears. Maybe Mom was right, and he is a cranky old bastard.

"Uncle Bob, how dare you talk to that young man like that! Here he is, out there trying to make the world a better place for all of us, and you yell at him?"

He hesitated. I thought he'd yell again and kick me out of his house, but he didn't. Instead he got real quiet and looked out the window, thinking.

"Yeah, Barbie, I guess you're right," he said, like he'd just realized what a jerk he had been. He fell silent again. Then he excused himself to use the bathroom. I stood and looked at pictures of boats and a lineup of sailing trophies on his fireplace mantel.

Afterward, we went outside to his back garden. It was lush with flowering hydrangeas and shrubs. He showed me his collection of cymbidiums. He was quiet looking at them, and I could see he was lost in thought again.

"These were Madge's. She had a few before she died and each year they multiply," he said. He pulled out the hose and watered them. "I don't know what to do with them, so I just take care of them all."

He had over one hundred potted cymbidiums and all of them were beautifully flowering. Madge had been his wife. She had just come out of a bad marriage when they met. Uncle Bob married her late in his life, maybe when he was in his forties. He was passionate about her. Then the unspeakable happened. After only five years of marriage, she developed brain cancer and died. I remember him sobbing at the funeral. I was little then. He never remarried and stayed devoted to her, even after she died. Her ashes were scattered on top of Mount Tamalpais, in Marin County. I wonder what that kind of devoted love must be like. I look for it.

We went on talking. He loved to sail.

"Maybe I'll take you out sailing some time. Would you like that?"

"Maybe, but I'm so busy, Uncle Bob, with school and work."

He seemed disappointed, but he didn't say anything more.

I liked hanging with Uncle Bob, even if he is a cranky old salt.

I'm sitting here in the Simple Pleasures Cafe. Pilar was on her way from Santa Rosa to bring me a futon she had managed to squish into her VW Bug for me. We had plans to go dancing now that I'm single again and I HAVEN'T BEEN OUT IN SO LONG! I never go out. But her car broke down on the Golden Gate Bridge. She was upset about it, so after squeezing the futon into my car, she managed to get her car going again and drove back home. I don't really have any friends since I work and study so much. With nothing to do on a Friday night I decided to come here, to Simple Pleasures Cafe, do my Spanish homework, and finish reading Aldous Huxley's *Brave New World*.

Simple Pleasures Cafe was crowded with the late night bohemian coffee-drinking crowd. A small band was playing. There was one available seat wedged in a corner with a table filled with beautiful women and one guy, all speaking German. I felt a little uncomfortable with them, like they were looking at me funny. I don't really take care of myself. I don't go shopping or wear makeup. I don't care about any of those things. I just want to get through school and live my dreams. I took the seat, opened my book, and read, ignoring them and their chatter.

One by one the women left, leaving just the guy. I didn't want to talk to him. I mean, here he is with all these good-looking women. They leave and he starts talking to me. I could tell his type.

"Why are you studying on a Friday night?" he asked.

I told him I was working my way through school. Then I told him about my upcoming trip to Mexico and Guatemala. He told me about his plan to cycle the Balkans, alone. I found that interesting. I knew nothing about the Balkans. He's Italian. He told me his mother is German, and that's why he speaks German. It turned into a nice conversation about culture, languages, and education. He asked me to meet him the next day.

"Maybe. If I'm here," I said. I wasn't interested in starting a relationship with anyone, even if he seemed interesting. I mean, I had just finished a two-year relationship with a jerk. I needed to finish school and get on with my dreams of traveling and writing.

The next day I found myself sitting alone in my studio, with my cat on my lap. I listened to the ocean just blocks away, where the Pacific meets Ocean Beach. I was spending so much time alone, walking the beach, collecting sand dollars, reading, and writing. I like hearing the surf at night from my open window. I keep it open just so I can sleep with the cool ocean air blowing on me at night. It's like listening to a lullaby.

Then I thought, maybe I do need to get out and make new friends. I'm only twenty-four years old and I'm living like an old lady, alone. All I do is study and work. I have no life. Besides, he sounded like a traveler. He could be interesting and perhaps inspire me.

I decided to go to the cafe when we said we might meet. I was fashionably late, of course. He wasn't there. Figures, I thought. So, I did my homework and read my book. An hour later, I looked up and saw a figure outside, in the dark rain, tying up a bicycle. There he was, wet through and cold.

"I'm really sorry. The bus never came. So I got on my bike and rode as fast as I could across town." He was dripping wet.

Maybe I had misjudged him.

His name was Ricci. We talked about traveling, photography, and our dreams. We talked about *Brave New World* and the control and domination of a dystopian world. He had gone to Santa Barbara University. We would have been there together had I gone! His parents wanted him to be an engineer and they got mad when he switched to political science. They put him through school and even sent him abroad, to Italy, to study. He said he had wanted to stay in Europe but his mom made him come back and finish university. He speaks three languages. I thought, how lucky he was to have all those things, and told him so. I wished I had such an education and parents who were concerned about my life.

There's something about him that feels special to me. There's something that scares me too.

May 1992

Ricci and I drive my beat-up VW bug north, along Highway One, California's two-lane coastal road along the Pacific Ocean, heading to Sea Ranch. I was to meet his parents for the first time. My car only broke down once, on a blind turn. We pushed it and got it going again.

His parents' house is unbelievably beautiful. The model Claudia Schiffer even did a photo shoot there once, for *Architectural Digest*. I felt a little uncomfortable, especially driving up in my poor car. I made a joke about the back bumper. Half of it is missing and the other half is crooked and looks like the wind-up mechanism of a toy car.

Ricci's parents are from Europe and very formal and sophisticated. They shook my hand and kissed me on each cheek. They spoke a lot of Italian together, which was nice to listen to. His mother had been a runway model before marrying and is drop-dead gorgeous. They spend half the year in their house in Sardegna. They have other homes too.

I learned they came to America when the Red Brigades, a Marxist-Leninist group, were active in Italy in the late seventies. His family was nervous about safety, as young people were kidnapping and assassinating people during a revolutionary uprising.

Ricci tells me his parents have harrowing stories of surviving WWII. They must be strong people. I think of my own family and how we could barely keep it together after my dad lost his job. Ricci's family survived war, famine, and death. They have so much to illustrate their strength.

We had a friendly conversation. I liked the way they ate together, so civilized and proper, everything carefully planned and laid out. Candles were lit and the Finnish Arabia dishware was clearly something valuable and respected. They know so much European history, and even the good kind of chocolate to buy. My mom just likes Hershey's, which they laugh at and say is bad chocolate. They tell me Americans don't understand these things. I felt so funny. I mean, what am I to them? I'm a girl from Fremont with a beat-up car. I felt that way, anyway. I can't offer very much.

Everything is perfect in their house. The art, the way the walls are colored and textured, and the artifacts from Rome. Even the way we sit after the meal to talk about life seems so elegant. His mom lights candles and you can see the ocean just down the hill. Ricci is lucky to come from such a family. I don't know what he sees in me, but there is something special between us. I can feel it.

Ricci teaches me new things, like how to put my fork and knife on my plate just so, after I eat a meal. He says his German grandmother taught him how to sit at a table. Nobody ever taught me such things about etiquette, except my dad, when he'd flick my elbows if they were on the table. And once, when I was five, he washed my mouth out with soap when I said "fuck" at the dinner table. I didn't know fuck was a bad word. Despite that, I still use the word.

Mom has told me that story over and over again, that Dad felt bad about it, but that he had to follow through with what he said, even if he didn't want to. Apparently, afterwards, I felt bad that he felt bad, so I climbed onto his lap and told him I still loved him. She says I was like that as a child, always trying to make others happy.

I tell Ricci all my dreams. I also tell him I want to teach. He tells me I'm better than that. Teachers don't get paid very well and he sees me doing something even greater. I don't know what he sees.

We have dinner at a Chinese restaurant when we get back. His fortune reads, "You'll receive a large inheritance one day." Mine reads, "Your eyes sparkle."

"You got the better deal," he said, smiling at me.

I think I'm falling in love.

July 1992

I did as I said, and returned to Mexico to travel. My mom and I hitchhiked through the mountains of Chiapas. She said she couldn't believe she was doing that, after years of telling me not to hitchhike. On her fiftieth birthday, we rode horses to a small mountain village for the village saint's festival, filled with music and banners, along with lots of drunk men. We walked among enormous stone heads of the Olmecs, a pre-Colombian civilization, history that fills your head with imaginative stories and awe. Mom almost cried when she left, wondering if I'd return safely. I had four more weeks of a solo sojourn, and I was headed to Guatemala.

Instead of a bus or train, I took a canoe down the trade route of the ancient Maya, the Usumacinta River, to cross the border into Guatemala. The boat came with a small outboard engine and a big-bellied captain who liked to drink whiskey. With a group of five random international travelers, we snaked down the river through dense forests and howling monkeys, along with rain, lightning, and thunder. Then the sun blazed down on us, bringing with it human-eating bugs.

The border control was a military base on the bank of the river guarded by lounging bare-chested Mexicans and big scary guns. We were frightened, yet not frightened, because there was such beauty in the moment, a kind of sensual mystery perhaps, when danger and adventure mix together. I was taken to one side, away from the others, and escorted to an empty concrete room with a singular desk and two chairs. I was the only one of the group who could speak some Spanish, or perhaps it was because I was the only single woman.

Why was I crossing the border? I explained the best I could. I was a traveler. I had leftover tags on my luggage from my previous trip, with dates that didn't match my passport. The guard looked at me suspiciously, and I suddenly realized I might be in serious danger, completely alone, nobody knowing where I was.

"I am a teacher and I have two children," I blurted. The words just came out. I thought being a mother might earn me some respect. I was right. I witnessed a shift in his demeanor.

He released me and I walked down a long path, with idle men watching, back to the canoe to continue crossing the border to Guatemala. Then, a big, muscled guard, dark hair matting his chest, got up and followed me. His eyes scanned my body as the other men watched him, some smiling, others laughing and pointing.

I stepped carefully into the canoe, the last one aboard, convinced we were escaping something that could rapidly turn bad. The guard leaned over and looked straight into my eyes, his face inches from mine. With cupped hands, he gently held out a secret parcel to me. Not knowing what else to do, I cupped my hands and felt something tiny. "*Cuidado*," he said. Careful.

The drunk captain shoved the canoe away from the bank and we floated away. The rain began to pour. Nervously, I opened my hands and peeked at what lay inside. It was a baby bird with big eyes. I looked behind me to see the dark guard and all his friends, who continued to watch me until we disappeared, the thick mist consuming us.

I breathed out, not realizing I had been holding my breath the entire time.

A baby bird in the middle of the jungle? In the palms of my hands? I felt a sense of responsibility. I hadn't asked for it. And how did I mistake the bare-chested man as dangerous rather than the kind young man that he was, handing me a present, entrusting me with the life of a beautiful, precious creature?

I knew I had to release the bird and trust it to the world. An offering of kindness and hope, I tried to think. It flew upward, toward the trees lining the bank, through the rain as the heat lightning flashed. I watched it disappear, feeling the weight of the world on me for some odd reason.

August 1992

I'm back in San Francisco now, and Ricci has moved in to my studio. I'm not sure how it happened. My parents don't even know he's living with me. He's getting ready for his bicycling trip through the Balkans. I sit in my Victorian armchair next to the open window with my legs tucked under me. We can share the rent and he can save money for his trip. He's asked me to take care of his things while he's away.

It's nighttime, and I feel the cool San Francisco air blow in. I pretend to study, finishing my final year of school.

But really I am watching Ricci go over maps of Albania and Romania as he prepares for his trip. In some ways, I feel he is already there. There's a wall dividing us, and I have this strange feeling that he will be the very last one I'll ever give my emotions to, like those that tickle and consume me now. But it's more than that. Somehow he'll do something that will change me. Call me crazy, but this is what I feel.

June 1993

"Here, you take it." Uncle Bob looked at me, expectantly.

I felt fear.

"No, no, I can't," I protested.

"Sure you can." He moved over to let me sit at the helm and handed me the tiller of his 29-foot Bristol, called *Lark*. "I'm here to catch you."

After a year of talking about it, Uncle Bob took me sailing aboard his boat. He was different on his boat, warm and smiling, especially when the wind blew across his face. We had left Alameda and were tacking up the Oakland Estuary to the San Francisco Bay, a narrow channel filled with shipping traffic, rowers, kayakers, and seagulls.

The tiller felt awkward in my hands. A puff of wind came along and Uncle Bob didn't do anything, but the boat did. I thought we would capsize.

"You have to feel it, the wind and the current," he said, as he adjusted the tiller in my hand. "You'll feel the groove. You have to feel it when you're at the helm. You're doing great."

"No, no, I can't do it." I was nervous, scared. Another sailboat approached and I had visions of losing complete control, crashing and dying.

"Here, you take it, Uncle. That's enough for me." I said. Relieved, I leaned back, feeling the salt air and gentle undulations of the Bay water. It felt safe with him at the helm. I felt safe with him, like he was watching out for me.

We had an amazing sail around the Bay. Great-Uncle Don was with us too, two brothers who seemed so at peace as we rounded Alcatraz. The wind blew hard. I held tight as the boat heeled. Grandpa used to sail with them too, the three brothers. Three amazing brothers. Uncle Bob told me they had done a lot racing. He used to design boats and build them too, with Grandpa, so I heard.

Uncle Bob smiled at me. "You like this, don't you?"

"It's fun, yeah."

"Why don't you take lessons? I'll pay for them." He smiled a lot with me these days.

"Uncle Bob, I don't have any time. I'm so busy with school and work. And sailing is an expensive hobby."

He seemed disappointed, but he didn't say it.

I sat up on the high side when the boat heeled and looked at the Golden Gate Bridge. It sure did look pretty. I found my thoughts turning to the ocean that lay beyond it.

June 1994

Okay, it took me over six years to do it, but I've done it! And every day I went to school I reminded myself why I was doing it. I swore I would never be like my father, uneducated and egocentric. I'm not an oceanographer but I am graduating, getting my degree in English, language studies to be specific, from San Francisco State University. I will teach, write stories, and travel the world.

It hasn't been easy, that's for sure. Worked my ass off. Worked at a law firm for a lawyer who had been a member of the Carter Administration. That felt good. Did my homework on the metro. My grades aren't stellar, but I've gotten my degree and learned a lot. No school debt. I even put money away in a retirement fund. I went to school and work with holes in my shoes at times, being careful not to cross my legs, so people wouldn't see the holes. I didn't have much of a social life.

BUT I DID IT! Now I'm off to China for a year to teach at Nanjing University. I can't believe I got the job. Fine, it only pays $150 a month, but I'll make it work. It's always been my dream to travel and I'M DOING IT ALL BY MYSELF!

I'll miss Ricci, though. It's funny how he's become such a big part of my life. I felt that connection to him when we met at Simple Pleasures Cafe two years ago. But it's been rocky. When he left to cycle through the Balkans, I met Robert. I didn't mean to enter a relationship. It just happened. Everyone said Ricci was taking advantage of me, helping him live his dream and never writing to me or calling me. I spent a lot of time sending care packages and taking care of his paperwork at home, but then I began to think that others might be right. I fell in love with him though. Maybe I was being selfish and self-centered. He was so mad when he got to Berlin and called me. He said I was trash from Fremont. I crawled into a closet and cried.

Really, I didn't mean to meet Robert. He was really kind and gentle. He saw me when I was standing on top of the Headlands overlooking the Golden Gate Bridge and the Pacific Ocean, one of my favorite places to be. Then he saw me down at Chrissy Field, where I was catching my breath after cycling.

"What's your phone number?" he said, after we talked a little bit.

"Do you have a pen?" I asked, thinking a friendship would be good.

He tapped the side of his head. "I will remember," he promised.

He did. He called me the next day.

He was from Beirut and introduced me to Middle Eastern food and art, which opened up a beautiful world for me. He was so respectful and had a nice way of looking at the world, despite having had to escape Beirut while bullets were flying.

Maybe what I did was wrong. I am a horrible person. It just happened. I didn't mean to hurt Ricci. He tells me he can't trust me. We're back together now, though I still feel him angry at me. I guess I deserve it. My trip to China will be good for us. He'll see that I can be faithful, even when we're not together. I feel I need to prove this to him so that he will trust me again, because he often says he can't.

We both have a dream to travel together and live unconventionally one day. Simplicity is our mantra after meeting at Simple Pleasures Cafe.

We've got it all figured out.

July 1994

I meet with Uncle Bob for our tuna fish sandwich and highball, like we often do. The newspaper is open to the day's stock trades. Everything is in order, including the hanging crocheted hot pads over the oven.

"So, Barbie, why are you going all the way China, for crying out loud?" he starts. "It's dirty there!" He goes off in his usual old-man crotchety, complaining way.

"It's adventure, Uncle. I love adventure and traveling. That's who I am!"

"I just don't understand it. You can have adventure here. You have everything here. A huge San Francisco Bay. I don't understand why you have to go all the way across an ocean for adventure." He swills his highball and gets up from the table. "They don't even speak English there!"

I know he doesn't mean what he said. He would miss me. I hug him. "I'll write letters, and I'll be back next year. Promise. Maybe we can go sailing again?"

"Yeah." He looks out the window. "Maybe."

November 1994

My parents weren't very happy at first about my going off to China by myself. Ricci was my advocate. He told them it'd be good for me. He understands what it means to be cultured and educated. We write to each other all the time and I really miss him. He's going to come visit me in January, for Chinese New Year, and we're going to Vietnam together. It's so amazing here. Don't ask me how I did it, but I managed to save up a thousand dollars for spending money, bought my plane ticket, and got a teaching job at Nanjing University, just down the Yangtze River, four hours by slow train from Shanghai.

The food is amazing and I want to experience EVERYTHING! I have a bicycle and my own apartment and I share a kitchen with other foreign faculty, from Spain and England.

I've got about 120 students and I'm teaching English and writing. I'm meeting all sorts of interesting people, not just Chinese students, even though they are wonderful too! I've met a really nice girl from England who went to boarding school and then studied at Cambridge, and lots of Spaniards, like Eva, Pere, and Gerard. And I'm studying Chinese painting with Hua Wen Yuan.

You wouldn't believe the pollution here though. The air is thick with dust and smog. One of my students took me across town to a farmer's market and showed me how to buy a live fish. The merchant shaved off its scales without even killing it. I didn't feel right about that. The fish flapped violently in the pink plastic bag as we rode our bikes back. My student assured me I had a happy fish. This is admittedly an ancient culture. Maybe they know something that I don't.

One of the most amazing moments was when I was asked to present a lecture to the university students about American culture. I had never thought about America's culture much before. Luckily, there is a basement at the university library full of old history books of American literature, great works filled with ideas and politics. It was dusty and cold there and I spent hours sitting on the concrete, cross-legged, reading and thinking what it means to be American. Here in China they ask me so many questions about our holidays, even about the symbols on the coins. Most of the questions I can't answer. Why do we have Halloween with witches and goblins? And what's the point of Valentine's Day, besides giving people Hallmark cards with chocolate? Why is there an eyeball on a dollar bill? I had to look up all these answers. I know so little about my own country and our culture. We never learned these things at school. Yet, here, in China, they know the meaning behind every one of their symbols. Everything has a story, even the way you hold chopsticks gives meaning to how clever in life you are. Food has symbolic value, like the little dumpling, and changes the way you eat, from merely stuffing your face to recognizing the richness of storytelling and joy.

I went through stacks of books and got an education on America culture while I was in China. I read ideas about the Wild West and violence in our cities. How we destroyed civilizations with ideas of progress and modernization. I thought about our heroes and our wars. I reflected on our value of self-independence, though one student told me that this idea, to China, means being selfish and that we are mean to our grandmothers and grandfathers by sending them off to retirement centers, like warehouses. There was much to think about. I didn't want to talk about fast food restaurants, traffic on freeways, and runoff ditches, but maybe I should have.

The End

The day of the presentation I was picked up by a chauffeur driving a fancy black car and we arrived at a grand lecture hall. Red banners were waving "Welcome American Teacher." There was a red carpet laid out, like the Academy Awards, and it looked like the Queen of England was coming. Oh my God, I thought. Students were hanging out the window, waving to ME! I felt like a movie star without having paid my dues.

How did I get here?

As I stood at the podium, a sense of dread came over me. Who was I to talk about America? I'm a nobody. I'm just a girl from Fremont who somehow managed to get a college degree and has the guts—or stupidity—to live on $150 a month in a place that doesn't speak English, just like my great-uncle had warned. But here was an auditorium filled with five hundred Chinese students, all waiting for ME to talk. I didn't recognize anyone, so that was good. This could all be kept a secret from the world.

I took a deep breath, opened my mouth, and began spewing my intellectually stimulating and passionate talk about values, history, literature, soul work of the American dream, history, ethics, and immigration. For nearly an hour I poured my heart and soul into the depth and richness of what I learned and what I believed. I was panting. I could feel my muscles twitch and sweat dripping down my back.

When I was done, I took a deep breath. The room was quiet, the audience still. Surely, I had inspired them with my wisdom and depth. They were stunned. Speechless. I knew it.

"Any questions?" I asked, smiling.

I scanned the room, eagerly awaiting the gush of meaningful, thoughtful ideas, comments, and questions I'd come to expect from these university students.

There was absolute silence. Finally, a single arm rose, halfway, hesitantly. A shy Chinese boy.

"Yes?" I was ready for anything. Bring it on.

"Excuse me. Do you like movies with Rambo?" All the other students sat up eagerly to hear my answer.

Rambo?

That night I sat in the dark on the front porch, listening to the cicadas. I had a terrifying feeling about the future, what lay ahead, as if an evil Chinese dragon would one day emerge.

Where do these thoughts come from?

June 1995

I came home from China almost completely broke, with just a hundred dollars in my pocket. Mom suggested I come live with them, but I'm not doing that. I couldn't do that. I slaved to get out of Fremont and I didn't want to return to a father still sitting in his armchair waiting to get his job back after thirteen years, a delusional dream about him standing up for what he believed against Ronald Reagan. And a mom who was codependent on him and working a job she hated. I could never go back. Everyone has gone on with their lives, so why can't he?

There have been no airplane crashes. Everyone is doing more than better. And Reagan beat the Soviet Empire after years with all of us worrying about nuclear war. He even ensured Gorbachev, the leader of the Soviet Empire, would "tear down that wall," the Berlin Wall, as he spoke again from the podium, freeing everyone in communist countries. The economy is buzzing and people are living big lives. What's the problem?

It's nice to be back with Ricci. Early yesterday morning his parents called from their home in Italy. It's funny, they never say, "Hey, how are you doing, Son?" It's all straight to business about financials or upkeep of their homes. I listen and admire the conversation. My family would never talk that way and I tell him that. They must really care about his future. He told me he likes the way my family talks. But we never talk about the important things that would make us financially secure or affect my future. My mom just calls to say hi and chitchat forever. Maybe he and I balance each other. We come from opposite worlds, don't we?

I told Ricci I got "Teacher of the Year Award" in China before I left Nanjing University. I also told him it seemed that many of the westerners who go to China are a little bit wacky. Then there were the jerks who go to China to get Chinese girls, the naïve girls believing in princes.

"So, your award wasn't really that important then? If the others were jerks?"

I stopped to consider this. "Yeah, you're probably right. It's just a silly piece of paper. I'm not really into awards and those things anyway."

We continued to eat our supper. I always appreciated him helping me see truth and not letting me get caught up in things that don't matter in the end. He helps me. Maybe we help each other.

I got a job pretty quickly. Ricci helped me with my résumé and gave me some direction too. He said, "Be a go-getter." I'm slow at these things. He even took me shopping and encouraged me to buy a blue suit, which I would never buy for myself. He put me in touch with an employment agency, which told me they could place me right away. I have an interview with an accounting firm, a place I would normally never work at, but everyone keeps telling me I'd be ideal for the job. I'm learning from Ricci. The job pays well, and I need money. Fingers crossed!

October 1995

I sit alone in a glass cage, crying. Yes, I'm wearing my blue suit, and, yes, I got the job at the San Francisco accounting firm and it pays a lot. BUT after a year of an incredible experience living and teaching in China, I find myself sitting in my private office like a fish in a bowl. I'm completely alone. Sometimes I'll see the mail carrier pass by on his runs. He waves to me through the glass.

They gave me a nameplate and said I was lucky to learn how to use WordPerfect. I'd be working for a very good accountant. He's demanding, but he has big clients. I was lucky to have so much responsibility, they said. Why is it that I don't believe them, like they are telling me to feel good about something I should run like hell from?

The job does pay a lot and I have to remember I need the money, though I didn't like how, after transcribing a letter and giving it to my boss to review and sign, he studied it and then looked at me over his eyeglasses. "Barbara, are you dyslexic?" I had misspelled a word.

Am I?

Still, I'm gaining valuable skills and working with the top accountants in the country on the thirty-third floor of one of the most important and sophisticated skyscrapers in San Francisco, even if I am only typing up letters in WordPerfect and sitting in a glass cage. It feels strange being isolated all day after having been amid millions of people every day. I miss China. I feel so alone.

Ricci introduced me to a woman named Bryna Stevens. She's in her late sixties and is a children's book writer. She also teaches piano. I told her I like to write too, and so she invited me to her writers group, the San Francisco Writers' Group, which has been around for thirty years. So I did, and I read and shared some stories I wrote about China with a room full of about thirty other writers. I had never read anything to a group before. Some people didn't even hate them, but they gave me advice on how to make them better.

Bryna encourages me a lot. Sometimes Ricci and I fight over little things. I don't know why, but we do. I want things to work out between us. Bryna helps me figure him out sometimes. He helps her with computer stuff and she'll complain about him. But that's her. She says she's not really Jewish, and she constantly claims she does things because she's not really Jewish. I find myself wondering if that makes her Jewish. I tell her this and she laughs.

I like sitting with her in her studio filled with piles of papers, writings, library books, music sheets, and crochet projects, stacked high. When I come to visit, she sits at the piano, plays a few notes, and starts talking about her father, growing up Jewish in New York, going to music school, of her born-again Christian son in North Carolina. She has a daughter who never talks to her and a son who was in an accident, became a paraplegic, and later died in Jerusalem. She's an outside the mold kind of woman. You could never put her in a box and wrap her up in a bow. She's a thinker and has her own way of doing things. Maybe people can't handle that. I like her a lot. And I'm learning from her.

April 1996

You won't believe what I'm doing! I just couldn't stay at the accounting firm. My boss was such a jerk, but I managed to make some money and now I'm working part-time back at the law firm (I love my boss!) and I got an internship at KQED public radio with Michael Krasny. I can't believe they trust ME! I mean, what do I know?

Michael has a two-hour talk show in the morning with guests who are writers, artists, politicians, and movers of culture. I get to interview people on the phone and set up the live broadcasts. I can't believe they are letting me—me!—do this. I worry they'll find out how dumb I am.

I lead the guests into the studio and sometimes I get to talk to them—these are big people in the world who influence the way we think and see the world. I feel so small.

Recently Mike Leigh, the film director of *Secrets and Lies*, was waiting for me to take him into the studio. I mean, here is one of the most famous film directors standing with ME for five whole minutes! What do I say? I didn't know. I opened my mouth to ask him a question so that we wouldn't be standing in awkward silence, but he asked me a question instead. He asked if I wrote. I told him I did, but that everything I write feels disconnected and mediocre.

He studied me for a moment before saying, "If it comes from you, everything is connected." I watched him enter the studio, his words echoing in my head.

Everything is connected.

Maybe it was the way he looked at me, but I could feel those words stick to my guts. Still, all of my writing is mediocre. Even Ricci tells me I miss periods and commas. Maybe I am dyslexic.

January 1997

I look out the window as the train winds its way through San Francisco. I remember my visions, my feelings, of nearly ten years ago when I first began my travels in foreign countries, how I dreamed that one day travel would become me and I could talk about the world, its beauty, and its craziness over a bottle of wine with friends from around the world, and figure out how to save it.

Save it from what, I wonder? Where do I come up with these ideas?

March 1997

It's been an amazing two years working at the radio station KQED with the producers and Michael Krasny, who knows how to interview the most amazing people of our time, politicians, artists, writers and journalists—the movers and shakers of our culture. They are real people doing real things. Taking chances. Living big dreams. Making big statements about the world and shaping the way we live. I got to produce a live broadcast performance on a panel discussion about religion. During the broadcast, David Minkow, the producer, told me to look for people who are unsure of their questions, seem timid, who don't raise their hands right away. They are the ones with the best questions, the thinkers, the ones who always question. The ones who look confident are often the ones who just like to hear themselves talk and usually carry big egos.

The panel discussion was good but what struck me as the most interesting was an audience member who raised her hand and asked why no one on the panel was from the Wicca movement. She said she was a witch. I was struck by that. A witch. I liked her and she seemed really kind. I guess she must be a good witch.

Anyway, I'm in the newsroom with reporters like Jason Beaubian and David Wright. I mean, these guys write stories about people who inspire others and events that shape our world. I'm so shy; I don't know how to talk to them without risking sounding stupid. Jason is really nice. He'll take me on his assignments to city board meetings and protests. He's even told me to get some ambient sounds for one of his news pieces, so my job is to walk around the city with a recording device and just pick up sounds of city life, which I love, because I love listening. Sometimes he'll ask me to get a quote from someone, like Nancy Pelosi, a politician who often speaks at rallies. I like her.

I swear I could sit on a park bench and watch the world unfold all day long. Some people call that lazy, but how many others do it in front a television set? I like how Bryna calls it "thinking about how it all ticks."

I'm writing some stories and I'm getting better. But I'll never be as good as these reporters. They've come from good schools, some of the best. And good families too.

I was in the studio learning how to produce a story with my voice. Cy Muskier, the engineer, and Raul Ramirez were coaching me while I read a story. The big fuzzy microphone intimidated me in the quiet, padded room like something designed for a crazy person, which is what I feared I was becoming later in the session. They kept telling me to repeat my story over and over again, telling me one thing or another was wrong about the cadence or intonation of my voice. Too fast, too slow, be more direct, and on and on and on. It was exhausting. After an hour of this I was so sick and tired of them telling me what to do that I looked at them like I wished they were dead. I hated them and thought maybe I'd kill them after I got out of that studio. No, I would just quit and walk out, and yell every expletive as I did it. "Fuck you!"

I read the piece thinking these very thoughts about them, wrapping each syllable around my tongue laced with venom and spitting it out at them.

"This is Barbara McVeigh, for KQED Radio," I finished, and continued to stew in these thoughts, glaring at them and daring them, in my mind, to say one more bad thing about what I had just read. I loathed them. What gave them the right to treat me so rottenly, so goddamn critically? I was ready to draw the pistol, had I one. They were quiet for a moment. Then they grinned.

"That's the voice!" they crowed.

So, I'm a real radio journalist! I've done a story about a lesbian comedian, Ellen DeGeneres. I even went to a lesbian bar to get the story. Ellen is an actor who just came out as gay on a television program and then got fired for being a lesbian. Everyone is in a tizzy about her coming out publicly, which is so weird, but that's our country.

The best story so far was last week, when Cy sent me to Berkeley after the Academy Awards. A film called *Breathing Lessons* about a guy named Mark O'Brien had just won an Academy Award for Best Documentary. I knew nothing about Mark O'Brien, except that he was disabled. So, I took BART across the Bay and walked the blocks through the Berkeley campus to Mark's studio. The door was slightly ajar. I pushed it open gently.

"Hello? I'm from KQED."

"Come in!"

I did, and that's when my jaw hit the floor. In front of me was a shaved head, drool dribbling down it. Below its chin was a monstrous cylinder concealing the attached body, an iron lung creating the breath of Darth Vader. It was not pretty. In fact, it was damn ugly. The head spoke.

"Hey, there! Come on in!"

Mark would have had to be blind not to have sensed my shock. He tried putting me at ease.

"Hey there, you're kinda cute. I'm looking for a girlfriend. Are you looking for a boyfriend?"

"What?"

He was flirting with me! It made me laugh, though I wasn't sure if I should have laughed. Would I insult him if I did? We began to talk. No, it wasn't just talk. It was one of the best conversations I'd ever had with another human being. Despite his handicap and extreme confinement, this man was more alive than most able-bodied people. He had lived an extraordinary life, confined to wheelchairs, breathing apparatuses, and cylinders for over forty years, since 1955.

He cracked jokes, told stories, and had opinions on what was happening in the world. He had managed to get an undergraduate degree from UC Berkeley and had been in graduate school until his health got the better of him. He wrote using a stick in his mouth to painstakingly tap on a computer keyboard, letter by letter, to craft stories, poetry, and essays. He had things he wanted to say and was determined to say them. He shared one of his poems with me. What struck me most was his compassion for others. And he could buckle your knees with a simple joke.

When I returned to the studio that afternoon I produced one of my best pieces I had ever written, inspired by a man who was so physically ugly but could create something so beautiful, with so much love and inspiration. I included his poem, and I listened to the broadcast later that day from home. I felt connected to it, in a very strange way.

"I wrote this poem about my mother," Mark said, "and all the dead, about two years ago."

A Dream Mother

Why is she taking me to the movies?
Serving me chicken and corn for breakfast.
Showing off her new dress.
Doesn't she know she's dead?

She's still a running character in my dreams,
Smoking Lucky, swapping dirty jokes
with the boss and Virgin Mary
Before the two of them roar off on a BVM Harley.
She always liked a ruckus.

Mark O'Brien (reprinted with permission)

Still, though, I'm not cut out to be a radio journalist for long. I'm not earning a living. Writing comes hard for me. Maybe I'm not a writer. Ricci tells me I should think about getting a real job. I mean, if they value me, he says, they'd pay me, right? He says I'm getting used. Maybe he's right. Maybe I'm just wasting my time.

March 1998

We were having a nice meal at Ricci's parents' house a few months back. Their place is so nice. It looks over the Pacific Ocean. Sometimes we harvest mussels down by the seaside and create magnificently beautiful dinners with candles and conversation. Still, it's hard for me to contribute.

I was telling his mother about the orcas in Monterey Bay. She laughed at me and told me that I was wrong, that orcas don't exist there, that they only live in northern waters. I'm often reminded of how I'm wrong and don't know as much as they know. True, I'm not from Europe. I don't speak more than one language, and I only went to San Francisco State, a basic college, I suppose.

Later, I looked up orcas and found out I was right, they are found in Monterey Bay. I emailed her this but she never replied.

Ricci told his mom he wanted to cycle through Albania again. His mom didn't look happy about it. I watched her. I could hear her thinking.

Interestingly, months later, his parents offered him a house. They'd sell the one in Los Angeles and use the money to buy him one in Marin. I wondered whether his mom was trying to make Ricci settle down, give him a sense of responsibility. In some ways I'd like to settle down too. I look at how comfortable his parents are. It's a nice way to live. They worked hard to earn it, and we could do the same. I told Ricci this. We're not married and he hasn't asked me yet either. It's been six years.

Recently, when we were at my parents' house, Uncle Bob shook his finger at Ricci and said, "Why aren't you making an honest woman out of her? Show her some respect!"

It made me laugh. My uncle is such a small, thin guy and Ricci is so tall. I love my great-uncle. He sticks up for me. And his comment did make me wonder why Ricci hasn't asked me to marry him. When I talk about it, Ricci gets mad and tells me that paperwork has nothing to do with our relationship. Maybe he's right. Paperwork doesn't mean anything when you care about each other, right?

He's asked me to look at houses and wants me to be a part of the decision to buy a house. I feel funny about it, since we're not married. I see how his mom looks at me sometimes, like maybe I'm after something more than just wanting to be with her son. Maybe it's just me. It's funny. I know people who want to marry rich guys, but I've never been one of them. I just want my backpack and freedom. But the house is such a gift, and imagine how we could do great things with people, community. How could anyone say no to such a gift? Ricci says we'll rent it out.

We've been looking at big homes. I told Ricci we should look at small homes. If we decide to live in the house one day, we could live simply, with little overhead, and then have time in our lives to do what we want and be free.

He shook his head. "Barbara, you don't know anything about real estate investment."

He's probably right. My family hasn't done anywhere near as well as his family. I'm sure I can learn a lot from them.

I hang out with Bryna a lot at Simple Pleasures Cafe and she plays the old wooden piano there, the same song over and over again. Then we talk writing. I still go to the writers' group, and I'm taking a photography class. Last week I took some black and white photos of Bryna. She loves having her picture taken and she's so photogenic. First, I took some shots of her teaching piano in her tiny studio. Her wrinkled, crooked fingers danced along the keyboard as a small girl with braided hair watched. Then we walked down the street; her San Francisco Cable Car earrings dangled as she swung her crocheted purse. Later, we headed to the Sutro Heights Garden. I had never seen this place tucked along the San Francisco cliffs, near Ocean Beach. Amid the Greek and Roman statues and structures we have fun clicking away and being silly, which she can do so easily, like a child, despite the fact that she's in her seventies. She lies down on the grass, her fingers prancing in the air above her, as if playing an imaginary piano high in the sky. I snap her picture.

"One day I'll play the piano in heaven," she declares. She turns her head toward me and smiles. I snap another picture.

The next day I stand in the dark room developing the images. Her dark cave-like eyes, as if she were dead and telling me something from another world, sends shivers down my spine. I put the picture away. I won't show her that one, I decide. She looks dead in it, like a ghost.

I think about the letter Bryna keeps on her piano, the one that has information on who to contact in case of emergency. My phone number is inside because she doesn't have family nearby. The writers group is pretty much the only family she has.

It's clear she loves children. Between her published children's books and piano teaching, she gives a lot to them. I can see that.

I hope one day I can write a book. Bryna inspires me.

July 1999

We move north to Marin County, a wealthy suburb outside San Francisco. I wear a ring on my finger. It feels right. I've waited for him for so many years. Now we're together, and when we discuss wedding arrangements he brings tears to my eyes. What's wrong with me? He gets angry at me and brings up inadequacies he sees in me—my career, my salary, the way I walk. Then he'll stop and be so kind, like he didn't mean it. He just gets grumpy. I do too sometimes, so I shouldn't judge.

I remember back to that time I sat looking at him, in my big Victorian chair by the window, an old one I used to have. He had been seated at his desk, and I'd sensed a wall dividing us, a premonition that he would someday ruin me. He would destroy my inner soul.

I'm probably just being dramatic because I'm feeling angry right now. I shouldn't listen to myself. I come up with the weirdest thoughts.

My interests are travel, writing, and taking pictures of this beautiful world. Why am I not pursuing them? Why are we not pursuing our dreams?

November 1999

I'm numb. I just don't feel anymore. I don't like myself. I don't like people. I don't like the colors, the textures, the sounds, or the languages. I yearn for something, something I fear I'm not smart enough to achieve. That's why I don't like myself. I've started working for a national lifestyle catalog company that sells home furnishings, creating images of homes you'd like to just dive into and live in. It's creative and I'm making some money to live on now. I work crazy hours and we don't get overtime, which I don't understand. Isn't that why we had unions? But they tell us we should feel lucky to have a creative job because it's a good job, and others would love to have such a job. So I don't complain.

I am headed to Toronto in less than two weeks to rekindle a friendship, a time, a memory. I am seeing Hua Wen Yun, a person who is reaching her dreams. I yearn to be around her energy, her vision, and her wisdom. I haven't seen her since my days in China, when she taught me how to paint trees and rocks with a paintbrush made with the hair of a goat or a horse's tail.

"Stand tall, like a bamboo, when you paint it," she'd tell me. "A bamboo can also yield to the wind."

She also told me my rocks were too soft, so I still practice those. At twenty-two years old, she left China all by herself and moved to Toronto without knowing a single person, except for a Romanian immigrant that Ricci knows. She had big dreams. Dreams to paint the sky, trees, and mountains and share that dream with others. She taught me to look at trees differently, to see their texture and lines, and maybe even their souls.

I pass my days of late looking at wedding dresses, searching for locations, and thinking about the ceremony next September. I listen to the football game echoing through our small apartment. Ricci sits and watches it alone. I really hate this place. But like everything in my life, I've let it go. I've given up. I'm tired. I work every day. I pay my bills and struggle to continue going forward. But it will get better, I promise myself. I'll save money and continue working hard. I believe this. Ricci and I have big dreams and our mantra is simple pleasures.

2000–2010

July 2000

My grandfather died just a few months ago. I found a picture he had of me sitting inside his plane, *The Keleher Lark*, he called it. Flying was his passion. I had curls in my hair, wore a little red dress, and had fat cheeks.

I remember the feeling of excitement as the motor started up and the propellers spun. I wanted to go way up high, and fly, not just sit idle on the runway. Hadn't my grandpa taken my brother and sister up? It's hard to remember. But I was always the baby, always too young. The others got the fun and then managed to get out before it turned ugly, or so it always seemed to me.

We all admired Grandpa. He was a self-taught engineer who didn't spend a day in college. He earned little as a mail carrier, but managed to raise a family thanks to my grandmother, who made each dollar stretch. Grandpa completely taught himself engineering, how to design and build a plane, and then later how to fly it. He'd have high-level engineers look at his designs and they would marvel at how smart he was. Grandpa always marveled too, at those who had fancy credentials but couldn't figure out how he made what he termed simple designs.

"They lack common sense," he'd say. He used to carry around a camera, filming the family, boats, and planes, in that order. We'd sit in the living room Friday nights eating popcorn and watch ourselves giggling, doing two-finger bunny ears over each others heads, not knowing what to do in front of a camera. Then we'd have to watch spanning of engine parts, propellers spinning, and airplanes at the local airfield, interspersed with images of Grandma sitting on a park bench, looking just perfect, like Audrey Hepburn.

Grandpa still talked angrily about my father and his job, up until the day he died. The years have been tough for my parents, having lost so much and having to rebuild their lives. Dad drinks and mom is still bitter.

"Your father followed his ego and wasn't a family man," Grandpa repeatedly told me.

I don't need my father for anything, I remind myself. I'm marrying into an educated, cultured family, a strong family. I have no intention of letting my dad walk me down the aisle, because he failed to guide me in the course of life. He doesn't deserve that privilege. I've had to find my way myself.

Am I embittered? No. I'm realistic. I love him but I give him very little respect and plenty of pity. It doesn't take much for a person to get out of an armchair and turn off a television set in order to live life. Or, for that matter, keep a job, be a father, and support his daughter instead of dragging her into the mess he chose.

I'm in love with Ricci and we're going to have an amazing life filled with our dreams.

We've got it all figured out.

September 2000

It was an international gathering of families up on a hill, overlooking the valley, with the ocean in the distance. We got married on a beautiful September day. Of course, there was lots of stress as these things go, but we did it, and we have dreams! Ricci walked me down the aisle and took the position proudly. Ricci has been everything to me. My dad stumbled, giving the speech, which was not a big surprise. Ricci's father, Dante, gave an elegant speech that made everyone clap. It's nice being part of a good family. They want the best for us, I can tell.

Ricci had proposed to me in Venice, on a gondola, as we approached the Bridge of Sighs, the historic place where prisoners had their last glimpse of freedom before heading to the chambers of prison, which is funny, as it's become a popular place to propose marriage. I have a beautiful ring, which also carries my grandmother's diamonds.

After the wedding, we went to Cuba!

Of course, it was my idea. We had to sneak in, since it's illegal for us to travel there as U.S. citizens, but that was the fun of it. Ricci was supposed to organize our trip, but when we got to Havana he told me he just hadn't had the time to do anything, because of our wedding and all. I understood. We'd been so busy. So, shouldering our backpacks, we walked through the hot muggy streets of Havana. He wanted to find a special place for us. We passed by many nice places, but he didn't like any of them. We kept walking. It was horribly hot, and we had to stop every two blocks, to rest.

Neighborhoods began to grow more disheveled and broken down, but Ricci kept walking. Policemen with submachine guns stood on some corners.

"Ricci, where are we going?" I had really wanted to find a nice place in the old part of Havana and enjoy some time together, have a few drinks and relax, but Ricci said that, because we spent so much on our wedding, it was best to be frugal in terms of where we slept. We'd spend our money on food and activities instead. I thought that seemed reasonable and I felt glad to be with someone resourceful and thinking big-picture. We finally found a place to stay. The room, next to a collapsed building, had a toilet with a plant growing out of it. I laughed so hard!

The cool rain was pouring when we went to search for a meal. Ricci's plastic bag of US dollars fell into the filthy gutter and he threw it on the table as we sat down at an eatery, exposing everything we had.

I grabbed the bag, intent on concealing it. He just wasn't thinking. He was tired, We were both tired.

"What the fuck are you doing?" he barked, and yanked the bag away from me.

"Ricci, don't show off your money!" I knew enough to know it was dangerous to show American dollars.

I wasn't sure what shocked me more, his action or his words. I was still trying to make sense of what just happened. "It's okay. We're both tired," I said. I tried to settle us both down. We had been under a lot of stress. It was our honeymoon. We needed to relax.

Later, we walked around Havana. It was an amazing place filled with music and happy people who dance late into the night everywhere. A group of giggling older ladies at a hair salon tried to drag Ricci inside one night. They were making a party and needed a guy to dance with. I encouraged him, but he didn't do it. He's shy. People here take the time to talk and simply meander. Old colonial buildings and 1950s Chevys give the air of old-lady sophistication, like that of a matriarch who stands for something just and true. And, of course, the mojitos! We hired a guide one night and he took us to the hidden dancing clubs. Ricci doesn't like to dance and told me to dance with the guide, so I did, watching him watch me. I tried to take his hand to encourage him to join me, but he refused. It was okay. We would find other things we like to do together. Life is so rich.

The artwork in Cuba is beautiful, though not filled with vivid reds and blues, typical colors one would think for a Caribbean Island nation. Instead, blacks and browns dominate the canvases. I find one by an artist named Choco. It's of a woman standing tall, embracing herself, hugging herself. I like it but Ricci says not to spend money. Still, I have to buy her, so I do. He buys artwork too, a sketch of a man's head with a spinning windmill inside it.

I don't understand why the United States says all these deprecating things about Cuba. People strike me as more educated and happy here than so many back home in the United States. It's strange.

Coming home I am apprehensive at getting caught. I remove everything related to Cuba in my backpack—coins, paper, receipts, everything. The tough U.S. Customs agent asks where I have been. I say I was in Mexico, which was technically true, since we passed through it in order to reach Cuba, so I haven't strictly lied. I feel so scared.

Why should I fear having seen another country and how they live? What gives my country that right? I thought I was free! Instead, I could have been fined thousands of dollars, interrogated, and put in prison had I been caught. It's strange when you think about it. I've experienced fear coming back to my own country.

July 2001

My parents and I had plans to meet in Italy for a week of travel together through Rome, Tuscany, and Milan, at which point they would return home and I would meet up with Ricci for a month-long cycling trip through Sardegna. However, his father fell ill the day before departure and was diagnosed with cancer, so we canceled Sardegna, and I went on without Ricci, since my parents' flights were nonrefundable. My parents had never been to Europe before. I was to go ahead of them and meet them in Rome.

We had lost our apartment shortly before the trip and so we moved in temporarily with my parents, back in Fremont. I wasn't happy about it, but I made a deal with myself that I'd find something about Fremont that I liked, so I spent those few weeks cycling all around Fremont. There was so much traffic that I decided to cycle along Niles Canyon, where in high school we joked about the White Witch and Zodiac Killer.

The shoulder alongside the two-lane road was narrow. Large trucks barreled past me in both directions, rattling my bicycle with their force. I was cycling fast when a large truck appeared up ahead, while another big truck could be heard approaching from behind. I tensed. I'd have to stay tightly within the confines of the narrow shoulder as the trucks passed each other, hoping they had sufficient space to do so without veering into mine. I glanced behind me at the truck bearing down on me and then ahead. As my gaze came to rest on the shoulder, I spotted a thick stick lying across it, completely obstructing my path. I was going so fast there was no way to safely stop in time, but there wasn't space to swerve around it. My heart began to pound.

Could I bunny-hop over it? How many years had it been since I did such a move on my bicycle? I didn't know what to do. As I bore down on it, within just a few yards, I was horrified when what I had thought was a stick turned out instead to be a huge, fat snake. I had no choice. I would have to ride over it. I held my breath and braced for impact, the roar of the truck behind me drowning everything else out. A split second before I reached the snake, it abruptly lifted its head and half its body, allowing me to pass, brushing against my leg just hard enough to affirm it was real. The trucks zoomed past and I stopped my bike, panting hard.

I turned back.

The snake was gone.

I sleep in my father-in-law Dante's studio in Rome. Tomorrow, my parents arrive. Across the street lives his sister, Ricci's aunt. Next door are cousins. This place allows the mind and imagination to wander endlessly. There's one singular work of art in the studio that appeals to me. It sits almost hidden behind a door, in a corner, on top of an old large cabinet, almost certainly from Dante's family's farmhouse outside of Rome. I study it. It looks to be over two hundred years old.

It's a portrait of a young man, possibly a nobleman judging by the way he's dressed and certainly not a farmer. He has soft full lips, and crinkled hair. I am taken by how similar the hair is to Ricci's. There's a hint of aristocracy, confidence. His eyes are big and brown, the nose somewhat aquiline, with a slight knob at the top. He's wearing a white fluffy blouse, donned with a bow under his chin.

A gilded gold frame surrounds the young man. Who could this person be, I wonder? Is this an ancestor of my husband, of my future child? Children?

The End

I look around. Why am I here? Because by chance I met a young man at a cafe in San Francisco ten years earlier? I was simple. I am simple. I feel that simplicity further accentuated when I'm surrounded by such historic, creative, and financial riches. How in the world can I contribute? I don't speak languages, and I'm certainly not as creative; nor do I have the financial means to match. I am learning, though. I can get by with Italian and learn more with each passing day. And, I remind myself, I also have a creative job, even if Ricci says it isn't a very good job. He says he sees me doing something else.

My parents arrive. We sit at a cafe under the sweltering Roman heart, in front of the Pantheon. A fountain splashes nearby and Chinese are selling trinkets.

My mother recites her list of people to buy for, fretting over forgetting someone. I tell her to think about herself and not to worry about everyone else. My father chimes in. He needs to find a gigolo doll. I look at him perplexed.

"A gigolo doll, from Rome?" I ask him. "What does that mean?"

"You know—one of those dolls you put on your dashboard and the head bounces as you drive."

I'm reminded of how American my parents are, uncouth, uneducated. It's embarrassing.

Umbria is beautiful. The air is warm. The hills radiate with their golden hills and I feel at peace, for this place shows me how strong I can be.

I see how childlike my parents are. I have trouble communicating with them. Perhaps it is an evil side of me that takes them around Italy, to demonstrate how uneducated my father is. He is not a learned man. Perhaps that angers me. I wish, as I have in the past, countless times, that I had a father I could be proud of.

But at least I have found what is meaningful in life for me. Education, inspiration, and travel. I want to share with them and wake them up to what is good in life. I still I feel I can get through to them.

I miss Ricci.

He understands these things.

After my parents leave, I continue on to France by myself and then to Portugal to visit a friend. Today I'm traveling alone and sit quietly high on a mountain, a throne of stone, of ages past, of Moorish ages past. I touch the rocks that were placed here a thousand years before, during the eleventh century. These stones will be here when my bones lie still in a grave after another thousand years. This place gives me strength. I touch the stones and lose my eyes—my sense of time fades. I feel the blood, the death, the lovers—it all happened here one time, long ago. I can imagine and feel it all.

Moments are beautiful because they are sacred. One has to respect each one because they will never exist again. And once you experience the sacred moments, they will be with you, a part of you. Maybe this is what love and life are all about.

Sometimes words are not what have value. It's the simple gestures—a touch, a facial expression. Sometimes it doesn't have to be a touch at all, but simply sitting next to someone. That's all. Feeling comfortable, secure, calm, and at peace.

I think of these things as I sit among the old stones.

August 2001

Ricci and I move into the house his parents gifted him. It's a big house, in San Rafael, with a lot of responsibility. I wonder how I shall feel once we settle down in what is now my own home, though it isn't really mine. His father wanted me to sign a prenuptial agreement in case our lives went awry.

I asked a lawyer about this and he said that it didn't seem right if you are working and contributing to a mortgage and upkeep. I told Ricci and he said not to worry about it. But, still, I worry. I didn't marry for money. Is that how they see me? I would be happy with a backpack and traveling, living our dreams. We talk about moving to the countryside and living simply.

One day.

September 2001

Ricci screamed at me this past week. I raised my voice to defend myself, and then he changed his tone. I'm finding that I feel shut in, controlled, punished like child. Why do I feel this way? What have I done?

I question for the first time whether it was right for me to marry Ricci. We've only been married for one year, and yet I've been asking myself the question often. He doesn't seem settled. Maybe we just need to find something we can do together. I mean, after all, married life is new and we're figuring it out as we go, this new way to live. He's trying to build his business, so I give it time and promise myself to be encouraging. We all get cranky.

Meanwhile the world is beginning to fall apart. Two towers burned and fell in New York City. The Pentagon was hit. Four planes were deliberately crashed. Terrorists. An evil has descended on our planet. I can feel it in my bones. People kill over ideals, freedom, and religion. How did this happen here? Why is this happening and why would anyone be so angry at our country?

March 2002

It's been a hard trip. I gave up my plans to visit Japan. I was missing Asia a lot, missing something I had found there, in China. But when I began planning a trip to Japan, Ricci decided he wanted to go back to the Balkans and drive through Romania, Bulgaria, and Albania. I thought about it hard and decided we should travel together, since we're married now.

I've been working with the home lifestyle catalog company, making good money. We've been living in the house, but relinquishing our dreams of traveling and living simply. I don't have much time to write and I miss it. I bought a little video camera for the trip, thinking maybe I might try to make a film. I've never done that before. Grandpa liked to make films, so maybe I'd give it a try.

The trip started off okay. We picked up a car in Germany, and visited his extended German family who all agreed we'd definitely be murdered on this Balkans trip. There is so much corruption and danger there, they say—gypsies, police, prostitutes, and worst of all, a new mafia that emerged after the Berlin Wall collapsed over twelve years ago.

We went anyway. We drove thousands of kilometers and many times I wanted to slow down, stop, and look around, but that wasn't part of the plan, Ricci insisted. He was concerned about our time and schedule, to ensure we saw all that we had agreed to see. We slept in the car a lot to save money. The roads were narrow and winding and I actually developed a blister on my hand from holding the "oh, shit!" handle. We met some of the families he'd spent time with on his previous trip, those who had lost everything after their governments fell and capitalism moved in—farmers, city dwellers, villagers. There's a sadness, a sense of disparity, among the people. I sense lost hope.

"The people have to learn how to compete," Ricci says. Yet, they look at us like the wicked capitalists. I think about this a lot. How much does a person need? Is it so bad to live cooperatively? People seem to have what they need *and* have their communities too.

I remember an old German friend named Tilman who was from the eastern side of Germany. I met him shortly after the Berlin Wall fell. He said to me then that, in East Germany, they had had what they needed. It wasn't so bad, not like the way we like to make it sound. There was a growing community of artists and they had time for one another. I think of the news as we heard it reported in America, especially when Reagan made speeches about how evil communism was. Anything can be evil, I suppose, if you make it bad. But there are so many people living in poverty in America too. I don't know what is right.

I'm filming the trip a lot. I've never done this before, but I like to capture faces, moments, and textures. It gives you license to listen and watch. I'm winging it because I've never filmed before.

We visited a monastery in Romania, but I had to fight for it. We had been driving for miles and miles when we passed a small inn.

"Please, Ricci, please, let's stop and stay for the night," I begged. We had been sleeping in the car and my blisters were popping.

Eventually he conceded and we went inside and spoke to the innkeepers. The wife walked with a limp. She made up our bed and cooked the food, while her husband offered Ricci a drink. They recommended we visit the local monastery, built in 1215 by Prince Radu Negru. Several hundred years later, the monastery served as a school to teach the children of the poor as well as those of noblemen and rulers. It sits high on a cliff, but first, they warned, we'd have to walk through the gypsy village, which was dangerous. The innkeeper gave us their big black dog Aragosh (Clown) to guide us for a safe journey.

Aragosh did indeed lead us. He guided us across the two-lane highway, over a bridge, and straight into the gypsy village, arousing all the gypsy children who armed themselves with sticks and stones.

"Gypsies and dogs don't mix," the innkeeper had cautioned us.

Aragosh snarled and barked ferociously during the standoff, creating a path for us to make our way to a switchblade trail. I actually quite liked the gypsies and I was more interested in making friends and not enemies, but Aragosh was in charge and once he'd chased them away, he set off along the trail, guiding us up the mountain. A woman came down the path, wailing. She wore a black veil. She had seen the Holy Mother, she told us. The mystery deepened as we ascended into the quiet of the dry woods.

Finally, we arrived at a wooden gate at the very top. I held my camera and scanned the old wooden door, the beautiful woodwork, and then over to a toothless monk who shook his finger at me, insisting I turn off my camera. I did as I was told.

He took us along the grounds and, in Italian, showed us kindly where they lived and told us something of who they were. I could follow along somewhat, content to let Ricci take the lead. The monastery is a convent for monks and the dedication day was on a Christian holy day, the Assumption of the Virgin, August 15. It's arguably the oldest monastery in Romania, written in Church Slavonic, and keeper of the grave of the oldest *voivode*, or "war leader," containing the remains of Nicolae Alexandru Basarab, the founder of the monastery.

The monk pointed to my camera and graciously gave me permission to film the grounds.

As we readied to leave, we looked for Aragosh to take us back to the inn. He lay nearby, with another dog. He refused to budge, so we had to leave him behind. We were a bit worried about facing his owner, having come back without his dog.

"Oh, that's his girlfriend," the innkeeper said, smiling proudly, when we explained.

We haven't run into any fellow travelers until this evening, when a Japanese man on a motorcycle stopped in and joined us for dinner. There were some local Romanian men there, drinking, and one of them kept eyeing us. He said something that sounded like he wanted to start a fight with Ricci. The innkeeper's wife, who had been watching, sat next to me to discourage any locals from picking a fight with her foreign guests. It worked.

I wondered why they would want to pick a fight with us—with anyone.

April 2002

Ricci hasn't spoken to me at all today. I guess we're in a fight, although it beats me what it's about. I decide to lose myself in my thoughts as we cross the border at Ruse, in Romania, and drive through the Bulgarian countryside. The rain is plummeting down.

Bulgaria's Rila Monastery is breathtaking. Built as a fortification against the Turks, its frescoes were painted to educate illiterate soldiers and villagers about the Bible. I stroll through the grounds, alone, stopping at times when the playful sun emerges from fluffy cotton-ball clouds to warm my skin through a thick sweater. The striped design of black and white stones and archways, the clock tower, the well, and the placid movement of the nuns and priests make this orthodox monastery one of the most beautiful I've seen. It has been a spiritual and literary center since the Middle Ages.

Such beauty as this can emerge from war and suffering. I have to remember this.

April 2002

We've reached Tirana, in Albania. Albania is definitely the strangest place of all. We enter it from Macedonia, and I quickly see how desperately sad the country is and has been. A whole forest was chopped down, leaving an exposed wasteland at the border, to prevent its people from hiding there and trying to escape across it. Former leader Enver Hoxha instilled fear in the Albanians with stories of how they'd be invaded by America. Funny, we had stories of being invaded by communists. We were, all of us, running in fear from each other.

Thousands of war shelters, like concrete pillboxes, are embedded in the landscape across the country. You see them everywhere—cow pastures, next to beaches, in the countryside, in the cities. They say there is one for every Albanian, just like we have a car for every person. Hoxha stripped away education too, so people are dumbed down, making it easier to control them. There is little trust between people. Now, Albanians push hard to make as much money as they can, because they now see how much we have in the west. Corruption is horrific and children are sold into prostitution across Europe. Now that many—men, mostly—have driver's licenses for the first time, cars, predominantly expensive Mercedes, have been stolen from West Germany and driven across the border. Everyone wants to look rich and be powerful. They see us in the west as being this way—they envy us our lifestyle and think we have it right.

We arrive at the country's capital, Tirana, to work at the National Gallery. They are interested in a project Ricci pitched to them about digitizing their artwork, most of which are social realist paintings from the communist period. Some have strong peasant women baring breasts and feeding naked babies. Faces are hard-edged. Deep entrenched eyes. I wander the halls and study them. Art can create such ideas and ways to be. These were made to ennoble people with an idea that the downtrodden are the heroes. It was a way to empower them, or perhaps at least make them more content with their lot in life.

But did it work?

I see the corruption. It is difficult to trust anyone, as people maneuver, trying always to position themselves favorably. One Albanian we met learned how to speak English by listening to American seventies music. He even wears the feathered hair of that decade. He tells me that while we in America might shop at a secondhand store, in Albania they shop at sixth-hand stores. They want what we have, or at least what they see we have that's desirable.

"We have poverty and violence in our country too," I tell him.

"But you have lots of money," he retorts.

Albania is the most horrifically polluted land I've ever seen. Yesterday we passed a river of plastic bags. It's so sad.

Ricci and I had approached the Soros Foundation for money for the CD digitalization project. Ricci is really good at creating support for the project. I see us doing big things one day.

At the National Gallery, when we started to talk money, the people there get a little strange, and there are questions. I see jealousy and competitiveness arising. They all want a piece of the pie, but there is no pie yet. Television cameras appear, and Ricci speaks, to officially present the project to a small audience. They have even rolled out the red carpet!

"Ricci," I ask, after his speech, "why didn't you recognize me, that I was also helping, that we are a team?"

"Barbara, you get so sensitive over these things. You should have said it yourself."

Maybe he's right.

I was so exhausted after all the driving and work that I desperately wanted a break. I plead with Ricci to head to a beach after having heard mention of Sarande, an idyllic coastal town. After so much driving, feeling depressed by the state of life in Albania, and talking to countless people who live perpetually with mistrust and suspicion, I just want to sit on a tranquil beach, stare at the water, and write.

We drive a two-lane freeway that was an insane four cars thick, passing the skeletal remains of myriad stripped cars. It feels strange, a disturbing glimpse of a post-apocalyptic future. As we drive in to the dusty desolate town, a plump middle-aged woman leaps out into the street, shrieking. Thinking she is a gypsy, our first instinct is to ignore her. As it turns out, she is panicking because her son has fallen from a construction site, and before we know it, she is in our car, with me attempting to console her as we drive her bloody, limp boy to the hospital, who is coughing and spitting up blood.

Ricci said it would be best if we didn't stay at the hospital on the chance she might claim we hit the child, in an attempt to extort money from us. I am appalled. You can't trust anyone here! That is how desperate everyone is. This must be what happens when a leader leads through fear, and controls people by suppressing them.

Edgy, we sit at a restaurant on the edge of the Ionian Sea. I feel myself start to relax ever so slightly, to be me again. Across the water I spy the misty island of Corfu. It had been a stressful trip, even down to our driving without car insurance. I wanted nothing more than a slice of calm and joy. My eyes are fixed on that far shore. Greece is just a short ferry ride away.

"Ricci, let's drop this trip and go to Corfu. Let's find a beach and just have some fun together and relax. Enjoy one another. There's been so much stress."

Ricci stares at me. "Barbara, you agreed to come here with me. Greece was not part of our plan. Not in the schedule." His voice is firm, his decision final.

I look again at Corfu. The mist is luring me with its siren call. I contemplate grabbing my bags and leaving Ricci. I could set out by myself, on my own.

I stop. We are married now, I remind myself, and he is right—I had agreed to join him on this trip. But, I think, glancing back to Corfu, while Greece wasn't part of the agreed plan, couldn't the plan change if we wanted it to? Is there anything wrong in being flexible?

I sip my beer, looking longingly at the distant island. Soon enough we'd be in Italy, at his family's house, in Sardegna. I was just tired of traveling. With weeping blisters on my hand and my right bicep aching from clutching the "oh, shit!" handle, this was hard traveling. We were constantly on the move. I thought of our house, back in Marin, the prospect of nestling into a comfortable home. Maybe I was growing up. Maybe it was time to let go of my dreams and settle down, become a family, with responsibility, like our parents want us to do. We'd work hard and save for the future, which is what we're supposed to do, right? We can still travel and live our dreams, right? We're lucky to have a comfortable home to go to, in one of the best places in the world to live, right?

I pull my gaze from Corfu and look at Ricci. I force a smile. "Okay. You're right."

May 2002

Have I sold my soul to the devil? Will I pay for this in my next life? After seeing starving children, mangy dogs, and desperate people who are no different to me in the Balkans, why am I privileged to sit quietly on the island cliffs of Paradiso, Sardegna, with the morning sun rising behind me?

It's beautiful here. I can feel a baby in me. Two weeks pregnant, I think. She'll be a girl. I know my body well. I dip into the cool Mediterranean water and look around at the private homes lining the seashore. We will have educated children who grow up in a beautiful world, with a strong family, one they can respect. That's where I'll pour my energy. Ricci will find his dream job, we'll pursue our dreams, and we'll be happy. One day, I'll write and teach.

We have it all figured out.

June 2002

When I get home to San Rafael, I spend days pulling together the film footage I shot during our Balkans trip. I figure out how to download and edit the film and even add some music. I have never done this before.

When it's finished, I show my little film to Ricci.

"Huh," he says. "Interesting."

I know it's pretty basic and I didn't expect a standing ovation. After all, I don't know anything about filmmaking. Days later, my edited film disappears. I am frantic.

"Ricci, my film is gone! What happened? I spent days making it!"

He looks in the files and shrugs. "The server does that sometimes. Did you back it up?"

I hadn't.

"Well, then, that's your fault, isn't it?"

"You told me to put it on the server, Ricci. Otherwise I would have had it on my desktop."

"It happens, Barbara."

I take a deep breath. Okay, I'll just have to make it again. That was my practice one, I tell myself. Things do happen. I'll be smarter next time.

August 2002

Uncle Bob died today. My mom called to tell me. I need a walk in the woods, to think about him, so I go to my favorite place, Phoenix Lake, and sit there, amid the trees. Phoenix Lake is beautiful when the light glistens on the water. I can feel him with me. I miss him already, my best friend. My smile is sad. My friend who always remembered my birthday with a card and a twenty-dollar bill.

I visited him in the hospital just yesterday. He seemed healthy enough. I brought him cut roses from our garden and he liked them. When the nurse walked in to attend to his needs, he got really upset.

"Leave me alone, goddamn it!" he shouted. "I don't need somebody treating me like a baby!"

The nurse eyed me as she walked out.

"Uncle Bob! That nurse was just trying to do her job. You be nice to her, for God's sake. Be nice!" I ordered. I was surprisingly firm with him, considering he was such an ailing man.

He looked out the window. "Yeah, Barbie, maybe you're right. Maybe you're right."

Mom gives me one of Uncle Bob's trophies. A silver plaque from the Saint Francis Yacht Club, "*Magic Bear* 1962 First Place."

"I think this should belong to you," she says.

There is something else, a black and white photograph of Uncle Bob sailing a boat across the Bay with his brother and boat designer.

I hold the photo in my hands and look at it for a long time. Uncle Bob had offered me sailing lessons once, and I had told him no, that my life was too busy. It's a regret now. I could have learned from a master. He would have taught me how to take the helm in the San Francisco Bay, the toughest place in the world to sail.

I miss my Uncle Bob.

January 2005

It's our daughter's second birthday. Ricci and I lie in bed this morning with a beautiful little girl between us. I rub my fingers through Ricci's hair.

"We are so lucky, aren't we?" I say.

Sometimes I don't think he understands how fortunate we are. I like to remind him.

At Ricci's parents' house, up north, we often spend time on the beach, harvest mussels, and make amazing meals. We go mushroom hunting in the coastal hills too. One time my mother-in-law and I discovered a whole grove of prized porcini mushrooms, each the size of a pumpkin pie. Anja was like a child, finding candy. She tells me at times what it was like growing up in Germany, after the war, surviving entire freezing winters on little more than potato-peel soup. The Russians had occupied their home after the war, forcing her family to live in the basement to survive. The soldiers stabbed the eyes of the children's portraits and butchered animals on their prized oriental rugs.

When the Iron Curtain was being drawn, they found themselves on the wrong side again. Anja's mother sent her and her two brothers out into the forest alone and told them to run west, that they'd be guided by old women in the forest, collecting wood. If children were caught by authorities, they could lie and claim they were lost. However, if adults were found running with the children, they would all be shot.

My mother often shared with me stories of the horrors of World War II and its Jewish victims, but no one ever talked about the German children. They, too, were innocent victims.

As a mother now, I could not imagine how desperate I would have to be to send my children away, out into a dark forest, alone. Anja doesn't talk much about it, though I have seen her eyes tear up when she does. I just can't imagine how strong she must be. I know she doesn't like how I am with my daughter. She never hugs Lucy and I find that strange, because I am always hugging and kissing her. But maybe I could learn something from her. My childhood was bad, but nothing compared to hers. And look how well she survived, and how she and Dante grew strong.

I see all that she and her husband have built since they married. They've got homes in Europe and several here, in California. They spend half the year in California and the other half in Europe. Anja tells me how much Dante makes her feel safe. She had to give up her career for him in Italy, as it wasn't considered proper for a man to have a wife who worked. She must love him so much, I think, to have given up her own pursuits.

Ricci and I are trying to find a balance and new direction. Ricci's business is struggling. He always seems angry with me for some reason. His dad's birthday was coming up and I said, "We should plan something for your father, for his birthday."

Ricci got quiet and then blurted, "You think too much about other people. You have to stop that."

He and his father fight a lot too. Maybe he's right. I think too much about other people. That can't be a good thing. We'll work it out. We're just in a rut.

We are falling into debt so I take a well-paying job managing household catalog work. I like working with creative people like photographers and writers. I like creating an inspirational world that you can dive into, even if it's color corrected and manipulated. I'm not excited about selling things, but you can't have it all. I'm making really good money, enough to help pay the mortgage, the *au pair,* and still save money. I think we'll drive to Baja, camp, and spend time together this Christmas, to travel like we always said we would. I hope to find time to write.

We have a German *au pair*. I totally love her. I chose a German *au pair* in honor of my mother-in-law, thinking I could help the German heritage stay alive. Ricci keeps telling me I'm not managing her well, but I'm just doing it differently than he does. Does that make it bad? He tells me if I don't manage her properly, she'll take advantage of us. I don't believe that, so I just keep doing what I'm doing.

I work long hours and it's hard finding quality family time. We've spearheaded and fostered a strong Italian community and Ricci speaks to our daughter only in Italian. I don't know why Anja doesn't speak German to Lucy. She has so much to give and I wonder why she doesn't. But never mind, she does cook amazingly well. She inspires me to keep my house organized, though I know I'll never measure up to her standards. I've never seen anyone so perfect all the time.

She gives me advice. Often. And I appreciate it. Life is good. We should feel lucky.

Even though I like my work, I'd rather be home with my daughter. I feel I'm missing out and the *au pair* is having all the fun with her at play dates and outings. Ricci doesn't like me working and tells me my job doesn't represent good values, but we need the money. He says we should move to Oregon. I don't know what to do. I can see he's not happy. I share ideas with him all the time about where to live and where to go. I've been all over the globe.

Ricci told his dad we want to sell the house and move somewhere that's more like us, simple, maybe buy land and build a place in the country. His dad got very angry.

"Look at everything we did for you, and sacrificed! I can't believe you want to sell it," his father shouted.

Ricci came home different after that conversation. I don't understand why his father doesn't trust Ricci. Shouldn't we make our own decisions? But they've done so well for themselves; maybe we're just not thinking straight. I mean, they've survived a world war and are giving us so much. We do have a nice house and live in one of the best places in the world. Everyone says so. We should be grateful.

I'm traveling a lot to the East Coast and Chicago. I get to see my little girl a few hours in the evening before she falls asleep, and I'm usually exhausted. I would rather be the quintessential stay-at-home mom, baking cookies, doing finger paints, and writing. I don't do much writing anymore. Ricci isn't happy that I am working, but he wasn't happy when I wasn't working. We were going broke. And he wasn't coming up with answers. At least we can pay the mortgage now, even if we now sleep in separate rooms. Everything will work out. I believe this. I have to believe it. We're just in a rut, I tell him.

I rock my daughter in the chair until late tonight. She's growing so fast. As the midnight hour approaches, I hear the helicopters above us. A man is scheduled to be executed in the prison down the street, at San Quentin. I hold my daughter closer to me. It can be such a cruel world and it makes it so much more real as I look at my innocent daughter and wonder what sort of world I am bringing her into. I am feeling acutely responsible for her and maybe the world, for some reason. I want her to know how beautiful life can be, from the smallest pollywogs to the great temples in Guatemala.

It's easy to let life get muddy and then find yourself stuck in it. Or to sit in a chair as poison is injected into you, until you're dead. That poison isn't just found in a needle. It can be inertia and sadness, or lost hope. I wondered how a person could inject another human being, knowing they are killing them. Why isn't that criminal?

I'm feeling like something is missing in my life, and I can't figure out what it is. Ricci and I seem so distant.

We need something.

February 2005

Ricci and I always seem to be fighting. Everything I do is wrong, he tells me—how I handle the *au pair*, the job I'm doing now. I attribute it to the fact that he's not happy about the business he's trying to build, and so he gets cranky about everything. I need to get into Ricci's head so I can figure out what to do, because what I'm doing now isn't working.

My mother-in-law agrees to meet me for lunch, to talk.

"It's been almost seven years. It's the itch," she says.

I listen. She has a strong marriage and I want to understand and learn what I can do better.

"Be strong, Barbara, be strong. Don't be sensitive." She had brought a book on astrology with her, which was decidedly out of character, but she was trying to help and I knew that.

"Pisces. It says you'll be a writer."

"That's what I want to be," I say.

"You will be."

"Maybe one day I'll write a good book of fiction, a good story. It's my dream, you know."

She gazes up at the blue sky. "I never liked fiction," she muses. "It's fake, made-up stuff. I like real stories about real people."

After lunch, I head back to the office. Maria, the editor, stops by my office to say hi.

"How'd it go with the mother-in-law?" she asks. She knows I am having marital problems. She's had her own problems over the years, and I have been confiding in her.

"Okay, I guess."

"Don't expect to get the kind of support you want from your husband's mother, Barbara."

"That's not true, Maria. She's family," I say. I hate it when people get into your business.

I travel to the East Coast the following week to print thirty million catalogs selling linens, sofas, tables, and rugs, inspiration to make a cozy home that is color manipulated and carefully laid out to inspire, and costs more than I could ever afford. I've spent days color-correcting to ensure the images convey quality and inspire people how to live a good home life.

Sometimes, when I stand in the middle of the massive press rooms with conveyer belts going this way and that, the roar of the motors hinders my ability to hear my own thoughts. These machines are pressing images and words onto millions of books that will be distributed, like Bibles, around the country. I'm in the belly of our economy, the entrails, the guts of what makes our country move and think and be. The epicenter of capitalism. What is real and what is not? I like the smell of the ink fumes. They make me feel dizzy.

April 2006

I've done it! I'm going to learn how to sail!

I have found a little nonprofit sailing organization in Sausalito that stems from the Oceanic Society. It's the cheapest deal in town. The boats aren't fancy, just a bunch of dinghies, really. But the idea makes me feel closer to Uncle Bob. I miss him. I miss that guy who always heard me and shared with me the simple things, like good conversation. He could make me laugh and feel good after we ate tuna fish sandwiches and drank highballs in the middle of the afternoon. And, he'd always remember my birthday. I really do miss him.

I could have learned from a master sailor. My Uncle Bob would have taught me how to take the helm in the toughest place to sail, as sailors say about the San Francisco Bay. He always told me, "You have to feel it."

Ricci is building up his business. He's trying. I see that.

August 2006

First, I stepped onto the dinghy. It rocked under me and I felt unstable, even scared. I held the tiller in my hands and when the wind came, the boat spun around and the boom nearly knocked everyone out. I apologized to everyone. Then I did it again. And another time too. Then I got tangled in the lines.

Then there was the day I tacked too soon and got stuck in irons. The boat's keel got wrapped around an anchor line of an old derelict boat in Richardson Bay. Nesting seagulls squawked frantically, screaming at us, mad. I was convinced someone was living on the boat and would start shooting at us. I'm not sure how I got us untangled and sailed away, free, with our lives. But I did.

Then there was the day when the bowline of the main sail came free and I only had the jib to sail by. I made it back to the dock okay.

Then came a day when I sat on the high side, with the tiller in hand. We were heeling hard and splash was flying. "Get ready to tack!" I shouted.

"Ready!" the crew cried.

"Tacking!"

The little dinghy crossed the wind and I set a new course, without getting stuck in irons. I was beginning to feel it.

Later that summer I got a call from Gary, one of the volunteer instructors.

"Barbara, will you help us teach a class? There's no money involved."

"Me?" And so I started to assist and show others how to take the helm of a little dinghy.

I like the idea behind this organization. It doesn't have anything to do with money. It's about people coming together and making things happen for one another. I like that spirit.

John Paul is one of the members. He's in his late sixties and he owns and lives on a thirty-four-foot Tartan called *Summer Solstice*. He has an English accent and a white beard. He's not exactly Ahab, although he shares that monomaniacal passion for sailing, and he has a swashbuckling anarchist flair too. I like him. I like him a lot.

There's also Wayne, who pretty much lives on the docks and wears the same pants every day. He teaches students every weekend. By the end of the summer, some might mistake him for a salty, raggedy, homeless guy, except he's got a smile and spark in his eye, and he knows how to say "Oh, yeah," a telltale phrase that means he knows where the good life can be found.

And there's Leah. She had to take the beginning sail class twice because she was so scared, and now she's out there, like Wayne, teaching others every weekend. People come together just to make it happen for each other. It's a nice way to be. We all put in and we all get to be free, sailing the dinghies around Richardson Bay.

I ask Ricci to join me. Maybe he'd like sailing too, I think. And before I know it, he's not just taking classes and teaching but off sailing in the ocean! It makes me happy to see him happy. It's like we're dancing, even if we're not doing it together.

November 11, 2007

I've just had a baby boy! He's beautiful. Labor was hard. I very nearly lost my uterus after Lucy was born, so they took special care with me, and it's a miracle he was born. I had a doula with me for support. She lit candles, chanted, and knitted a hat during my labor. I'm sure the nurses in the labor room thought we were witches. I found such joy in it!

My wedding ring had to be cut off before delivery. The doctor was worried about the circulation in my fingers. Never mind. It's just a symbol, right?

My baby boy is perfect. I nurse him straight away. Lucy comes to visit. I feel like a family now. His name is Kyle, but I like to call him Ocean.

Ricci says his business is getting better and predicts that I can quit working at the household catalog company and become the quintessential mom, baking chocolate cookies without rushing, and create a nurturing home. Perfect!

September 2008

Nearly a year, nay? How the days ebb and flow. I'm but a jellyfish pulsating along with the current, following it listlessly. A big blob, without thought, nothing more than tentacles touching what drifts near me, hoping it's some yummy morsel that will see me through another day.

What can I say? I was on a sailboat feeling the wind, and with that fresh hope we were moving along. Not close hauled, but perhaps on a reach. Beam or broad.

I don't know about the tides tomorrow, next week, or the year after. Right now this ebb is filled with inertia. Where's the humanity? I'm calling for it. Ah, but I forgot. I lost my mouth too.

My daughter has started kindergarten. And each time I go to the classroom I look at all the information they're intent on pushing on her. It doesn't feel right to me. I know it sounds crazy, but I feel I can do it better. I hear about a homeschooling community. I see how free and happy the children are. They are learning too.

Lucy has only been in school for one month, but she's changed already. She's no longer that calm inquisitive child I knew her to be. There's a nervousness about her. She comes home and bursts out crying, acting out unlike she ever has before. I've become the taxi driver, getting her from here to there, packing and unpacking lunches. I'm losing my daughter. I can feel it. Is this what school and life are about? I question it all. More importantly, Ricci isn't happy. But when did we ever ask for this kind of lifestyle?

I thought we wanted to be free and live unconventionally.

What happened?

January 2009

He packed the car and took the kids. A night of camping, he said. But as I stood in the driveway, barefoot, waving goodbye, I knew it was much more than that. His eyes did not meet mine. Instead, they stared at the road ahead, the road away from me. A practice run?

I sit alone, and feel quiet resolve. The black crows circling above break an internal silence I've carried for so long now.

We had started talking about living on a boat and voyaging. There are other families around the globe who cruise like that. It'd be a grand adventure together, living simply and enjoying life. Now I find myself wondering whether he has already started without me, and he cannot hear my calls.

I don't know what he wants.

The redwoods have stood the test of time. I envy their deep roots. Mine just can't seem to get past the surface of this place I've tried to call home. My home has been one where I'm not heard and everything

I do is wrong. I've cast a blind eye to it all so I can curl into bed and watch a mountain stand tall outside my window, where Uncle Bob scattered his wife's ashes. How he loved her.

My only place of comfort is inside my head, where stories play out, one by one. I try to jot them down as more than mediocre and disconnected thoughts. In between, I feel moments of warmth, breathing softly and knowing he or she is my flesh and blood. Motherhood should not be like this. And, yet, it is so utterly complicated. What am I to do?

Be strong, Barbara. Don't be so sensitive. That was Anja's advice. I try to remember her words.

I'll go sailing soon. That is where I feel free.

May 2009

We've reconnected!

We're going to sail around the world. I contemplate the ebbs and flows of life.

I pull Lucy from school for three weeks. We drive three thousand miles across the country to Florida to look at boats, to find our cruising boat, a home we can create, in order to sail and follow our dreams, to live simply. Boats are cheaper there than in California.

We sleep in the car at truck stops, all jumbled up at times, to save money. We look like a bottle of specimens. Bare feet on the front window. Knees scrape against windows. A foot in my face. Some nights we stay in cheap hotels and eat cold cereal in Styrofoam bowls, using plastic spoons and cups. I'm not sure which to feel worse about, the bad food we're eating as part of our free breakfast deal, or the piles of garbage bags I spot, filled with those Styrofoam bowls and plastic spoons, as we drive away from the hotel. It is a cheap price and I begin to see the cost of being cheap. My stomach gurgles each time.

When we arrive in Pensacola, Florida, we find a beach of white sugar that tickles our toes. That's how Lucy describes it. We jump into the roaring surf. We feel free! Until a terrific storm, with thunder and lightning, makes us run like ants back to the car.

We look at boat after boat, at dock after dock. We meet with people who have had adventures sailing the seas, while our adventure consists of being eaten alive by every bug that crawls and flies in Florida. It's a conspiracy.

We visit Tarpon Springs, and marvel at Greek seamen hauling in sponges. Sea sponges. Piles—heaps and mounds of them that grow on the ocean floor. A sponge to wash your body costs six, seven, or eight dollars, depending on the size. I find myself wondering at the real cost to our oceans.

We don't find a boat. We'll keep looking. We still have our dreams.

June 2009

"It's the French style," he says to me, as he kisses me on each cheek.

"Italian too," I remind him, as my husband seals the deal with kisses from the Frenchman's wife.

We have a boat! *Fayaway*, a Ranger 23. A small boat for the San Francisco Bay. She'll be our practice boat for the big one with our new French boat partners.

I can't ignore the guitar music of the African American woman who sits by our cafe table as we sign the paperwork over a cup of afternoon coffee. She sings about women's power.

Fayaway was the name of a Polynesian native in Herman Melville's first book, *Typee*. She didn't know sex was viewed as original sin, according to the story.

She is powerful. I like sailing her, holding the throbbing tiller in my hand, as if she is teaching me something more than how to fly with the wind.

I read Melville's book and get mad. How have Christian missionaries gotten away with going to new lands, conquering native cultures, and painting them as barbaric? Surely, this is a crime. Melville believed Europeans should have left the native cultures in peace, and that the islands would have been better off left undiscovered. I believe he's right. But I confess I like discovering *Fayaway*. She's the perfect-sized boat to explore the San Francisco Bay.

September 2009

My daughter's assigned first grade desk sits empty, and I feel a lump in my throat, because instead of driving her to our local public school, one noted for its academic achievements, "California Distinguished," and containing her kindergarten friends from last year, we decide to take an alternative route. We went fishing that day and got hooked—by a creative group of homeschoolers. Our homeschooling journey has begun as we dive into a world filled with boundless local independent schooling choices, as I'm now discovering, all while we prepare for our voyage around the world.

This homeschooling community of parents is tired of a system that puts so much pressure on our children. And the children are learning beautifully! Lucy will do an all-day nature class with eight other girls. She'll get dirty, rain or shine, and even run barefoot through the mountains. It was one of my most joyful moments, picking her up from her little school that a mom put together by finding a willing teacher and seven other rebel families. Lucy and the girls came running down the hill, laughing and singing, with sticks in their hands and feathers in their hair! They looked like a group of hippies and Lucy exuberantly shared with me all the wonders they discovered, including banana slugs, bay leaves, and blackberries. I reflected on her kindergarten days, cooped up in a classroom for hours, with noise and so much stimulation stapled to the walls, like drilling in information, images of ways to be. Now, her imagination is free to wander and it's coming from the inside out, and not from outside in. These kids already have so much richness. They know how to ask questions and be curious, when they are allowed to do so.

We're not slave to a hardcore schedule, dragging ourselves out of bed at the command of annoying alarm bells, rushing through breakfast, racing to school with her little pack in fear of facing the school clerk and creating tardy excuses about traffic issues or how we're guilty for having lingered too long. It's so freeing and feels so right. I'm connecting to so many sources, teachers who share their passion of rich literature, living history, and the arts. I also have more time where I can sit quietly with my daughter and talk about silly things and serious matters. I feel like I'm living life.

Ricci has gotten involved in beekeeping, which has been great as we all embrace learning. We're cultivating honey, making candles, soap, and balms. Homeschooling is changing the way we live our lives from one of rushing and doing to one of creating and nurturing. It brings you back to life.

The End

I make a road trip with the kids. Ricci has been voyaging up the coast with a mentor, to get practice. The kids and I visit the caverns of Shasta. I didn't even know there were caverns in Shasta and I've lived in California all my life. Then, in Oregon, we sit in front of a volcano, Mount St. Helens, and marvel at its power, imagining what it must be like inside, during an eruption—the power and exhilaration that earth can create. We sleep in a tent, the three of us, and listen, giggling, all the next morning to the birds.

We arrive in Port Townsend, Washington, to greet Ricci at the ferry, and we are all so excited to see him and hear about his adventure sailing up the coast. I knew he'd love sailing. He puts arms around me and we are off, ready to go camping together as a family. But the next day, dark clouds descend, as a torrent of irreversible words spill, things he can never take back, such as how I have no ability to do anything except be a mother, which in his opinion, is a base occupation. I can't understand where it all comes from.

He says he has passion for sailing and intends to pursue that, even if it means he can't support us. I don't know how to respond. Maybe he is just in a bad mood? I let it go. Of course he must be in a bad mood. I can't imagine how tired you become when sailing on the ocean, right? And he's found passion. That's the very thing I've been hoping for.

But I convince myself that it's getting better.

Ricci has lots of stories to share about what it is like out on the ocean. And we're practicing with homeschooling, so we are prepared.

We're finally getting out of our rut. See?

We have found a magical wonderland! The Port Townsend Wooden Boat Show. Children sing songs, like "What Do You Do with a Drunken Sailor?" at the top of their lungs and all the sea salts descend for merriment and work. There is a large room filled with wood and saws, nails and hammers, and over fifty people all working on their one-foot-long boats. Tall masts, schooners, swoops, and more. It is boat-building frenzy, complete with bruised fingers and egos. We left with sufficient wooden fodder to inspire us to take to the seas, even if we start our dreaming in a bathtub.

March 2010

"I aim to give their soul back to them," the sailing instructor explains to us about his downtown students, the ones who leave behind the "what people tell you to do" modern world and strip down into the "what you must do to survive" world of the ancient sea.

We meet him during a stopover in Alameda, as he heads south with a crew of new students who will either turn green riding the ocean's swells or risk injury with newly stretched grins.

We sit chatting with him on his pristine "glass" (fiberglass) boat, securely fastened to a dock, on the edge of a big city. In our minds we, too, drift to this lullaby blueness he so beautifully describes: killer whales breaching, surging fifteen-foot swells, and no schedules except to listen to and feel what Mother Nature presents.

Ricci and I have just come from viewing a lien sale in a nearby harbor. We still seek our dream boat, our 37-foot home for the next two years. A lien sale, a sale for abandoned boats, is, we discover, another world—nearly an underwater world. How some of the boats avoid sinking is either a miracle or just a matter of days. Shipwrecked vessels manage a more noble demise than the sad, broken-down, forgotten beauties, as one in particular had been. She was a *Tayana*, a boat we have had in mind. With their teak detailing, slim lines, slow but steady, the boats are highly reputable. We had hoped to find a deal. Instead, we found a tired lady, one severely abused. Whoever had been living in her had swilled more beer than a factory could produce. Rubbish filled her cabin like a beer drinker's swollen gut. Her mast was rotted, and her teak detailing sagged like crepey pale skin.

"I'll take her," a man had volunteered, gold chains rattling about his neck. "I'll strip her and chop her up." He smiled a toothless grin.

I cringed.

A dark-skinned woman with a partly shaved head, a ponytail popping out of the top, scanned the boat and gave the hull a gentle kick. Her frumpy figure and crow eyes revealed an older age than what the rebellious purple hairstyle might suggest. Her words surprised me.

"Who ever lived here had pain," she mused. "I'm sorry for him."

We viewed other abused boats, and they, too, were filled with similar amounts of refuse: rusted bicycle and machine parts, rotted cardboard boxes spilling over with the moldy remnants of clothing, blankets, and sleeping bags. The stench was unbearable in places.

I wondered why people would live in such a pack-rat way, hoarding unnecessary objects, like clinging to a retired vacant purpose. Though on some level I could understand. I had since become eager to clear out all the unnecessary clutter that had quietly, like a slow leak, seeped into my life—faux fragrant candles, dusty corporate attire, friendships worthy of only meaningless chitchat, muddled static voices selling me one thing or another, none of which I needed. I was struggling to sort out the meaningful, worthwhile pieces.

"My name is Soul," the dark-skinned woman said to me. She took me by surprise again. "You can see me dancing on YouTube."

I had my two-year-old son in a stroller. She bent down until she was face to face with him and lifted her back leg like a skater flying across ice. "I can dance on the water. The Coast Guard leaves me alone because they just think I'm crazy, but I really want to show people how fun life can be."

That night I watched the video. She stood in a bare wooden skiff, small motor rumbling, as it made repeated wide circles against the backdrop of city buildings. She moved, contorting her torso, with stiff limbs, struggling for grace, gripping a cigarette between fingers. Then, with a unique combination of surfer movements, tai chi, and a bit of Egyptian belly dancing, she bounced along her own wake with large curved lips and a laugh louder than her two-stroke engine.

I felt my soul twitch with envy. At that moment, I knew that Ricci and I needed to find the right boat as soon as possible, so we could leave the ties of our earthly life and enter the big vast blue. We needed this. We needed our dreams.

At least, I knew I did.

April 2010

It's a Green Gulch Zen Meditation Center work party in Mill Valley. Children run barefoot through a garden of lavender, apple trees, and grasses. The gong rings. I relish the quiet. We've been arguing a lot again, over things that don't matter. I put spoons upside down in the dishwasher. I use too many cups. I should use the appliances more efficiently. I should stack shoes in the hall better.

I don't understand.

I've got two small kids and it's enough to make sure they get what they need with food and diaper-changing. Ricci's still building his business. Maybe he's just cranky. I needed the Zen garden, some quiet time. He wouldn't come.

I sit on the cool earth, harvesting purslane, a succulent leafy green. A Brazilian man, Sidão Tennucchi, works the same gardening bed as me. He likes to talk. And I like to listen. He speaks about his love affairs, his heartbreak, his life. He has such passion for women and love. I wonder about love, and what it is, because I am beginning to forget what it means. Or is it passion I miss?

We have still not found our boat and our life is becoming more mundane. Other than the various sailing trips on the Bay, we weren't moving forward.

Kyle falls asleep in a wheelbarrow. Lucy and her friend Sara find the remains of a dead deer and squeal with its discovery. Before we leave, Sidão introduces us all to his two friends, also Brazilian. I am chasing Kyle at this point, so I can't chitchat. One Brazilian in particular stands out. He looks like a pirate with his bandanna and earring. He doesn't say much but I feel him watching everything. He is older, maybe in his fifties or so. There is something about him that I find disconcerting, uncomfortable. In fact, he scares me.

I go to take a picture of the girls, Lucy in her little cowboy hat and Sara with her lovey, her favorite stuffed animal. As I snap the photo, this pirate-like man steps into the picture, between the girls, like a ghost, a spirit, and smiles at the camera.

Later, I look at the picture. There was something about it that feels strange to me, like it is trying to tell me something I need to know. Who is this pirate who disturbs me so?

May 2010

I am excited to get back to the sailing organization in Sausalito. Now that Kyle is a bit older, I can return to teaching sailing classes. I missed the community. We still haven't found a cruising boat, but we are still looking.

After my first weekend back on the water, sailing the dinghies and feeling exhilarated, sweat and salt in my hair, Wayne approaches me. He

The End

looks dejected, which is unusual for him. He is always out there getting people excited about the little boats that carry so much joy for us all.

"There is no director. The organization has no money. It's in the red. Nobody wants to put in the work."

What?

The news shocks me. I stand on the docks alongside him, looking at the small boats jostle with the choppy water as they knock rhythmically against the dock.

"Maybe I can help," I hear myself say. I like bringing people together. I can't imagine this little organization failing. I love sailing and it has introduced me to a whole new community of people I enjoy. It helps me to feel connected to Uncle Bob, whom I still miss.

I talk to Ricci about it, knowing he has found a connection there too. There is an upcoming board meeting in San Francisco, so Ricci and I bring the kids.

On the drive, I tell Ricci about the concerns for the organization. I tell him I think I can take on the organization part-time. There'd be a little money for us, I said, and I was confident I could do it. He listened, without saying anything.

We arrive at the Fort Mason office, a dusty old forgotten room with stacks of sailing books, an old typewriter, and sailing files from the 1990s. The existing board of directors and a few others who care about the organization have only bad news to share, about sinking boats, rising debt, and the mounds of paperwork that need to be done. It sounds virtually hopeless. To find a responsible director who will take all this on for $15 an hour, with no benefits, and deal with cranky, passionate, and opinionated sailors and more, is a lot to ask these days, especially since smart people are making the bigger bucks in San Francisco as tech businesses grow. People have money but they don't have time, and our organization needs people with time and spirit. There was a kids camp too, in San Rafael, that required overseeing.

I don't know much about it, but it sounds like something I wouldn't mind helping out with. I open my mouth to speak, but Ricci speaks first.

"I'll take on the director's role."

I look at him, startled. Then I tell myself that perhaps this will be good for him. For us. He's finding passion. I hear it in his voice. We could manage the organization together, I think.

"If you want to take it on," the board members say, "it's all yours. There's no money."

"I can help," I offer.

Ricci smiles. "Barbara, you've got two small kids to watch. You can't take on the organization. That's impossible."

I hesitate. He's right, I say to myself. There is no money to be made, and running around with two small children is a lot for me to handle already.

He is smiling, and that makes me glad. We'll make it happen together, like dance partners. To build up a nonprofit sailing community and lure people who want to sail and are willing to sacrifice time and commit to scrubbing decks, organizing supply cabinets, and stitching up sails takes great energy, time and passion. It can feed you in ways that money can't.

To run a volunteer nonprofit sailing organization takes guts and balls of steel, as we would come to know, maybe more than Sir Francis Drake, Magellan, or Columbus had. At least they got regal ships, blessings from royalty with ambition for gold. We had broken dinghies, no money, no support, and no false hopes of getting rich. We just want to survive the rest of the season. And once we do that, we will still have our dream to sail the world.

July 2010

"Ricci, if we are going to sail together, I need ocean experience, and this is a great opportunity."

John Paul and Kenichi, another SEA member, are planning to take *Summer Solstice* voyaging to the Channel Islands and have invited me to join them. Ricci has voyaged up and down the coast, but I haven't yet. I need to get out onto the ocean, for experience.

The summer season had started for the sailing organization and Ricci was just beginning to pull it together.

"Ricci, it's just a week or two of sailing. You can watch the kids. I'll get others to help you. I need to do this," I insist. "If we plan to go cruising around the world, I need ocean experience."

He isn't happy about it, but he doesn't say no. I prepare meals for him and the kids, line up friends to help him every day, and pack my bag with gloves, harness, warm clothes, foulies, head lamps, and my journal. He drives me to the San Francisco docks. I can see he's mad. I lean over to kiss him goodbye and he pulls away.

Baffled and irritated, I say, "I don't get it. I've supported your voyages." He looks straight ahead, his expression stony.

In contrast, aboard *Summer Solstice*, the energy is good. John Paul has taken charge and his English accent conjures up images of good old-fashioned adventure, pirates and hidden treasure, as I mentally prepare myself for the ocean where whales breach and albatross fly. There's nothing to be gained by thinking about sinking, crashing into a container ship, or falling off the boat in the middle of the night. Be positive, I remind myself with a grin. Always be positive.

I am quiet while we prep the boat, still grappling with why Ricci refused to support me on this voyage. I had supplied him with apple pies and sincere "bon voyage" kisses when he'd left. I couldn't figure it out.

We head out, sailing under the Golden Gate Bridge and into the undulating big blue of the Pacific Ocean. It is blowing a good thirty knots northerly, our sails are raised, and I am viciously barfing over the stern.

Of course.

"Don't mind me," I say to JP and Kenichi in as upbeat a tone as I can manage, my stomach heaving. I am determined not to take medicine. I would will myself to overcome the sickness.

Normally the wind is southerly this time of year, with a wind that should be at our back, making for a nice, easy ride downwind, but that hasn't happened. Instead, we have to "beat" into the wind for hours and the waves are strong. I take the helm as one wave after another crashes into the bow, drenching me like someone heaving buckets of salt water into my face. I am pleased to discover I am not afraid.

"Bring it on," I splutter, wiping my eyes. The nice lady on the radio keeps repeating her recorded weather report about an easy ten-knot breeze off the coast. She's lying. I barf again and have a few choice words for her, and her false report.

We aren't making headway. After hours of battling, we are exhausted. We haven't even rounded Pedro Point, which isn't far into our journey at all. We eventually give up and return to the docks, wet and tired.

The next day we have a hearty breakfast and voyage out again, fresh and determined. This time, I don't barf.

There's magic sailing down the coast, feeling removed from all the noise of life, recognizing how meaningless most of it is—chatter, bills, appointments, media, waiting for permission to proceed at intersections when there are no other cars.

Here you feel free, knowing you are negotiating only with nature, that higher spirit, one you must respect, listen to, and watch. I imagine all the past voyagers who looked at these same contours of our coast and heard the faraway whispers of waves crashing on sand. I think of them meeting the natives, listening to their drums, and sitting by late-night fires, under the stars. We have a marine layer, so all is gray for us. My hair is becoming saltier and my soul thickens, the more I listen to the murmurings of forgotten voices of past mariners and natives. They still echo out there, I think, if you listen.

Night comes, and with it my first solo night watch. John Paul and Kenichi go below for some shuteye, and I stand alone, in pure blackness, penetrating darkness, fifty miles offshore. I can't see anything except for what I call illuminating eyeballs. A boring scientist might correct me by calling it bioluminescence, these lights bobbing around the side of the boat. I prefer eyeballs. Somehow it makes me feel less alone as I try to muster confidence, trusting there are no lampposts to crash into.

A lamppost?

Well, then, maybe a whale.

As I sink into the dark rhythm, faraway voices emerge, like distant voices on a playground. Who can explain voices at sea? A strange combination of wind and water? I listen. I swear they are there, just out of sight, as I feel the heartbeat of the water. Why is it so easy to reminisce on the fantastic here, reminded that we are but flotsam on a mysterious tide, riding on a huge ball moving through outer space?

We arrive in Morro Bay four days later. New, thick knots wrap and tangle my hair, and I lick my chapped lips with joy as we arrived at port. My first step on land is like stepping onto a boat. There are new rules to abide by, whether you want them or not.

I am greeted by a litany of phone messages. Ricci shouts, insists I come home. He is doing too much.

I feel guilty. I'm a mother. Sadly, I find a bus and say, "Bon voyage," to my mates as they continue on to the Channel Islands.

"You okay?" Kenichi asks.

I shake my head. "I don't know. I don't know."

Ricci has found passion. Even if it doesn't bring in money, I see a spark in his eyes. I drive him to the docks.

"Go sailing, honey," I urge him. "Forget work. Find your passion!" He is heading off to conduct a private dinghy class to a couple from out of town.

"Believe me, one day you're going to be happy about this," he says.

I drive away hoping he is right, praying he is right. I have our two kids in the back. I have them to care for. Maybe Ricci had been right. Running an organization with two small kids would be too much for me. Already I feel I am losing spirit. My hair is becoming more ragged, along with my clothes. When I was sailing, I didn't care. But while I am stuck in traffic, driving home, and look at my growing wrinkles in the rearview mirror, I do care that my life seems to be passing me by.

We still don't have our boat, our finances are tanking, with Ricci running the nonprofit that pays so little as our house in the fancy neighborhood begins to rot. It's getting harder to keep up. We have taken a loan on the house, so at least we won't starve. The kids are being homeschooled in a dynamic community that's showing me a powerful way to educate and challenge the mainstream way of doing things. Life is education. They are not sitting in classrooms getting stuffed with information to regurgitate. They are alive, being in nature, learning about science, rich literature, and art. Lucy spends only seven hours on academics a week, and I see her filled with such spirit, laughter, and love for life. This gives me a lift, and I'm holding on tightly to it.

August 2010

Ricci, the kids, and I sail out to China Camp in San Pablo Bay to celebrate the annual heritage festival. It used to be a Chinese shrimping village until the early 1900s, when the shrimp disappeared. (Is that any surprise when you consider the vast numbers that are harvested?)

A century ago, runoff silt from the California Gold Rush era washed down the Sierra Nevada mountains, tumbled through the delta and piled into San Pablo Bay, creating shallow muddy waters. A deep shipping channel is dredged for commercial ships that load and unload at the nearby sugar factory. Add mercury to the mix, which they used during the mining days, and you have pretty much a disaster in the San Pablo Bay. In addition, there's a rock quarry just north of us, where you can hear occasional blasts that make you shudder, and an enormous oil refinery across the bay, with vast twisting pipes and towers, along with a wall akin to those ringing medieval castles. To the east sits the remains of the last whaling station in the United States. Big leviathans were hauled from the ocean right up until 1972 and chopped into dog food.

People talk about San Francisco Bay, not San Pablo Bay, separating two peninsulas with the likes of a rib, the San Rafael/Richmond Bridge.

People like to go where the good is, not the ugly. You don't see many people sailing in San Pablo Bay, except for the salty wooden-boat characters who join us here for the festival. I think of these things as I rock on *Fayaway*. The water feels ill to me, like it's telling me in words it's been abused, discarded, and forgotten. Then I see something beautiful, like a hawk flying by with a fish in its talons and I'm uplifted. Later, we find a buoy covered with slimy green algae, living shells with eyeballs poking out, a tiny crab that fits in my daughter's hands, and other life that reminds me of my childhood days playing in the runoff ditch and finding my treasured pollywogs.

I hear Chinese dragon dancers and beating drums on the beach. Other historic boats are anchored here, along with the impressive Chinese junk *Grace Quan,* and, from the Maritime Museum, the *Alma*, which used to carry potatoes, eggs, and other cargo down the Petaluma River. At night the sailors emerge from the water, like crabs, to land on the shore, and old sea salts from a hundred years ago pull out mandolins and spin yarns. Last night, looking at the stars, I felt we were a million miles from home, when in fact we are merely ten miles as the crow flies. This is practice for the big voyage, I think.

The next morning a bearded man comes by in a motor boat. "Ahoy!" he cries out. His name is Captain Richard Gillette and he is aboard *Pegasus*, a beautiful wooden 51-foot Alden. He invites us for coffee.

The End

There were other sailors onboard too, sun-kissed, sleeves rolled up, feet bare. The small chitchat was warming, just like the coffee. Everyone shared something they had: fruit, muffins, or milk and cereal.

Captain Gillette takes inner city youth sailing on *Pegasus* and he invites us to crew for him some time. I like the idea.

We sail back to Sausalito under a gorgeous sun and wind. Ricci is at the helm. The kids sleep down below, and I am sure we are crossing heaven, becoming a good sailing family.

October 2010

Pegasus definitely has magic. A long bow sprit. Pure white. I've never crewed before on a big boat and this 51-foot Alden is a sophisticated lady. I'm terrified, like a new crewmember wet behind the ears, headed to the South Seas. But I listen and I follow. A rush of information is delivered to me—emergency procedures, flares, life jackets, radio, foulies, stowage, hand signals, knots, lazarette, fender positions, man overboard instructions, mizzen, how to manage the youth coming for the day.

Then we hear those youth as they approach. They're loud. I hustle into position with a warm smile, ready to welcome them to a day of adventure. My smile falters when I am greeted by anger and attitude.

The youth are mostly African American and Latinos, all exuding an air of mean toughness and trotting past, donning cool looks as they enter an unfamiliar place, the docks in Berkeley, California.

I had been given the instructions to ensure PFDs, personal flotation devices, are secured on each child.

"What are these, bulletproof vests?" one demands. He refuses to put it on. "It'll mess my style." He is about fourteen, and would scare the shit out me if I found myself having to pass him on a dark street, alone.

A girl gets sassy about her hair.

I convey my concerns to Captain Gillette.

"Some of these kids have never seen the Bay," even if they live close by, Captain Gillette says. This will be their first voyage on the San Francisco Bay.

The kids still won't put on the PFDs. Some are laughing and not listening. Captain Richard Gillette takes his position on the boat.

"You!" He points to the meanest of the bunch. "You see this dock, and this boat? If your head gets between them, it'll pop open like a cantaloupe. Ever see the guts of a cantaloupe? It's messy. I am the captain of this boat and you will listen to me. Understood?"

The kids got really quiet. Still, you can't remove the twinkle in this captain's eyes no matter what words spew from his mouth.

They don their PFDs and get loaded, top side, all tethered in. I am reminded of stories of the slave trade. I can understand their fear, as some begin to show it, an association that I would never consider in relation to myself. Possible? A young girl, maybe thirteen, one of the shyer, quieter ones, sits next to me, close to the aft. She's wearing multicolored barrettes in her hair, above a round face with eyes wide, gripping tightly.

"It's going to be okay," I say to her.

"I'm scared," she whispers.

Soon we're out and the tough kids no longer look so tough. There's a growing nervousness, bad jokes are passed around, and hands clench lifelines. Sails are raised, and we fall off, catching the 15-knot wind that fills the main nicely. The boat heels, and shrieks of fear and laughter also give rise. Spray hits us and a cormorant stretches his neck and glides by after a seal pup pops his head out, starboard.

Little by little, I see wonder, as these hardened kids of the modern world melt back into joyful children. I see laughing faces, and they talk about what they see and how they've never seen such things before. A teacher leads them in song. "What do you do with a drunken sailor? What do you do with a drunken sailor?" and they open their mouths, fully releasing voices at the top of their lungs with a rhythm that pulsates with the boat. Another youth, maybe sixteen, takes the helm at Captain Gillette's invitation and I see his eyes light up, like a fire in his spirit. He takes us close haul, past Alcatraz, with the Golden Gate Bridge in sight.

"Give them real responsibility and they rise to it," says Captain Gillette. "They just need someone to believe in them."

I think how amazing it is, how a voyage can heal when, for centuries, voyages would kill not only life but something even worse—spirit. Once that's killed, it can take years, decades, even centuries to restore.

I think back to my own teenage years and how much anger I harbored for the world. I was a good kid but I, too, carried anger and attitude. It protected me from the mean world, didn't it? I came from a bad family and so I lived into it. I saw things I didn't like. I wonder whether it's their story too.

Then I get this crazy idea. I wonder if it's the bad kids, the ones acting up, rebelling, who are actually the good kids. They are pissed off at a system that feels bad, but they can define it when they're told to learn it. They see the untruths, the meanness around them, but they are told what to do, and to just do as they're told. There are many untruths around us, giving value and prestige to people with money when they use it to build castles, like kings, telling those without money that they live in poverty, without, that they are the "bad" ones. What is poverty, anyway? If you have a roof over your head, food on the table, and a community of good people, isn't that enough? You make yourself happy. It doesn't take money to be happy.

I'm happy sitting on a boat, with a little food, salt in my hair, feeling free. This is happiness. Pure happiness.

The girl with the barrettes looks at me. "Really? We have to go back already?"

I think she had been feeling free too.

I sign up to skipper in the Sausalito's Women's Skipper Regatta. I had skippered the year before with our boat partner Beatrice, from France. We had received a standing ovation when we crossed the finish line. I also won the largest trophy. Nobody needs to know that we were so dead last the committee boat nearly gave up hope that we'd ever cross the finish line. But we did, and they clapped joyously because they could finally get back to the yacht club for a well-deserved drink.

I had the only all-female crew, so I got the trophy, even if my one French crew hardly spoke a word of English and we had no clue about racing. We just followed everyone else, before getting stuck at the end, when the wind died. Receiving that trophy was an act of courage—I did not feel I deserved a trophy at all. But I remind myself that nobody needs to know such secrets. My large trophy gets polished and sits behind glass at the Sausalito Yacht Club and nobody needs to know, right?

Right.

They spelled the name of the boat wrong.

I want to redeem myself. My cousin Donny and second cousin Stacey agree to crew for me. I didn't even know them before I started sailing. They used to sail with Great-Uncle Bob and Uncle Don. They carried the secrets, I believed. The family secrets. They'd show me things I didn't know, even if they don't sail much anymore.

Donny recently sold his Ranger 23 boat to Arianne Paul, Uncle Bob's dear old friend, who is like blood. She is sailing blood, which might be deeper than family blood. It can get sticky. I am connecting to a family heritage I didn't even know I had, and it is a heritage I can be proud of.

Donny, Stacey and I board *Fayaway*, and I start the engine. I'm nervous, but I can do it, I keep chanting. I am meant to do this, aren't I? I am going to win a race, a big fat trophy from the Sausalito Yacht Club, the right way. I know Uncle Bob is with me. I can feel it.

We raise sails and head down the Sausalito Channel to the start line, out in the Bay and close to Sausalito Yacht Club. I am at the helm, feeling the wind, feeling powerful, with the tiller in my hand.

"Uncle Bob, this one is for you!" I shout, in pure Hollywood style. He is listening.

"Stacey, would you mind pulling in the line over there?" I ask.

"Is that enough?"

"Uh, maybe just a little bit more."

Moments later, I ask, "Don, what do you think I should do?"

"What do you want to do?"

"I don't know. Do you think we should raise sails now, or wait?"

It goes on like this. Who am I to skipper when they know so much more than I? But we are all fumbling and I begin to doubt their crew ability.

We start talking a little about Great-Uncle Bob and Uncle Don.

"Barbara, you shouldn't romanticize the way Uncle Bob and Uncle Don sailed," Stacey says. "All they did was yell at one another."

"What?"

Donny chimes in. "Oh God, it was hell sailing with them. They forced me on that boat when I was a kid and still they'd find a way to blame me if we lost a race. I was just kid."

"Really?"

We tack a few times. Then we raise the sails.

"Stacey, could you pull that line in just a little bit tighter, please?" I ask. I don't want to sound pushy.

"I think I was no more than sixteen when they forced me into the cabin mid-race to stitch up the ripped sail. I wanted to puke but they wouldn't listen to me. God, it was horrible."

The lineup for the race starts. Women are at the helms and they have fire in their eyes. I am smiling. I have Uncle Bob on my side and they don't know it.

We tack, we jibe, we start working together better. The gun fires and we're off, on our first upwind leg, looking good.

See?

"Um, Donny, what do you think? Should we go that way? I think the current is stronger over there." There is a moment of silence. He's looking.

"But then again, the wind looks stronger over there, so maybe if we go that way, it'd be better, don't you think?"

That's when he launches.

"Goddamn it, Barbara! Who's the skipper! You are! Shout those orders and stop being so goddamn polite, would you?"

I am stunned into silence.

"Pick a goddamn point," he adds, "and just do it!"

Fine. I think. I am now totally pissed off.

The wind picks up and we start to fly.

"Fine!" I shout. "You got it. Pull that line a little faster next time, will you? I'm tired of being polite, if you must know. You guys are both moving so goddamn slowly. What kind of crew is on this boat anyway, for God's sake?" I am screaming now.

"Well, what the hell are we out here for if we're not going to sail and win that goddamn trophy! What do you think we're doing? Going for a day sail?" Don retorts.

We are heeling pretty well and I am finding the groove. Arianne Paul is ahead of us. She is no longer sailing family. She's the enemy, and you don't let the enemy beat you because then they'll have the laurels at the yacht and hold it over your head until your dying day. Even worse, their picture will be on the wall and yours won't. It's a horrid state of being. Even worse, they might get written up in *Latitude 38* and you won't. I am finally getting the big picture.

"Fine! I don't care about your opinion. Get ready to tack!" I shout. I am now angry. I will disown Stacey and Donny after this race. They're not family. They are distant cousins and that doesn't count. Why did I ever want them on my boat? *My* boat.

We round the mark and Don has to climb onto the deck to fly the pole for the jib. He starts complaining about his bones.

"I don't want to hear any complaints. Just get it up!"

"I'm a goddamn seventy-year-old man! I'm going as fast as I can!"

"Well, it's not fast enough."

"Well, then next time choose your crew better. I'm what you got, so stop complaining."

There we are, suddenly, neck and neck with three other boats, rounding another mark. I have the inside lead. We are like mustangs, just feet away from one another, feeling each other, the energy of the wind and water driving us. We enter that slow-motion dream, feeling every hint of wind and using it. Feeling and using every bit of current and wake. Not looking at the other helmsman, but still looking at them, feeling their moves so you can calculate and defend yours.

Tick, tock, tick, tock. It's like that.

I have the helm and I'm not afraid. The moment comes and you whisper commands to your crew, so others outside your boat won't hear your secrets. On cue, you tack hard and fast. *GO!*

We round the mark. As the inside boat around the mark we have every advantage. We could win the race. Then, just like that, it all comes untied.

Just like that.

A line comes undone. We lose the wind and our sails begin to flutter and die. The other boats, including Arianne's fly past us. She waves to us. The horrible smile. The one you want to give the finger to. That adrenaline bubble bursts and we give one another looks of dismay.

What just happened?

The confidence disappears.

"Not my fault," says Donny.

Stacey looks guilty, but it's not her fault either.

"Okay, let's get moving. We're here to have fun and not to lay blame." I try to lift their spirits as well as my own, because there is no fun in being on a boat where everyone is blaming the other.

"Speak for yourself. I'm not here to have fun. I'm here to win a race," Donny said.

Is this my family?

Donny looks at me, "Always remember. If you win a race, the crew gets the credit. If you lose, it's the skipper's fault."

"So now it's all my fault?"

"You said it. Not me."

We don't win a trophy. But after a drink or two we manage to laugh about it all. We even take a picture with Arianne Paul, just to show sailing blood is thicker than winning a trophy. It's a little trophy anyway. Why would we want it? I had skippered my first race without crashing into a boat. I met a family I didn't even know I had.

Still, I can't deny this feeling that I am being led to something. I can feel it in my gut. Maybe there is a bigger trophy out there, waiting for me. One day I'll win a race. One day.

December 2010

We sit in the garage, all twenty-five of us. Instead of holiday Christmas noise, we create a spiral of evergreens, with a candle in the center. It is quiet and still. Reverent, some might say. One by one, the children walk the spiral with a candle, illuminating it, and walk out of the spiral, placing their burning candle on the ground until the entire spiral glows.

So simple. So beautiful. This is a winter solstice with the homeschoolers. It's all I need for a holiday season, I decide.

Homeschooling has opened the world to us. Teachers teach in small groups and the children have so much time to wonder and dream. One parent has converted her garage into a classroom. We share resources, use the library, and explore. My daughter has memorized "Jabberwocky," by Lewis Carroll, and the children sing this at the top of their lungs in the backseat of the car, and it makes me smile.

We're raising silkworms and discovering mulberry trees in the park, connecting that to silk stories and history of China and fashion. We're making candles with beeswax and raising honeybees. We'll harvest the honey and watch the action of the crazy bees as we laugh and lick the honey.

I've converted my dining room into a classroom, and we find people with their own passions to share with the children. For some weeks I invited all the old ladies from the neighborhood to join us for a knitting group. It wasn't about the knitting, I discovered; it was learning about their life stories. One lady had lived in Germany during World War II and her parents sent her to London for safety, until the bombs began to drop. Then she was shuffled to a lady who lived out in the countryside, where she learned to knit socks for soldiers. I listen to their stories and they become so real. They're not the manufactured, politically correct stories you find in school textbooks.

I also have calm in my life, as a community of mothers come together to create a rich education for our children. Why are children stuck in classrooms?

Ricci and I continue to spend a great deal of time on *Fayaway* and on the docks with the kids. They look at the jellyfish and nap in the bow.

Ricci is working hard to get the sailing organization ready for next year. He's been sailing in the ocean, and even singlehandedly to the Farallon Islands. I am so proud of him. It's like we're dancing, I tell myself yet again, even if we're not always partnering together.

2011–2012

April 2011

It was decided. I would skipper in the Corinthian Yacht Club Race. We were always racing with others, but this time we needed to do it together, Ricci and I.

"I'm the skipper this time," I remind him. He agrees.

We are running late.

"Ricci, we need to get to the docks and prep the boat."

"We have plenty of time, Barbara. Everything is ready on the boat. We can raise sails on our way to the start line. It'll take time to get there. You'll be fine. Don't worry."

Well, I was worrying, and he wasn't hurrying. I am wrong, yet again, it seems. We get to the docks to *Fayaway*. She is such a beauty, all twenty-three feet of her.

We are off!

I amp up the outboard engine, wanting to get to the race early, take note of the currents, who was racing, and feel ready for the start of the race.

"You're ready, Barbara. Don't worry about anything."

I look at my watch and am stunned.

"Ricci, the first gun just went off! We're running behind!"

The timing had started and here we are, still raising sails on *Fayaway*, far from the start line. The main sail had been reefed and is now twisted and stuck. We are still in Richardson's Bay, in Sausalito, and need to go against a strong current to Raccoon Straight, in front of Angel Island, otherwise all our efforts will have been for nothing. Finally, Ricci gets the sail up and I crank the engine.

We are racing to reach the race.

I hold the throbbing tiller. I am the skipper, I remind myself, and him. I see the boats. They are like raging mustangs, tacking and jibing, positioning in front of an imaginary line. We have to cut into them.

They are bigger than us. A lot of bigger. And we are on a port tack, which means we have to watch out for them. One boat is coming at us, the stand-on vessel, which means we are the give-way vessel. In other words, we have to get out of their way.

"Ricci, I'm going to jibe around." I wait for Ricci to say "Ready!"

He doesn't. He doesn't even look up.

"Ricci? Are you listening to me?"

The End

He is doing something with a line.

"Ricci!" I shout. He doesn't react. He isn't listening to me.

"Starboard!" the other boat shouts. They are about to crack us in half, all sixty feet of them.

Ricci looks up, whirls around, and yanks the tiller from my hand.

"Barbara! You need to jibe!" he barks.

What? Is this a comedy act?

"That's what I just said!"

We do jibe, just in the nick of time and miss getting crunched by a hair-raising twelve inches. The skipper of the other boat raises his fist in the air at me. That single act has just ended any fun I might have had at the yacht club after-party. I wouldn't dare show my face to him now, after what had just happened.

We are starboard now and the race is about to begin. There is nothing more exhilarating than being part of the lineup of a sailing race. The sheer energy of guts and will, along with wind and current, makes you more alive than anything.

"Ricci, we need to tack. Now. *Now!*" Ricci is looking elsewhere. Again, he isn't listening to me.

"Barbara, you need to tack."

"Ricci, you aren't listening to me! That's what I just said!"

"Go, Barbara! We're losing time!"

I pull myself together and get into the upwind groove. Water is churning. There are so many boats.

"Barbara, you need to get upwind more."

He tries to wrest the tiller from me.

I don't want to listen to him anymore, but I do. He scrambles around and pulls lines together. And we settle into a long tack the best we can. This is my first race as skipper for a sail around the entire San Francisco Bay with the big dogs. I don't need a trophy. I just want to complete the race, and I tell him that.

"Barbara, you can do better than that," Maybe he is right.

He hangs the radio in the companionway, where it dangles. Not a good idea, I think.

"Ricci, I prefer the radio somewhere else. Can you put it in the sink, or keep it on your body?"

"It's not safe there, Barbara."

I take a deep breath. I am tired of arguing. We sail in silence. He keeps a watchful eye out and I tack when I think it is time. He didn't think it was time.

"Wake!" I shouted. A small wave is coming toward us, from a passing boat. Ricci, down below, is just coming back up when the radio whacks him in the head and knocks him down.

"Goddamn it!" He yanks it off the line and throws it down. His head is bleeding.

The race is over for me. A part of me wants desperately to laugh off the whole day, but another part of me doesn't want to laugh.

"We're going home," I announce. "I'm done with this race."

This makes him angrier, but I am not listening anymore.

When we arrive at the docks we are both silent, not speaking to one another. Leah, from our sailing organization, is there, her normal cheerful self. She looks at me and cocks an eyebrow.

"That good, huh?"

She doesn't bother to ask how we placed.

One day I would single-hand a race, I decide. By myself.

Homeschooling is going amazingly well. It's funny how people ask us the silliest questions, like whether are our kids are getting socialized. Of course they are! Others ask if we are worried about them learning the right things. Of course, they're learning! The bigger question to ask is what they're learning.

Lucy knows more botanicals than most adults, never mind kids her age. Birds too. She loves them. She spends hours drawing and reading. We attend cultural heritage events, insect fairs, do old-fashioned rug braiding, and she transformed into Ariel in a Shakespearean performance.

As a family, we raise silkworms and read about Chinese history and culture. We discover lifecycles and the beauty of delicate eggs after the worms become moths, have sex, lay eggs, and die. We even discovered a whole grove of mulberry trees by a children's park. At dusk, we sneak over and pick leaves, afraid of getting caught. Who else would know these were mulberry trees, with a full history related to white worms with a visible heartbeat, silk robes, and a Chinese empress named Hsi-Ling-Chi of the year 2640?

We begin to see a web of nature around us as it relates to our history, our stories. I'm waking up to it just as fast as Lucy is learning it. It's an education for me as well, recognizing how we are connected and how our forgotten stories are no longer shared.

Lucy brings home some soap root.

"What is that?" I ask.

She tells me how the Miwoks used this root for washing, and its toxins to stun fish in order to catch them. She uses the fiber to make little brushes, and carries it around like a treasure. It is a treasure. The nature in our mountains not only tell stories but also weave a full narrative about our history, our medicines, our habits, and their beauty. They are our living museums.

We start attending hikes with a nature leader named David Herlocker. He works with the Marin County Open Space District and teaches us that hiking has nothing to do with reaching the top of the mountain. The magic happens when you stop along the way and look around you. And so we stop all the time to discover little trap-door spiders living in the earth, cicadas, and a Jerusalem beetle that died because of a horseworm parasite. The connection between the lives of the creatures, the tiniest ones, and the world becomes bigger. I think of my pollywogs.

This is education, though it's more than that. It's learning about a world most adults don't even know exists, or care about. It's rediscovering our sense of wonder and awe. These mountains are a living museum of history, science, and wonder. I see how the children thrive and the adults marvel. I see the world with new eyes.

May 2011

"Sheet in!"

I hear the command amid the loudly clapping sails, rushing wind, and clambering of sailors on deck.

Captain Richard Gillette has invited me to crew with *Pegasus* for the Master Mariners Regatta, a historic race with schooners and scows since 1867 that plied the San Francisco Bay. Right-of-way encounters and individual duels were usually settled by bare knuckles, the throwing of coal, or with buckets of sea water, so the stories say.

The countless wooden boats chop the water into a fuzzy white soup as the wind howls through the San Francisco Gate. We are ready to round the upwind mark near the St. Francis Yacht Club. As we heel, the water washes over the deck.

"Ready to tack," Captain Gillette shouts.

I know what that means. I am preparing the mizzen line, the big thick rope in my hands, like a snake trying to get away, when I look up to witness an incredible sight. Mere feet away are other heritage wooden boats, some 20-footers, others as much as 72 feet, with full sails flying, filled with salty, bearded faces, stout women, all manic, doing the same thing.

Skippers shout orders, crews pull lines while others duck under booms as the wind gusts and sails swing from one side to the other. Helmsmen nobly hold tillers as spray flies across their bodies, and they take it all without wincing. I feel like I have entered a dream, a distant memory, a sight that has been part of the San Francisco Bay history for over a hundred years.

And here we are, in front of the St. Francis Yacht Club, the place where *Magic* had been in 1962. Magic got me here, I think, and feel a tingle down my back. This is my heritage. It's stunningly beautiful.

The wind in the sail captures you, the discord of shifting sails from port to starboard creates sublime peace, with air filling and pulling you to a perfect course. Balanced by wind and water, aligned with all the elements around you, it's like a symphony of music, song, voices, and more, and you are part of the energy, a part of it all.

"Keep sheeting in!"

I have my hand on the winch handle, working hard and rotating it with all my strength, feeling the tendons in my back and shoulders grind, grunting, together with all onboard.

When I look up, I see a sailboat, an old wooden one, with tall white sails, moving by us. It catches me by surprise, and I hesitate, feeling something inside me move.

"I think that's my uncle's boat," I say out loud, to anyone who might be listening.

Skylark. Did he have a boat by that name? Wait, wasn't that the name of my grandfather's airplane? The facts muddle in my head, and I slip into a timelessness, a dream, the task before me becoming obscured and unimportant. Or was it a ghost, a spirit of something powerful trying to lure me to somewhere I couldn't see?

"Barbara, keep sheeting in!" somebody yells.

I snap out of my reverie to see all eyes on me. The crew and captain are counting on me, I realize. I start cranking again, determined to disregard what I saw and felt. We've lost time because of me and I see some disappointed glares. I haven't stuck to my part of the deal, sheeting in. Did I get lost in a daydream? What moved me so? The guilt, letting everyone down, was profound, and I felt that too.

After the race we voyage down the Oakland estuary to Alameda, where Uncle Bob had lived, and not far from where he had kept his boats. The last time I had sailed this stretch was with him, ten years before, not long before he died, following my first sail out into the Bay. I remembered sitting next to him when he offered me the tiller.

"Here you take it," he urged.

"No, no, I can't." I remember the fear.

"Sure you can." And he moved over to let me sit at the helm and handed me the tiller. "I'm here to catch you."

I sat at the helm. It felt awkward in my hands. I worried the boat would capsize. Why did I think that?

"You have to feel it, the wind and the current," he said, as he adjusted the tiller in my hand. "You'll feel the groove. But you have to feel it."

"No, I can't do it." I was nervous, scared. Another sailboat was approaching and I had visions of losing complete control. Crashing and dying.

"Here you take it, Uncle. That's enough for me," I said. I leaned back, feeling the salt air and gentle undulations of the bay water. It felt safe with him at the helm. I felt safe, like he was watching out for me.

Pegasus arrived at the docks in Alameda, at a yacht club for the end-of-race celebration. We had a rough go at docking. A young man on the dock took our bow line and was trying to control the big heavy wooden boat, an impossible task. He wasn't listening to Captain Richard Gillette's command.

"I've got it," the young man insisted.

The captain raised his voice and issued a direct command unlike anything I'd heard.

"I am in charge of this vessel. I am the captain of this boat. You need to do what I tell you. Do you understand me?" he barked. He was responsible. He took the responsibility highly. I admired him for that.

I get off the boat and walk into a historic wonderland. This is a true celebration of local heritage, not only of old wooden boat history and stories but of people too, those who carry the spirit of the ocean and live by it, not dressed in character to act but truly revealing themselves and their love for the water. Old salts with rough faces and hands walked the talk.

Those who have sailed oceans, sometimes singlehandedly, mill around like honored guests visiting landlubbers. I can tell they'd rather be in the midst of 30-knot winds, sea spray flying, than look put together in the modern safe world. This is where you demonstrate your guts and honor, by rips in your pants, sunburn on your face, and salt-encrusted hair. Anything less proves you are just trying to look pretty, a sign of pettiness and lack of courage. I walk the docks looking for *Magic*, my great-uncle's old boat, the one that had been in the photo my mom gave me, along with his trophy. But the boat isn't there. I have no idea if she even exists anymore.

The award ceremonies are not pompous. They, too, seem real, recycling last year's leftover trophies because this year someone forgot to order them. They had probably been out sailing, so all was forgiven. A good laugh about it was more valued than a shiny cast metal piece from a factory.

Dungareed men and children with matted sea salt hair dance together with a spirit of being outside of any modern realm. These folks carried Jack London, Henry Melville, Jonathan Swift, and Richard Henry Dana in their hearts, eyes, and words, understanding that it takes a good philosophy of life, passion, friends, a simple fiddle, drinks, and shared food to feel alive, while they ignore egos and money, elements of that underworld some call the modern one.

This is my heritage.

My heritage.

One I never knew about. Nobody had told me. This is where I come from. My grandfather. My great-uncles. My heritage.

I walk around, watching, listening, feeling. It is the most beautiful sight to me and I am connected to it. My family is connected to it.

I call Ricci. I want him to be there with me. I want my kids to see their heritage and admire the beauty of the wind passing through the banners, listening to the music of the halyards play a tune that's been alive since wooden boats have sailed the seas.

"Ricci, are you coming? Bring the kids. I want them to see this."

"Sorry, Barb, I can't."

"I thought you said you would." I am surprised and a bit let down. Why didn't he want to come share this special time with me? I was discovering a side of my family that I could actually be proud of. I had never known of it. I wanted my children to know of it.

"Yeah, I'm sorry. I'm busy."

"Busy with what?"

"I said I can't."

"Okay. Can you come pick me up after?" It was a long way home by public transportation, a mere thirty-minute drive by car versus a four-hour trek in the dark of night by trains and buses.

"Nope. Can't do that. You can take the bus, or find someone to bring you back to Marin."

I would have done it for him. Why couldn't he come to me?

We hang up. It's already getting late. I ask around for a ride back to Marin. Most of the sailors are going to sleep there, on their boats. Finally, I find someone to take me to BART in Oakland, which would take me to San Francisco. I can't help but watch the wind blow garbage, paper bags, around the dark empty streets as I wait alone on a dark corner for the last bus in San Francisco to take me back to home to Marin. I feel very alone.

But I also feel salt in my hair. And I like it.

July 2011

The sailing season is in full swing. It's not easy running a nonprofit with so little money and such humble boats. People like to go where it's attractive, impressive, where they can talk about fancy boats and yacht club bars. We've got small stinky boats and a wooden dock. The marina here in Sausalito doesn't like us either. They're going upscale, and although we're honest and nice, we're salty, so they've put our little operation on the outskirts of the marina, and told us we're not allowed to hang up any signage. The new board of directors is not entirely supportive of Ricci's work, but he's building a community, I'm teaching classes and writing about our great sails. And people are joining us. They come, one by one, but they do come.

I take note of the people who sign up for lessons. More often than not, they're getting a divorce, or looking for something in their life to hold on to. I love teaching those who have no confidence, only to later see them shouting orders and reveling in feeling free. I'm determined that we're going to make this organization into something powerful, even if it's not fancy.

Ricci and I still talk about sailing around the world, but right now we just have to get through a sailing season. I see the fire in Ricci's eyes. And we're doing it with our kids. They come to the docks and hang with us in the boat. It's like voyaging and dancing, isn't it?

I was teaching a dinghy class in Richardson Bay the other day, when I met a ghost. A small wooden boat approached and I noticed an image of a bear at the top of its big, billowing white sail. Curious, I sailed toward it and got close enough to ask those aboard, "Hey, is that a Bear boat you're sailing?" I had recently learned about these boats that were originally crafted in Sausalito by two Portuguese brothers during the early 1930s. I had been thinking about Uncle Bob.

"Yes, it is."

"You wouldn't happen to know anything about a boat named *Magic*, would you?"

"That's us. We're *Magic*."

I lost control of my boat. It spun around and the boom nearly lopped off the heads of my students. I was stunned.

"You're *Magic*? That's my great-uncle's boat!"

"Who was your uncle?"

"Robert Keleher."

"Robert Keleher! He was the best racer ever! That's your uncle?"

"Yes!"

I felt like I was looking at my uncle in the cockpit, sitting there at the helm, smiling. A shiver went down my spine.

We promised we would connect again, in the future, and they invited me to go sailing with them. Imagine!

October 2011

We did it. We got through the season. Not only that but we have a full board of directors, even though they aren't the most savory of sorts, and they still have a growing mindset to change us to a fancy-pants racing organization. They do not understand the meaning of community, nonprofit, give-back, except for the likes of John Paul and a few others. But the organization hasn't closed, we have dock space and classes, and there exists a spirit to make things happen.

Now—big drum roll, please—it's time for our annual board meeting, and a room full of sailors have come to participate and support all our efforts and the success of getting through a season against all odds. Our boats have gotten fixed, we are out of the red, we have new members, and, most of all, we have plans for the next year.

Members like Helena have volunteered weeks of teaching and brought food and drinks to share. Wayne have been taking photos and videos. Kenichi, John Paul, and others are out the docks every weekend doing what needs to be done. Frank and Cathy have offered a hand. Ricci, along with another board member, secured a new donated trawler to act as our clubhouse. We have had so many great events throughout the year, including a dinghy race to the Presidio Yacht Club near the Golden Gate Bridge (where a big boat with a helicopter on top nearly ran me over, causing me to lose the race. Okay, fine, I was losing anyway, but they made me look worse when I nearly capsized in their wake.) We don't need a stinking yacht club. We aren't exactly the prettiest bunch of sailors, but we have salt, vigor, and guts.

Our board meeting is about to start. I stand in the shadows. After all, I'm not the director, just the director's wife. And I stood for Ricci. I can see what this means to him. We have invested a tremendous amount of our own money, are verging on debt ourselves, and I want to see him fly.

The president stands up and faces the eager, sun-kissed faces of sailors.

"Hi folks, thanks for coming tonight. This is great. But I want you to know the organization is broke. We've got no money."

Wait, what?

The president was sabotaging the organization! I watch those eager, delighted faces diminish into sadness, anger, and despair. He went over the numbers, and, yes, according to the numbers, we were broke. Chris, another member of the organization, starts to speak. He advocates changing the organization to a racing organization, and on, and on, and on. Interest piques but the spirit has been deflated. I am stunned. We had pulled ourselves out of debt, fixed boats, grew membership, developed new programs and we were still sailing! Couldn't they have spoken to that?

Ricci steps forward. He is not tight with the board, and he has struggled with them all year. Ricci knows he can't talk. Bad blood has been building. But Ricci has brought someone else in to talk and share a message. It is one of those guys from the other side, one of the fancy yacht clubs that has been helping Ricci to teach classes.

"You guys have no idea what you're trying to do. You have a treasure. There are racing groups, competitive groups out there now, leagues ahead of where you are. It's there and it's done. You have to cultivate what and who you are. You have history, nonprofit history with a community. Thirty years of it. That is where you should be sailing from. Stop trying to be like others and find yourself."

I watch Ricci and feel so proud of him. He has stuck it to them. My husband. He believed this and he was watching out for the little guy. That was who I have been standing by. This is who I love.

But despite the good intentions, the organization has begun to nosedive. Once you break spirit, it's tough to get it back, especially the second time around.

In the trawler, a number of us sit together late one night pondering what we could do. Our spirit is gone too. We are surrendering.

Carrie says, "Hey, look, we've got five hundred dollars in the bank account. Let's just have a rip-roaring party and retire. We can find other things in our lives besides running a sad little sailing organization that nobody wants that's on the edge of the boondocks, right?"

I keep asking myself why I am so tied to this organization. Why does it mean so much to me? My uncle, I thought—that's why. Even if he's dead, his memory keeps me going. My heritage. The one person in my family I feel connected to. The one I could sit at a table with a tuna fish sandwich and a highball and talk life, love, and politics.

I wanted to give this sailing heritage to my children. I want them to feel free, like I feel when I'm sailing. What's given Ricci a sparkle in his eyes.

What should we do? The sailing season is over. We'll have to get through the winter season and start again, next year.

September 2011

I drive through the city streets now and watch people. After this season of running a little, stinky-boat nonprofit sailing organization, I see people differently. I see our entire country differently.

I think about the few people trying to build this little organization. It's about sailing—or is it? People come in order to feel free, to feel the wind in their hair as they ply around the waters of the Bay, to feel connected and experience awe, to feel alive. Most are looking to take charge in their life, search for community, or maybe find that certain something we all want in our lives, but just can't grab it.

Here's a cheap organization that doesn't require money, or at least much money, but what it does require is for people to bring their own spirit to create the organization. But people don't want to do that. They want to go where the good already is, they want to come and take, and be happy with a deal, feeling proud of that. But to get real value, you have to give of yourself to it—it's a democracy of sorts. If everyone comes and merely takes without giving, the organization falls apart and nobody has a boat to sail. Nobody gets to feel that freedom.

I watch how Ricci and others, like John Paul, Frank Lawler, Leah, Wayne, and more, put so much of their hearts and souls into the organization, and how much others gain from their selfless contribution. But then those who benefit aren't giving back. I see how easy it is to complain about the organization, complain about the way other people do things, without taking it to the next step and offering to help, to do something themselves. It's easy to complain. But it's difficult to give, to "do." Those who do stick their necks out and do something have to watch their necks, and don't receive the respect they should. Why don't we respect those who stick their necks out for the rest of us?

I drive through the city streets and watch people. This is how our country runs these days, I think. People come and take. I walk through the department stores and see why. Discounts, freebies, sales—we are trained to think this way, how to get the most for the least, to reward ourselves with a deal without considering why we should get that deal. It's everywhere, this message: how to get away with the most we can.

The irony? We are not getting away with it. We are not free. We are enslaved by a system where we spend all our time and effort trying to get something for nothing. Our consumer learning is silently teaching us all the wrong values and habits.

I think about this. A lot.

March 2012

As the days pass, Dante, my father-in-law, becomes more and more ill. So many doctors, worries, and more. The costs and the care Anja puts into him is substantial, staggering. I tell Ricci we should spend more time with them. He's their only son. It's the right thing to do.

I don't see my family much, but then again, I don't want to. When I see my parents, I only remember the pain of all those past years after dad was fired, and how they couldn't hold it together. How my father chose his priority, and how I suffered for it during my childhood.

Dante has a doctor's appointment and I drive him to San Francisco, where we will meet up with Ricci and Anja. We cross the Golden Gate Bridge and look at the sailboats. A flotilla is headed out to the ocean.

"Aren't they pretty?" I say. I can tell he has something on his mind. "Ricci is really pulling the organization together, you know. It's great, watching him sail. It's given him something. I see it in his spirit."

Dante turns to me. "You know, Barbara, you're doing a great thing for Ricci."

I know what he's referring to. Dante sees it. Ricci is doing something that makes him happy, the happiest I have ever seen him. It shows. Even if Ricci isn't around much, leaving me with the kids most the time, it is so good to see that sparkle in his eyes and hear him talking big for a little nonprofit sailing organization. And, yet, it was not without its worries.

"Unfortunately, we're going to go broke, Dante. We don't make any money doing this."

He looks back to the boats headed out to the ocean as he contemplates my words.

"Life has a strange way of working out," he says. "Keep going for your dreams."

I look at him in surprise. These are unexpected words from a sophisticated engineer who has accomplished so much with his life, learning English at a late age, immigrating to the United States, and building an impressive level of financial stability for his family. Ricci has often said he feels like he's failed his father by not being a doctor, a lawyer, or an accountant, society's tags for success. Yet, clearly, his dad just wants his son to be happy.

So do I.

We sit in comfortable silence for the rest of the ride, me wondering for the first time what regrets Dante might have, what he might feel he has missed in his own life, now that he is reaching the end of his. He has always made me feel comfortable. Such a kind man. He has our best interests at heart. I believe that.

But I am also tired. We are going broke and this little sailing organization is sucking us dry. Our garage has become the storage spot for the entire organization, complete with derelict boats, sailing books, sails, lines, boxes, and more. It is taking over our lives. I am tired.

"Ricci, we can't go on like this. Let's move."

But he isn't listening to me.

April 2012

The donut. It's round. Circular. The circle of life. Sweet. Some warn we should stay away from donuts. They are too rich with fat and sugar. I never did like to listen to people.

I want a donut.

There is a bakery in San Anselmo and the place lures me. Maybe because it has been forgotten by those other than the forgotten old folks who talked about the forgotten days, and chipper kids stopping by after school for cheap donuts. My grandfather liked donut shops. We'd get a box of them when I was a kid, a Saturday morning treat, and I'd lick the chocolate off the bottom of the pink cardboard box. I could sit quietly in a donut shop and recall those lingering childhood memories.

I look around. The bakery has its own cobwebs, much like our home, spun in every corner. The walls are decorated with faded Christmas-wrapped packages even though Easter has just passed. Dated linoleum is peeling. None of this bothers me. Forgotten places can be the keepers of our stories, if you take the time to stop and listen.

I come with my kids to sit at the "I Spy" table, a box with scratched Plexiglas and dusty diminutive horses, cars and sailboats. A game. That's when I spy a familiar face.

"Hey, I know you." I say, loudly. The pirate stands upright, guilty-looking, like I had found him out.

"Green Gulch," I prompt. "The Zen Mediation Center, a year ago. You're friends with Sidão Tennucchi, right?"

He relaxes and nods.

It is José Neto, the Brazilian guy in my photo, the one with the bandanna and dangling earring, the one who had disturbed me for some unknown reason. His behavior strikes me as odd, and I wonder whether he is a bank robber or some other kind of criminal.

He is seated with an older guy who reminds me of my grandfather. Maybe it's his parole officer, I think. The two of them made no sense—a rebel-looking pirate and straight-laced grandpa, each eating a blueberry muffin and drinking cheap coffee. Instead of feeling disturbed, I was now intrigued.

The kids and I sit next to them and we chat casually about Sidão and his poetry, his passion. I asked José if he is also a poet. He isn't.

"I play the guitar."

Coincidence? As it happened, I have been looking for someone to teach guitar to Lucy, my daughter. We had found someone, but he was more interested in showing off his playing than teaching someone else. A good mentor is hard to find.

"Do you play around here?"

He hesitates. Maybe it is shyness. Or maybe he isn't that good.

"I play for Steve Winwood."

There's this thing that usually happens when associations with big names are revealed. The dynamics alter. A chasm builds. A wall. Takers reveal themselves. But I wasn't interested in Steve Winwood, my thoughts flitting back momentarily to my days at the record shop, stacking and sorting his albums. Yes, I'm curious, but my curiosity lies in why a guitarist for Steve Winwood would sit in a forgotten bakery and act shy about his work.

Neto gives me his email address and suggests maybe he can give Lucy lessons after he finishes touring, later in the year.

May 2012

I've started teaching. That was never the plan, but life has its share of surprises. I'm teaching a little nature program at Phoenix Lake with a group of girls. A homeschooling mother asked me to do this after seeing I was more interested in playing with the kids than talking to the mothers when we gathered our children together. And I do love playing with the children. And, of course, I love nature!

I had been getting dirty and wet moving stones to build damns in the little creek with the kids, marveling at all the multicolored rocks and digging into the sand. I found some bay nuts and showed the children how to make dolls with acorn caps and leaves. We created tiny villages in the hollows of bay trees. I discovered some miner's lettuce and we nibbled on it, while the mothers voiced concern about the possible danger and poison oak. I knew better.

The mother even wants to pay me! I told her I feel guilty about taking payment for something I enjoy doing so much, that I feel I should pay them to enjoy their kids. I get paid to play! Oh, I love life.

My little group meets in the woods each week for hours at a time. The entire forest is our classroom, filled with science, literature, and music. I'm on a discovery and I'm learning as fast as the children. Last week we sat on stones and for thirty minutes observed an ant manage a large crumb as it walked across a stone, found a pinpoint hole and wiggled in, butt-first, before disappearing. How fun was that!

The children make ink from oak galls by smashing them and adding hot water and iron, a chemistry project to demonstrate how humans have made ink since the Middle Ages, right up until the early twentieth century. We then read the Declaration of Independence and I ask them to figure out the connection between it and the ink project we'd done. The answer? The authors signed the Declaration of Independence with oak gall ink. Imagine! Then I teach them about the life inside an oak gall and its significance to our natural wonderland and our American history.

This is just the beginning. Why are children in classrooms when you can play and discover life and meaning around us instead of inside, subjected to stale textbooks and follow-up tests, with checkboxes and grades? The hills are filled with forgotten stories and significance! This is how our schools should be run, I think. I'm having as much fun as the kids. Now, we need to find some pollywogs and get dirty!

I hold these classes outdoors, rain or shine, and I feel like a kid again.

July 2012

Ricci has been working hard every day in the garage, cleaning and rebuilding a derelict sailboat covered in algae and dead tube worms, which were caked on the bottom, like concrete. It's been a labor of love, a passion for him, so I don't want to stop him. It feeds him in ways that other things can't. I see that and I want to take that stand with him.

I am reminded of my grandfather with his airplanes, and how he'd spend days in his garage building airplanes he would later fly. I understood passion, like your body, soul, and mind stretching for the dream. (Though my father's dream about getting his job back was just plain delusional. There is a point where you have to be real.)

Neighbors walk by our house and see the disarray on our driveway and turn up their noses. I'm having a hard time facing our neighbors. They just don't understand.

The sailing organization is barely surviving. The one youth sailing program needs reshaping, but the adult program in Sausalito is officially dead. There is no more energy. People are gone now, they've moved on, and now it's up to the youth to keep us going. I'm helping Ricci full tilt, dragging our kids back and forth with me, cleaning the yacht club bathroom, washing leftover stinky clothes for the Goodwill donation bin while we hold weekly Friday award events, with barbecues, which means schlepping groceries, cleanup, and squeezing more and more leftovers into our bulging fridge. The only thing that keeps me going is seeing the smiles on the children as they sail their small boats across the Bay.

"You give them real responsibility, and they'll rise to it," I recall Captain Richard Gillette saying.

We're going deeper into debt each month. But, I remind myself, Ricci's got passion and that makes me happy, even if our garage is overrun with boat parts, old decaying sails, life jackets, buckets, and assorted junk. Our house, the one his parents gave us, is falling apart due to neglect and lack of money. Rot and mold festers.

I found a mushroom growing behind the toilet. White carpets have dark spots and trails. Every week I remove cobwebs from corners. Yard plants are dead. Used boat parts line the garage racks and the side of the house.

But our dreams are still intact, right? We'll get through this. I want to believe this. I have to believe this. But I'm overrun too. I'm feeling weathered, and I'm looking more and more weathered. Worry keeps me up at night and it's taking its toll. My stomach aches and churns. It's going to be okay, I keep telling myself.

Ricci finishes the boat and it looks really good. He wants to take it camping with us down south, to Morro Bay, so we trailer it the five hours south, rig it, and spent about twenty minutes sailing it in the harbor. Without a safety boat in such a tiny boat with no engine and two children, I am too nervous to go far. He keeps telling me I worry too much, and that I need to relax. Maybe he's right.

We end up cutting our trip short and bring the boat back closer to home, to Tomales Bay. I know he really wants to share it, to sail together. After all, we had big plans to voyage down the coast, around the world, and be the cruising family. However, I have to start facing the fact that this dream has been reduced to keeping a nonprofit sailing organization afloat while it sucks us dry, and we need to be happy with a dingy little sail.

But that's okay, right?

We arrive at the boat launch of Tomales Bay. Conditions are a bit rough—lots of wind and chop. There are some white caps on the bay and the water is ocean cold, because the bay leads straight to the

Pacific Ocean. I knew we would have just twenty minutes in these waters before hyperthermia sets in. It's important to be aware of the danger and know what to do.

We arrive at the north end of the bay and observe the conditions.

"Ricci, the wind is too strong. We don't know these waters. It's a small boat."

"Oh, you wankers!" Ricci exclaims, upset and frustrated. He had worked so hard on this boat and we had driven an hour with it, in hopes of a short sail. But it was not safe.

"Ricci, we don't have a chase boat if we get into trouble."

"You're always thinking the worst, Barbara."

Am I?

I feel guilt-stricken. Maybe I am. I look at the water again, and then at my children. It doesn't feel safe. My daughter shakes her head. She's scared too.

"We're not wankers, Ricci. It's not safe." He gets mad.

We drive further south, along the bay, and arrive at another boat launch where Ricci insists the wind isn't quite as strong.

"Look at that. We could sail straight across the bay to that beach. It's not far."

"Okay," I say, still apprehensive. I have my radio and intend to keep it on my body.

We get the boat ready. The kids are in wetsuits, and we launch the boat without a problem. Ricci is right. I should listen to him more, and not myself. It isn't bad once we raise the sails. Across the bay we go. No, we fly! He smiles from the helm.

"See?"

He is right. It is blissful. The children laugh as our little boat flies across the bay. We feel free, young. A little family crossing the bay, all of us smiling, Ricci too. We arrive on a sunny beach, which we have all to ourselves. For two hours we enjoy each other, laughing, building sand castles, and feeling delightfully removed from the world, something we have wanted to do all these years. And in this moment we've done it, no more than thirty miles from home, as the crow flies.

I think of what my Uncle Bob said to me, when I was leaving for China.

"Barbie, why go all the way there when you have everything here?" I smile. He was right.

We eat lunch, me in my sarong, and I think about those faraway Polynesian Islands we'd dreamed of sailing to, because I feel as if we have reached them, if not by latitude certainly in spirit. I watch Ricci tweak the boat he has worked so hard on. He is a beautiful man, and I am grateful.

I didn't want to leave that beach in those moments, really I didn't. Finally, we had found paradise and a place to enjoy one another and our two children. Finally, we were out of our rut and on track as a happy family.

But the time inevitably comes. We need to head back to the modern world.

"Shove off," Ricci tells me, "and when the water is deeper, I'll put in the rudder."

It is a reasonable enough request, but it makes me nervous. I'm always nervous, I chide myself. I need to trust.

We raise sails and begin to move, but Ricci is struggling to get the rudder into the aft groove.

"Barbara, slow the boat down. I can't line up the bolts." The wind picks up and catches the sails before I can react.

"Ricci, I can't slow it down." We're heading fast to the open water, with no way to steer.

"Barbara, slow the boat!" But I can't. Ricci keeps trying and failing to position the rudder. A wave washes over us and the rush of water fills the boat, nearly capsizing us.

"Lucy, bail as fast as you can!" I hand her a Tupperware container. Ricci was still leaning over the back, trying to secure the rudder. I try steering the boat with the jibs, using the weight of our bodies. The wind is getting stronger. Water is everywhere. Kyle is white-knuckled, holding on tight. Lucy bails frantically, but she's doing it windward, so all the water she empties comes right back at me. "The other side, sweetie! Bail on the other side!"

The boat flips abruptly, without warning, and we suddenly find ourselves plunged into the frigid water. Our possessions float away with the strong current. I pull the frightened kids close to me, next to the boat.

"Are you okay? All okay?" I ask. I double-check their life jackets and then check to see if I still have the radio. It's still here, on me. "Ricci, I'm hailing for help."

"Goddamn it, Barbara, that's ridiculous!" he yells, as he scrambles to the top of the hull, grabbing lines and flexing every muscle in an attempt to right the boat.

But it isn't ridiculous. His words shock me as much as the cold water. I had been taught to always call as soon as someone hits frigid water. Call to alert authorities, not necessarily for a rescue, but to let them know what the situation is, in case it worsens. It makes perfect sense to prepare them. And our situation is indeed getting worse. The boat has turtled, meaning the mast is stuck in the mud. We are far from shore. The wind is blowing harder and the current is strong.

"I'm calling!"

"Fine, but call 'pan-pan' only." Pan-pan, called three times, is the standard maritime alert signal of a distress situation where no immediate danger to life is present.

I hail, "Pan-pan, pan-pan, pan-pan, this is sailing vessel *Tick-Tock*. Do you read me?"

We had never named the boat and the name *Tick-Tock* just comes to me in that moment. I am worried about time running out. After twenty minutes in these cold waters, hypothermia sets in, which can be fatal. I am calm and collected, doing exactly what I have been trained to do in such situations. We aren't calling "mayday," but we are alerting the Coast Guard to a possible dangerous situation.

I am shaking from the cold, my numb fingers trying to push the radio buttons. Ricci stands tall on top of the hull, pulling and grunting with all his might, neck muscles popping. I have never seen such a contorted expression on his face.

The boat isn't budging. I look at Lucy and Kyle, both who are wet and miserably cold. I circle near them so the current won't push them away from us.

"Are you guys okay? Cold?"

Lucy nods.

"Hold tight and don't let go. We're going to be okay," I say.

The End

"*Tick-Tock*, this is the Coast Guard. We read you. Where is your location?"

"Our small sailboat capsized in Tomales Bay, just off Heart's Desire Beach. We are two kids, two adults. We're wearing lifejackets and we're trying to right the boat. Can you stand by?" My voice is surprisingly calm and even. A fireman had once told me to always tell them you have kids, that it puts a faster beat into their walk.

"*Tick-Tock, Tick-Tock*, can you give us better coordinates?"

I couldn't. It had all happened so fast.

"The boat isn't righting. Let's swim for it!" Ricci says.

I'm appalled. "No, that's the worst thing to do! The number one rule is to stay with the boat!"

"Barbara, the beach is right there!"

What was he thinking? It wasn't just "right there." The current is strong. With two small children and me already shivering, I know it's the wrong thing to do. He was ready to pick a fight now? No!

It's hard for me to stand my ground, even at the best of times. For some reason, I am always willing to believe someone else has it right, and not me. Not today.

I grab the radio and make the call. "Mayday, mayday, this is *Tick Tock*. We need a rescue."

I hold onto the kids and look Ricci straight in the eye. Despite my conviction, my training, I can't help but wonder, am I being a wanker? Ricci thinks so. I clutch the kids tighter.

I have named the boat well. Because in these minutes, along with the whistling wind, I can hear the slow—painfully slow—*tick-tock* of time. The sharp cold settles into my fingers and toes. They are sufficiently numb that it is difficult to keep grip of the radio. Ricci drags the kids up, on top of the hull. We wait and wait.

Guilt is setting in. The beach fun we had, our carefree afternoon, is reduced to a senseless whim. I look at my kids on the hull, shivering, and am grateful we are in a bay and not out in the ocean. I put my head down and try to keep warm.

Tick-tock, tick-tock.

I hear a motor. I listen as the children are rescued first. There are voices, strong, kind voices. Someone grabs my life jacket and lifts me out of the water. I scramble with my legs, the best I can, against the metal side of the small motorboat. I am unable to manage anything else. A blanket is thrown on me. I'm warmer, secure. A face in front of mine looks me in the eye and talks to me.

I look around. The kids are huddled together in a corner of the vessel. I close my eyes, as a shiver I cannot control takes over my body. We arrive at a beach and my legs collapse as my body falls to the warm sand. The children are being escorted into an ambulance.

They are okay, they are okay, I keep repeating, under my breath. I can do nothing for them.

"I can't stop shivering," I say to the rescuer. He gives me another blanket and says something, but I don't hear his words. I think I might throw up, but I don't. Then I hear him.

"In another five minutes, you would have had a helicopter rescue," he says.

We are taken to the fire department where the kids drink hot chocolate and watch basketball with the firemen. Ricci heads back with one of the rescuers to retrieve the boat and meets with us later. He walks in with a smile.

"Got the boat!"

It's strange. We have dinner and there is laughter. We survived an adventure of a lifetime. Ricci seems proud, and, oddly, I feel proud too. The grave reality of it all doesn't sink in until later, after the adrenalin dies down.

"Ricci, were you worried about what happened?" In the several days that have passed, the episode has grown heavier in my belly. I have nightmares about all the things that could have gone wrong. What if I had lost the radio?

He shrugs. He wasn't worried, he said.

Anja has often told me that Dante makes her feel safe. I do not feel safe. I have never felt safe with Ricci, and I suspect I never will. What does that say about us? About me?

I want to get out alive. I want my kids to get out alive.

July 2012

The organization is assuredly dying now. The adult program in Sausalito can't survive where we are, at the end of a dock with no permission for signage. The youth program needs full attention. It's difficult to find board members who are interested in anything beyond their own cheap sailing. We need leaders who believe in community, who aren't working 70-hour per week jobs and taking fancy vacations, only to come to this sailing organization to get a deal.

We've spent the entire summer on the youth program, the one program that has hope—a program where kids can play, explore, and sail without the sole goal being to engage in competitive racing. I've been helping Ricci every day. We rush back and forth between home and the docks, often dragging the kids along with a car packed with hamburger buns, bins containing boat parts, youth counselor paychecks, invoices, salt-sodden lost clothing from the campers, and more. I'm packing and unpacking it almost every day, when I'm not mopping up the mess in the yacht club bathrooms made by the youth sailors or stealing precious time to clean my own house.

I take photos and write about the camps as often as I can, and that feels good. I stop and look at the youngsters sporting broad smiles as they sail close-hauled, hiked out, and I remember what it felt like to learn to take the helm. It makes me happy to see these children play with the wind and water and feel free. There's no competition. It's pure play.

Every week we hold celebrations for the youth sailors and also run a new program we've created, which we've called Sea Explorers, a week-long program mixing science and kids, in conjunction with the Romberg Tiburon Center.

Ricci has done it again. What a hero! He has found a place in San Rafael, at Loch Lomond Marina, to relocate the adult sailing program to, from Sausalito where it's proved virtually impossible to survive. He did it without board approval. We're being rebels and doing what's right for the organization and not people's personal selfish motives. The board members don't care about the organization's mission and what it stands for, or at least should stand for. We need a new board that understands community and will watch out for each other, and not compete against each other. We plan to meet the founder, Jane, a former sea captain. She's retired, so we think she'll better understand and share our commitment and vision.

"You go," Ricci tells me. Jane has just moved to Benicia, the sweet little city by the mouth of the Delta, returning to the Bay Area after living in northern California for ten years, running a farm.

We meet the same day of the Delta Do Dah, its flotilla of boats with spinnakers flying, like big bold Odyssean spirits voyaging to the source of the Bay, providing an epic backdrop as we talk. Ricci and I had originally signed up for the flotilla but we've been so busy trying to save the organization that we just couldn't manage it.

Jane strikes me as tough, but honest, a straight-to-the-point sort of person, no bullshit. This was originally her organization, her baby. She started it thirty years ago, growing it out of the Oceanic Society, back when she was busy being a mom, a sea captain, and who knows what else. I explain all that we have done over the years.

She left the organization ten years earlier, she tells me, when there were political problems. She decided to fulfill a dream of living on a farm, so she moved north. The organization had been going south ever since, except for the work Ricci and I and a few other committed souls, like John Paul, Leah, Wayne, and Helena, had put in. We needed help now. We were desperate.

Jane looks at me hard. "Are you active?"

"Yes," I assure her. "And I intend to stay active. I want the organization to survive. My great-uncle was a sailor. It makes me feel close to him." I don't know why I added that.

She looks at me intently. "Do you have guts? Do you *really* have the guts and are willing to do what it takes to make things happen?"

"I do."

Wasn't that what I had been doing? What we had been doing?

"Good."

December 2012

Ricci and I are in terrible debt. The house is falling apart with rot. The garden is a disaster. I tell him I want to move. I want to simplify. I don't want to take care of such a big house. It's too much. All I do is clean, cook, and rush around for everyone, while I watch every penny and never spend any on myself. I'm looking more weathered, with perpetual sea salt in my hair and crow lines that are becoming deeper. We fight more and more about this.

"Please, let's sell this and move to the countryside," I beg. "Live simply, so we can do good things with our lives."

He is exasperated. "All you do is complain."

José Neto agrees to give a guitar lesson to Lucy. I scrape together enough money to make it happen. José has a little cottage in a big garden behind a house. Inside are stacks of music and posters of him with legacy players, Steve Winwood and others. Lucy sits down next to him and I watch them pluck the first strings as rays of light shoot through the room. I go outside and sit under a massive bay tree, remembering the days I'd climb such trees and sit alone, quietly, watching the life around me and feeling the wind swirl between my body and the tree. Feeling connected to something. The guitar music drifts outside, singular notes that pop like bubbles around me.

I pull out a pen and write whatever comes to mind. I imagine José inside, with my daughter, that fatherly comforting feeling he exudes. I miss it, feeling safe. When have I ever felt safe, I wonder. I remember my chapped lips, Blistex, my father and his job. My mother, and her crying. My husband, and his incessant complaints about me. I have only my children. I hesitate.

Do I?

I am losing myself and everything I believe in.

Who am I?

I am curious about this guitarist, José Neto. I know he plays with big names but I have never heard his name. I used to know of so many classical guitarists, like Andrés Segovia, Christopher Parkening, Ottmar Liebert, Los Romeros, Paco de Lucía, and many others. Who is this person who has reopened the door to my past, memories of thirty years ago, making me feel things I haven't felt in years?

I look him up on the internet. There is no Wikipedia page for him, but I do find a few old write-ups, *The London Times* and other concerts reviews. He is called legendary. A master. A consummate guitarist.

"[A]s soon as he touched his custom-guitar, sending a shower of harmonics into the silence, he rendered all musings about categorisation redundant ... he demonstrated just how much musical territory, opened up by Hendrix in the 1960s, still remains for subsequent generations of guitarists to explore."
— *The London Times, 1996*

I discover a recorded outdoor performance of his band, Netoband, in Fairfax. He played a solo on his white guitar. I watch. Earrings in his ears. A bandanna. He does look like a pirate, a rebel, but gentle, all-knowing. I listen to the performance and the music fills me, spilling into every crevice of my being, every corner filled with cobwebs, like the bakery where I'd met him again. Forgotten places. Forgotten stories from my life. I witness his passion as he plays. I want that too. I listen more.

I read a bit about Steve Winwood and Harry Belafonte, and listen to them play, but it is the others, Flora Purim and Airto Moreira, Brazilian jazz greats, I listen to most, remembering those treasured imports at the record store before being ordered to dump them because weren't moneymakers. The musicians seem almost forgotten now.

I learn about José's daughter, eighteen-year-old Flora, who was killed in a car accident. It must have been about the same time I first met him at the Zen Center. I listen to an acoustic piece he played called "Lua Dances," over and over again. I can't stop listening. It speaks to me in a strange hypnotic way. I read about the bakery he and his wife Maria used to run. I could see they were good people. They called Neto the pie-eating Jimi Hendrix.

I listen to José's performance again, a performance at a street festival, nothing terribly fancy or special, one would say, yet it brings me comfort. Or am I being lured by it?

I find myself listening to it often. In the middle of the night, I wake up and listen. I sit in the bathroom and stare at myself for hours. Ricci eventually knocks on the door.

"Are you okay in there?"

"I'm just meditating," I reply, but, really, I don't know what I'm doing. I just stare at myself, nothing more.

Who am I?

The End

I have been so concerned about Ricci finding his passion that I feel myself lost.

I lie down to take a nap. Afternoon light is streaming through the windows. I gaze outside, at Mount Tamalpais, close my eyes, and feel unfamiliar energy gently swirl around me, embracing me.

Please take care of my father.

I open my eyes. Take care of my father? Who said that? I look around the room. Everything looks the same. But something is different. I felt that energy. I know I did.

I pull out my own guitar. When the kids were little I would often take it out, and they would dance wildly while I strummed. I pick up where I had last left off, *Greensleeves*. I could still play it.

Maybe it's time to turn the page. Time to learn a new song.

Or is it too late for me?

2013–2014

January 2013

I sit on the floor, folding my son's laundry. The pile feels like an endless stream. I can't match the socks. Some are missing. Some have holes. My son's socks represent my life, I think—nothing matches up anymore.

Ricci walks in and stands in the doorway.

"I can't keep up, Ricci. This house is falling apart. There's no money." I am worried, as always, about the bills, and I am weary of the stress that seems to grow as frequently, as fast, as persistently as the cobwebs in every corner of the space we occupy. Ricci is indifferent to it all.

"I cashed out a retirement fund last December," I remind him, "to pay the property taxes. We are buried! I'm not living life; I'm barely surviving!"

He stands there. I'm not sure what he's thinking. I hold a striped sock in my hand that has no partner.

"You have to get a job, Ricci, a job that pays. Or we need to sell this house. One or the other. I can't keep up like this. I don't want to keep up like this."

Angry words burst forth from him, a torrent that washes over me.

"If I get a job, you have to get a job. All you do is complain," he fires at me.

I look at the tired-looking sock as he rattles off why I am to blame for the sorry state of our finances. It is full of holes. Why have I been so intent on keeping this sorry sock when what I should do is throw it away? I try to let Ricci's words wash over me, but they soak in and I feel my insides churn. My eyes are still fixed on the damn sock as the words churning inside me burst forth.

"Ricci, you have no idea what it's like to grow up broke. You have no idea. Living in poverty is not glamorous, and yet you make out like it is. I had to work for years to go to school. Do you know how hard that was? Running around, working my ass off, with holes in my shoes? I've now cashed out a retirement fund I managed to save when I was a full-time student, working full-time, all in order to pay the mortgage and property taxes on this house." I was fed up. "Get a job that pays, Ricci. We can't financially support an entire organization anymore."

I scrunched up the sock and threw it to the side, where all the other unmatched socks lay. It was time to purge.

Him too.

"You quit?"

I stare at Ricci. Admittedly, the organization has no more money, not even to pay just Ricci, so his quitting comes as a bit of a relief, but we had given our word to help the new board members, including Jane, through the next season.

"I gave them two weeks' notice and told them they are not to call me after that."

I gasp. "Two weeks?" While that might be the standard for a corporate job, the sailing organization was anything but corporate. The board members would have questions, many questions. Most of those on the board have never run a sailing organization before. Boat registrations, legal issues, repairs, camps, lessons, community relations—the list goes on in my head. "We brought these people in to help the organization. We can't leave them stranded. It's setting them up to fail, Ricci."

"I believe I have been very generous."

He had been. We both had been. I knew that. But two weeks?

"Maybe I should step in and help."

"No, Barbara, they will suck you dry." Ricci says, his voice angry.

I think of our argument the day before. Had I brought this on? Is this my doing?

"Ricci, the organization will fall apart. We spent three hard years building it up and going into major debt ourselves for it. You can't put that on the board. Some of them are our friends. They will be the fall guys, the ones to blame for a failed organization."

"Again, I think I was very generous."

I can't believe it. Surely there's a better way to handle such a transition.

Ricci will not budge.

Jane is understandably furious. I attend the next board meeting, to gauge the state of things. Jane launches immediately into words of anger.

"He pulled us into this! What happened to that big speech he gave us about the values of sailing? There's hardly any money. How are we going to survive? How dare he just walk out on us like this!"

The board looks demoralized. If the organization fails, it's on them now, not us.

"Goddamn Ricci! Look at all the things he hasn't done! Those boats aren't even registered!"

I understand her frustration, but I also understand Ricci's perspective. He's exhausted. He needs a break. He is totally burned out. Yes, I am tired too, but he has done so much, I thought. A story is building, however, that Ricci is the one bringing the organization down.

"Now, wait a minute," I say. "Ricci didn't register the boats for a good reason. And be reminded, this organization wouldn't even be here if it weren't for him." I might not be happy with his actions and how he'd chosen to do what he did, but this is my husband, after all, and I've watched him work his tail off to save this organization. Nobody is going to make my family look bad after all that we have done. We are a good family in this community. We are not a bad family.

Jane continues her diatribe, intent on positioning Ricci as the fall guy. Not only that, but the entire Bay Area sailing community would hear how he and I were the ones to bring the organization down. This is a tight community that extends not just through the San Francisco Bay Area but also internationally. If I let the organization fall apart now, I think, it's like disrespecting my uncle, and my heritage.

I look out to the water.

What should I do?

My great-uncle was the first person in my family that I honored and respected, who had gifted me with a heritage I could finally be proud of, a connection to value, and an entire community of people—sailors—I respected. And this treasure of mine could all be shot down by a measly nonprofit sailing organization of dinghies.

After the board meeting, Jane and I sit down on the docks. I am reminded of that first day I sat with her in Benicia, with the backdrop of spinnakers fully filled, headed downwind during the big Delta Do Dah.

"Jane, you're the founder. You can come back and help set it straight. You're retired and you've got the time. You know how to run operations, an organization. We need help. "

I remember her having looked at me and asking whether I intended to stay involved. I had told her yes.

"You have to have guts, Barbara," she'd said. "Guts."

Now, here we are, months later, sitting on the docks, water lapping, and she's asking me for help. Some children sail by us and I watch them laugh and play.

"Barbara, you could take the director's job," she urged. "You know how to run the organization. You've been doing it with Ricci. We'll pay you. Run the kids' camp. This organization will fall apart if you can't take the job. There's no other person qualified for it."

She's right. Who else is going to take on a job for $20 an hour that runs you ragged for an entire season? It takes guts.

Or stupidity.

I gaze at the water, trying to clear my mind of noise, in search of a clear answer.

What would Uncle Bob do?

He'd do what's right. He would keep his word.

Who do I listen to, my dead uncle or my living husband?

The noise clears. I know the right answer.

February 2013

I sit outside the bakery, eating a chocolate donut, thinking again of how my grandfather loved donut shops and finding odd comfort in that. My spirit is worn so thin. After three years of running this sailing organization with tiny boats, we are broke, nearly $100,000 in debt, our house is falling apart, and we are back to arguing. Ricci was angry.

I have spent so many summers volunteer teaching and running programs. Ricci had been paid the equivalent of what I had made twenty-five years ago, when I was a full-time college student. The efforts had fed us in ways no money or food could, but we had been sucked dry.

Jane's words ring in my ears.

"Barbara, nobody else can run this organization this summer but you. You're our only hope. I can support you, but you need to run it. We'll pay you, and give you a title."

Ricci and I had talked this morning.

"Don't take the job," he said, standing over me while I did the dishes. "Go work for a real environmental organization if you want to do something for the world. The sailing organization is a backwater group that will never amount to anything."

"Ricci, I helped you all last season with the summer camp. You even said yourself it'd be a good summer job for me, side money, while I'm with the kids. Now you're telling me not to take the job? We need money, Ricci. You're not working. I can do this job, with the kids. I know how to do it."

Furious, he wheeled around, strode into his office, and slammed the door.

I finish my donut, lick my fingers, and picked up the phone.
"Okay, Jane, I want in. I'll take on the job for this season only."
That night, at dinner, Ricci spoke again.
"I'm not going to help you. You're on your own if you do it."
"I helped you. You won't help me now?"
He didn't answer. I told myself that one day he'd understand why I had to do this. It was the right thing to do. I knew it was just his anger talking. Maybe one day he'll look back and admit I was right, and we could maybe feel again the way we did on Heart's Desire Beach.
Or maybe not.
I was gambling. I knew that too.

Lucy's guitar lessons continue, and, as always, I sit and listen and watch. Shadows of their fingers move against the wall. I hear the bay tree rustle outside. There is something unusual about José. He isn't one to live on the surface. There is depth to him, one that does not reveal itself with words, but maybe it does through music. I listen carefully to hear what is being spoken.

After the lesson, I hand him his payment and he seems reluctant to take it. I insist.

He still unsettles me.

April 2013

I sign up and pay for The Buckeye Gathering, a "get back to the roots of civilization, get connected to nature and people" event. People camp out on Native American land in northern California to celebrate and honor primitive ancestral arts, eat together, make art, whittle reeds for flutes, learn to slaughter a goat with respect, and sing by the fire, under the stars. The big rules—no modern technology, no alcohol, and no drugs.

I buy three tickets, one for me and two for the kids. Ricci says he has things to do and doesn't want to spend the money, but I need to get away and feel the simple way of being, before launching into the intense sailing season I'll be taking on singlehandedly.

I understand why he's against it. Ricci is still not working and our finances grow ever grimmer. It's arguably not a sensible idea to pay to attend this gathering, although it's not terribly expensive. I went ahead, rationalizing that it would be my one getaway this year, plus, I'd actually earn some money for a change, over the summer. I need to remind myself that I am human and not a machine. I already know what it is going to be like when the sailing camp heats up in May. All my energy, day and night, will be consumed by running the ship. I need a deep breath, connection with the kids, and renewed energy.

More than that, something is calling me to it.

I keep to myself during the event's first few days, listening to faraway drum circles, staring into the sky at the circling hawks, and sitting among a circle of women potters who have just collected clay from the nearby stream. Who knew that clay doesn't just come in a box, labeled Michael's Art Supplies! It's the simple reminders of who and what we are that excite me.

My kids sit with me as we learn how to make pots Anasazi style, coiling clay like snakes and shaping them into small vessels. I learn that the Anasazi were the ancestors of the Hopi, those who lived in the Four Corners region. The Hopi had a prophesy of the Fifth World, the world beyond materialism. There was talk about a blue star marking a new beginning, a world beyond materialism.

I think back to that blue sea star at Santa Barbara University.

When I am not sitting around, cross-legged, watching people, I lie in my tent and stare at ants crisscrossing the nylon ceiling. I wander to the river and take a cool plunge as mothers sit with their naked little children on the shore. Cottonwood blossoms float down onto the water like snow, collecting around me. The noise in my head, the arguments, the incessant spin, is easing, drifting away, replaced by the subtle gentle rhythms of nature that surround me. A bird. A fence lizard, shuffling leaves. Drops of water falling as I lift my hand to rub fingers through my long, tangled hair.

Even here, I can't get the sound of Neto's music out of my head. I close my eyes and I watch the full solo performance. How he moves onstage. How his sad eyes look out to the people. How his fingers move across the frets and his fingers pluck the strings. How many times have I watched that video? Why can't I get the music out of my head?

My thoughts inevitably return to my life and my unhappiness. Why? Why am I not grateful, content? Am I spoiled? Do I have too much?

But I don't want all this. I didn't ask for it. And my voice is not being heard. More than anything, I can feel my marriage crumbling.

Why? What can I do to save it?

What is wrong with me?

I take a walk up a hill where woodcrafters and herbalists have collected, mingling. The trees feel strange again, an uneasy quiet that draws me into its dreamlike state.

There is a young boy sitting at the foot of an oak, whittling a stick with a big knife. He looks up at me and makes a motion of slicing his neck.

"Huh?"

He points behind me, and I turn around.

There she is. A strong, gentle mama, strung up by her neck. A man collects blood from her neck, quietly and reverently. A woman slowly strokes and milks her exposed teats, the little beads of milk dripping into a metal bowl. I hear another noise, one of distress. Her kid in the adjacent pen is crying. Her mother has just been slaughtered and the last vestiges of her life are being drained out of her. This is me, I think, looking at the goat. I am being drained dry.

As I stand and watched the languid eyes and body hanging limply, I feel something swirl around me, an energy.

I was the best goat I could possibly be. I was the best mother I could possibly be. But it wasn't good enough. I wasn't good enough. World, please be kind to my baby.

She went through me. For a moment, I was her.

I head back to the tent along the dry dusty road and begin to sob. Why am I crying? I see to my left a teepee, one reserved for women only, and so I enter, relieved to find no one else inside, only crystals, books, journals, and herbal tea. I sit down and pull out my journal. I scribble, *If I were to die tomorrow, what would be my biggest regret in life?*

In big bold letters I add: *WRITE.*

But what do I write about? Some pathetic woman who can't figure out her life? Divorces her husband? Comes from a dysfunctional family? That's been done, to death. I have nothing to write about. And everything I write is mediocre and disconnected anyway.

The next morning the organizer speaks about the week, sharing his vision of it and how we have created a beautiful week together, people bringing their best skills, art, and energy to share with one another. I find myself agreeing with him. This week has transformed my life in more ways than one.

He shares a story about the night before. Someone had been smoking a cigarette by the fire, something that was not exactly condoned. The individual tossed the butt into the fire.

"You see, you have to ask what is the intention of your acts," the organizer says. "Are you throwing away the cigarette, or are you offering tobacco to the fire?"

The act is the same, he points out, but it is the difference in the energy and outcome that reshape the way we live our lives.

When it's all over, Ricci is there to pick up the kids. He's upset.

"Why didn't you answer your phone? I've been calling you all week!"

"Ricci, it's a primitive gathering. No technology. You knew where I was."

The kids get into the van and he slams the door shut, yelling a litany of words before he speeds away, leaving me standing there, alone, in the road, as the dust flies in his wake. He is taking them to Sea Ranch, to visit his mother for a few days.

It feels bigger than that.

I climb into my car and drive back to the house, back to my life. I drop my luggage and head straight into the garage filled with half-empty paint cans, tools, camping equipment, boxes of stuff, bins of paperwork, school supplies, shoes, boots, bicycles, and stacks of things to sell at some future garage sale. I grab the ladder, being careful not to knock down three suitcases, containers of camping gear, rubber boots, unused skis, a rubber inflatable boat, and any other items in its path.

We did not buy these things. They grow and multiply, like fungus. I swear to it.

I find it, what I'm looking for. There, in the rafters, in a dark corner, sits an unlabeled box.

I pull down the box and sit cross-legged on the cold concrete floor. I look at it and it looks back at me. I break its seal and all my old journals, notes, and pictures spill out.

I read radio stories I had written for KQED public radio when I was a pigtailed intern for Michael Krasny.

There are stories I wrote about Nancy Pelosi, a congresswoman who later went on to become the first female Speaker of the House.

There was the story about Ellen DeGeneres, when she first came out of the closet. I had gone to a lesbian bar in San Francisco to get that story, after she had been fired from a national sitcom for publicly revealing her sexuality.

I think of how far society has come since those days. One bold person makes a statement and, twenty years later, we have legalized gay marriage. It's possible to change, and change big. It can just take one person.

I think back to my nature student who proudly has two mothers. She was the most delightful, well-balanced, loving child. It just takes courage and a dream, I suppose.

I rummage through the pile. There is the story I wrote about Mark O'Brien, the one I am most proud of. I recall the morning when editor Cy Musiker shouted the assignment to me across the newsroom and I cringed, followed by the shock I felt when I first laid eyes on O'Brien, a severely disabled man who was yet more alive than most able-bodied people. He is dead now but his face is still vividly etched in my mind, those sparkling eyes and flirtatious words.

My legs cramp on the cold concrete and I stretch them.

There are no excuses.

Those were Mark's words.

There are no excuses.

I repeat them out loud. His words give me pause.

There are no excuses for not doing what you want to do, I think. I try to remember his poem, his reading of it, his lips moving.

The End

Adreammother

> Why is she taking me to the movies?
> Serving me chicken and corn for breakfast.
> Showing off her new dress.
> Doesn't she know she's dead?
>
> She's still a running character in my dreams,
> Smoking Lucky, swapping dirty jokes
> with the boss and Virgin Mary
> Before the two of them roar off on a BVM Harley.
> She always liked a ruckus.

***

Why is she taking me to the movies.
Serving chicken and corn for breakfast.
Showing off her new dress.
Doesn't she know she's dead?

She's still a running character in my dreams
sucking Lucky, swapping dirty jokes
with the boss and Virgin Mary before the
two of them roar off on a BVM's Harley.
She always liked a ruckus.
Mark O'Brien

She always liked a ruckus.
 I am feeling something, something long forgotten, but I don't know what it is. A time, perhaps, when I was inspired by people, including a man who couldn't do anything but lie for years on his back, trapped inside an iron lung, and write by painstakingly using a stick in his mouth to type about the beauty and foibles of life and humanity.
 I carry the box upstairs, to my office, and pull up other old diaries and pieces I've written on my computer. I begin to read about a part of me I had forgotten. I read about my dreams of the life I would live, one of traveling, writing, and learning about people around the world.

I thumb through pictures taken in Guatemala of my mother and me, riding, carefree, in the back of a pickup truck, and through the mountains of highland Mexico, Mayan land. We were having so much fun together. I was braless and we were laughing. I had nothing but a filthy dirty backpack to my name.

I dig out pictures of my grandfather flying the plane he had designed and built in his garage. He was a postman. He didn't have much money, but he had a dream, one he never let go. He taught himself how to make it happen and he did it.

I thought of my sailing uncles. They were never happier than when they were sitting on the rail of a sailboat, flying through wind and water, across the San Francisco Bay. They lived lives of integrity and filled their lives with the music of their dreams.

I listen to Neto's music and then sit down to write. I hesitate. The blank page stares passively, lifelessly, at me. I have nothing to write about. I pull up short stories I've written. Maybe I should start with fiction.

"Barbara, you should be happy you have a big kitchen." My mother-in-law's words echo in my head.

Why am I not happy? Do I ask for too much? I never asked for a big kitchen.

I listen to Neto's songs again. They comfort me.

June 2013

People say that sailing toughens you up. Trust me, running a nonprofit sailing organization will make you tougher than any sea captain. It's an organization that doesn't lure people with promises of big trophies, fancy boats, or high-level contacts or prestige. In a world of racing, we don't race. We play instead, an idea that may, in some eyes, mark us as trivial, not serious, even downright lazy, without purpose. But we have lots of fun, and I'm not afraid to say it.

These weeks I've been running like a mad woman, rushing between the docks and home. Ricci is still looking for work and hardly speaks to me; neither will he watch the kids while I work. I don't have money for sitters, and we don't have a local community that trades kids or a neighborhood where kids can safely roam freely. The kids figure out the formula fast and park themselves in front of a television set while I'm still willing to bend my media principles.

"Kids, this is the summer you'll remember that you got to watch movies all summer long. Don't get used to it," I tell them.

Meanwhile I rush back and forth to deal with parents, kids, counselors, and boats, all for $20 an hour and, more importantly, stand by my family name. We will not be the fall guys, I keep telling myself. We are a good family. Boats break all the time, consistently. Then, there's the yacht club bathroom we get to use. How can you expect thirty kids to keep a bathroom pristine when they walk in sodden, wet, and tired? It's a set-up-to-fail situation and so I'm in there, mopping the floor, to ensure the yacht club continues to like us.

My other babysitter is the neighborhood pool. While the kids swim, I make lists and review rosters, and field a phone call from a crazed mother. I hold the phone two feet from my ear as little Ian's mother launches into a tirade about sharks eating her son and how irresponsible we are to allow kids on boats to sail in San Pablo Bay.

"My son capsized! It's dangerous! I can't believe you let kids sail out there!"

The next day Ian scrapes his knees after running across the lawn and taking a tumble, and I get another call from her.

"You guys are absolutely irresponsible."

Life is dangerous, I want to tell her. And nobody gets out alive. Instead, I just return her money and belay my tongue.

Not all parents are the same. Emily gets knocked in the head with a boom and calls her dad to tell him, in accordance with our policy. Her dad asks if she thinks it has knocked some sense into her. She laughs and gets back to sailing. She is better than most of the other kids, with a high level of confidence.

Sara scraped her feet badly against some barnacles, despite our repeated urging to wear her shoes. She had three bandages on her feet to remind her why shoes were a good idea after that, and she never forgot again.

Then there was that first day, when all the kids were sailing upwind, back to the docks, against 20-knot winds while the parents watched in horror, convinced we were trying to kill their children. One mother who couldn't see her child came running up to me.

"Where's my son?" she cried.

I fought the impulse to tell her I was sorry, that he had been eaten by a shark, but at that moment her son tacked, turned a corner, and she saw him at the helm, coming toward us, his huge grin rippling across the water.

"Oh," she said, feebly, and looked at me, not only relieved but also surprised. It was as if she were seeing magic for the first time and it then dawned on her that it was I who had created it for her.

Why are we so afraid to let our children experience life? Maybe because we adults have forgotten ourselves?

There were graduation ceremonies, repeated trips to pick up hamburger buns, new pins and cleats for the boats, battles with renegade counselors over an extra fifty cents an hour, relationships with the aging yacht club liaison, keeping the harbormaster happy, putting up signs on fences, designing, printing, and distributing brochures. The list goes on, without an end in sight.

I was flying.

Still, I must maintain a delicate balance. Jane has my back, running the ship, but I still need to monitor her tongue. She continues to find reasons to blame Ricci for anything and everything.

"Jane, the organization wouldn't exist without Ricci's work these past years," I repeat, feeling like a broken record. He is my husband, my family. Nobody is going to take us down.

I want to give back to some people too. There are some sailors who give so much to the organization, while others complain yet do nothing to resolve the problems they gripe about. It's easy to complain, I think, and it creates a false sense of elevation. The ones who give are those who stick their necks out, adding their own spirit to the mix, improving the situation for everyone. There were three people I wanted to give back to.

John Paul Watts was one. He has given so much to so many people, including me. I'll always remember his birthday sail in 2009. We had sailed a flotilla of boats to Angel Island one midwinter day, and as we crossed the bay, a freak squall with thirty-five-knot winds and hard rain hit us. Then, as freakishly as that storm had descended on us, it disappeared when we reached the island. The sky cleared into a scene reminiscent of one of Michelangelo's frescoes, complete with heavenly

The End

blues and billowy clouds, along with the most resplendent Technicolor rainbow ever painted. In acknowledgment of everything he has done for us, with the help of Jane and others we have created the John Paul Watts Fund to help kids who can't pay for sailing camp, to give some children a chance to connect to the beauty of this marine world.

Carlos Grana is another one I'm anxious to recognize. He had, I was told, sold his successful language business at the age of 38 and plunged into following his dream of becoming a film director. He had no experience and started from complete scratch, even moving to Los Angeles from San Francisco. He once made a promotional film for our organization without asking for anything in return. I want to give back to him. I see him struggling and striving to live his crazy dream. I admire the guts it takes to do that. I still don't know what to do for him.

Another is Frank Lawler. Over the years, I have caught him red-handed at the docks, fixing boats without any expectation of acknowledgment or reward. He simply did it because he felt he could. I am anxious to find a way to honor him.

August 2013

Today is to be a magic day, literally as well as figuratively. The Maritime Museum in San Francisco is hosting a Bear Boat sail-in as part of the Louis Vuitton America's Cup pre-races, and I am participating, sailing *Magic Bear,* number 65, my uncle's old boat, which was the sixty-fifth Bear boat ever constructed, alongside owner Tim, of the Mahoney Family. The museum has the number one boat, *Merry Bear,* the first ever built, which they have carefully restored over the years, and other Bear Boats are sailing in to illustrate the beautiful wooden-boat heritage of our San Francisco Bay. I can't believe I will be sailing *Magic,* as I didn't even know *Magic* still existed when I first started sailing years ago. I still display my uncle's trophy that my mom gave me after his death on a shelf.

Magic does exist.

There is always so much fuss over the America's Cup: big money, big boats, and a big trophy, a race that captures the international top dogs. But I didn't care about that part of it. For me, it was about something more profound.

We prep the boat at Sausalito. I look at Tim.

"You know how special this is to me, right?"

"I think I do." He had sailed a lot with his father, and understands the connections you make when you sail together. But it's not just that. You feel your dreams, freedom, maybe even your soul, just like that sailing instructor had told me years before.

We raise the sail, and I watch it rise, as if setting a spirit free, in flight. Tim gives me the wooden tiller right away and we tack across the bay. I am reminded of a black and white photo in Diane Beeston's book, *Of Wind, Fog and Sail: Sailing on San Francisco Bay*, and fancy that we look just like it. Jane gave me her copy of the out-of-print book the previous year and I treasure it. Today, it feels even more sacred.

Magic is solid, a thick, strong lady with palpable warmth, worth, charm, and reverence. She has a soul.

Traffic is heavy, as sailors, ferries, motorboats, and yachts head out to watch the big races from all corners of the bay. I don't care about the fancy racing boats. I only care about this very moment, holding the tiller and hearing Uncle Bob's words, "You have to feel it," inside.

I am at the helm of *Magic*.

Gauging by his eyes and hesitant reach for the tiller, Tim is starting to get nervous. The Youth Red Bulls, on speed-demon catamarans, are bearing down on us, one by one. We are the give-way boat, while they are stand-ons, meaning it's our responsibility to move out of their way, and we have to move fast. I am not worried. I know exactly what to do.

I am smiling big as I weave in and out of their downwind practice leg. Their youthful vigor and big sails dash within feet of us.

"Looking good, kids!" I shout.

Tim is still concerned.

"I've got it, don't worry," I assure him. And I do.

When we arrive at the docks of the Maritime Museum, others Bear Boats are gathered from across the San Francisco Bay Area. Everyone chitchats about bilges, races, and history, but not me. I lie on my back, on the wooden docks, gazing into a sky filled with tall masts, not unlike church steeples. The halyards, like wind chimes, make their music. Soft clouds and light fog move across the big blue, and I feel connected to it all—my past and everything I thought I was and have become. A mother, a wife, a real sailor. I have a heritage, something to be proud of, a family member who bequeathed me something to be proud of. I don't care about the big races that drive big egos, the fancy trophies, or the money. I have found something much deeper for me, something real and profound.

On the way back, Tim takes the helm. I sit on the high side, getting splashed occasionally, and feeling the rhythm of the pulsating *Magic*. The fiery hues, the rich warm reds and golds of the sunset, dip behind the Golden Gate Bridge, a reminder of how good it feels to be alive.

This was my trophy, I thought, all this, what I had needed from Uncle Bob.

And, yet, I feel something else is coming.

The America's Cup is in full swing. I watch a few races, and although they are amazing to see, with their fancy boats and world-class racers, I have other business to tend to. I have finally figured out how to acknowledge the contributions of fellow member and volunteer Frank Lawler. I found a pewter cup for two dollars at a secondhand store and called up Frank, who's a former metalworker.

"Frank, do you think we can make a trophy out of this?"

"Sure. I can do something with it. Bring it over."

He created a little trophy, complete with the words "1st Place" hammered by hand into a strip of metal and wrapped it around the cup. I filled the cup with chocolates and officially designated it as the First Place trophy of the inaugural Frank Lawler Regatta 2013.

A group of sailors have collected on the docks, kids and adults. I had never run a regatta before, but since nobody else is doing it, I figured nobody would complain. I mean, what could go wrong?

Ricci refuses to come, but I am convinced he will make an appearance. He saved this organization, after all. Can't he see what I am doing? I will not let his name—our name—be dragged through the mud. I could sit around, get my nails done, and focus on looking good that way. Instead, I am running around, biting my nails, trying to ensure everyone else looks and feels good.

After some confusion about where to start the race, how we would conduct it, and so on, Frank blows a whistle and the flotilla of little boats—the Picos, Catalinas, chase boats, and our trawler *Descalza* are off!

It is one of those beautiful days that makes you think how thankful you are to be alive. The winds are at about 20 knots and sky is an unremitting blue. Currents are pretty strong with chop and San Pablo Bay is ours!

Kids are racing against the adults across the bay to China Camp, where the Chinese heritage festival is being celebrated, where Ricci and I first met Captain Richard Gillette. The wind is blowing so hard that the kids in little boats are flying, the adults doing their best to keep up.

Wayne capsizes and is shivering violently when picked up in the chase boat. The smile on his face says it all. "Awesome, man!"

I sail with Chris, who grew up with the sailing organization. Now an adult, he takes care of both his parents and his severely handicaped brother, so sailing is a way of returning to his own life. We intentionally stay behind the pack. We are less interested in winning than watching the joy on the faces of thirty crazy adults and youth as they race ahead of us, across San Pablo Bay, in pursuit of the first Lawler Regatta trophy.

I am having more fun watching this race in San Pablo Bay than the America's Cup, in San Francisco Bay, which is in full swing, complete with helicopters and international yachts, and adulation for whomever manages to take home the coveted historic trophy. Even Queen Victoria had once yearned to win the prize. Here instead, on San Pablo Bay, I feel a satisfying rebelliousness, as if we are pirates, taking what we want as ours, and giving our hearts and souls to do it. Oh, yeah, this is the good life.

At the end of the race, a disagreement breaks out, an emotional dispute about the exact location of the finish line, who had crossed it first, and who might have cheated. One complains it was an unjust race, and I am blamed for not making it clear enough. Another complains at how there is only one trophy, nothing for the second-place winners and their contenders.

I can't believe it. They are serious! Stricken with guilt, feeling responsible for all the ruckus, I resurrect some dusty old plaques from another century, race, and place, and repurpose them. To my relief, everyone is now content, as the three winning youths hold up high the prized two-dollar cup from a secondhand shop (that part is top secret, of course). The chocolates inside it are rapidly consumed and we snap photos in *paparazzi* fashion, eating, drinking, and cheering.

I write an article for *Latitude 38*, the West Coast sailing rag. The big boat of billionaire Larry Ellison dons the cover as winner of this year's America's Cup, and, inside, our rag-tag kids are pictured holding their coveted trophy from a simultaneous little boat race in the San Pablo Bay. It's the inside guts that count, I think. Oh, it's fun being a rebel, a pirate in the fancy-pants system!

I am still trying to come up with an idea to honor fellow member and selfless volunteer Carlos Grana. I have been watching his emerging evocative film work featuring women, lots of women. His camera captures flesh, eyes, the freedom of the trapeze, looks of rebellion. The music and imagery tantalize—they are sensual, dangerous, and bold. His artistry is growing and I admire what it has taken for him to follow his dream against all odds. Carlos has guts.

"How did the race go?" Ricci asks that night.

"It would have been better had you joined us."

The organization has made it through the season. I survived as well, barely. I sit on my sofa as sharply edged sunbeams pierce the dirty windows overhead and slice through the air, like a cheese grater. And I am the shreds of cheese that remain. There is nothing left of my whole self but pieces of my body and spirit after everyone has taken what they wanted. The dust drifts in the light and I gaze up at spiders lurking in the ceiling corners, taunting me. They are more at home here than I am. Mindlessly, I watched the dust dance.

What is wrong with me?

I'm nothing more than fragments, exhausted. There is nothing left of me. Zilch.

Ricci doesn't speak to me much. The few times he does, it's unpleasant. He's still mad, I guess, that I worked all summer for the organization. But we'll pull through. We will. We always do.

We decide to put the kids back into public school. We are broke and have no other choice. I no longer have the juice in me to homeschool. Still, I'm not happy with the decision we've been forced to make as I've seen what public school has become. It's all I can do to muster up the energy to buy frozen pizzas for the kids for dinner and tell them they're lucky to be getting a meal.

We are a good family, I say out loud.

I'm not sure anyone is listening.

September 2013

It's a California Distinguished School, I remind myself, to reassure me yet again about our decision to stop homeschooling. That means it has been recognized by the State of California as providing an exemplary, quality education program. What does that really mean in today's world, I wonder.

The last four years our lives have been spent on boats, docks, immersed in nature, or in small groups of students being taught literature, art, and science. We have been free. Poor, but free, creating our own structure, living by our ideals instead of some mainstream life governed by corporate bosses, rules, schedules, monkey suits, alarm clocks, impeccable grooming, yet admittedly without corporate pay.

My daughter stands close to me at the school introductory day, not in fear but more in a state of awe. We are both awed. The school is generating so much energy to make the day seem special—big speeches, free candy, children doing a rah-rah dance. Why is everyone trying so hard to make the idea of learning literature, science, and math into something special? My thoughts flit back to my first day at my old accounting firm, when I received my gold-plated nameplate and was told how lucky I was to work on the 33rd floor of one of the fanciest buildings in San Francisco.

I wanted to run then.

I want to run now.

But where do I run?

Lucy had first been required to take a placement exam. I bring her into the school office, acutely aware of how I have likely been labeled the crazy mom who foolishly homeschooled her daughter. In a way, it is as much my own self-worth and teaching ability that are on the line as my daughter's knowledge.

"Just be honest and do the best you can, Lucy," I say before she heads into the back room. I sit and wait, anxiously, worrying whether my decision had adversely affected her, whether I had done right by her or not. It had felt right at the time.

She returns an hour later, looking despondent, and the poker-faced clerk takes her paperwork, examines her answers, and marks it.

I can't help myself. "What did she score?" I ask.

"I'm afraid I'm not allowed to say."

"I've been responsible for her education," I say. "And I'm her parent. I have the right to know," I add, trying not to sound rude.

The clerk glances around and lowers her voice to a whisper.

"I can't tell you the exact score, but she scored in the top percentile."

"Top percentile! Really?" I pause. "And that was with just seven hours of academics a week. Homeschooling." I am elated. I feel validated.

There is an uncomfortable silence, accompanied by looks of disbelief. I walk away, feeling relieved and happy.

Within weeks, my daughter changes from being happy and grounded to more and more withdrawn. She's tired, cranky. She doesn't like school. There's homework every night. Hours of it. I watch carefully and I don't like what I see. It's not soul driven; it's ramming information down these children's throats. I witness my daughter's spirit dwindle as she cranks through all her assignments, homework, checklists, essays, and more homework. She needs a computer to complete assignments. My feelings of helplessness grow.

Today's school paradigm is a social experiment. Who says mass education on this corporatized level is natural, healthy, and valid? Who says requiring computers in class is natural, healthy, and valid? My spirit rises with questions, followed by anger, but what do I do with it all?

I feel powerless.

Over the ensuing weeks, my mind, body, and spirit re-establish balance, and I read up on public education to discover we fail to question, or fail to ask the hard questions. Technology has pushed its way into the classroom. Is this really right, I wonder? Or it just business?

So much stimulation surrounds the children. Competitive sports dominate school grounds, and shouts from kids can be heard after they win a game: "We are number one!"

I read about the push toward standards and standardized testing. Ronald Reagan's name appears and I learn about the "No Child Left Behind" campaign that ties educational subsidies and funding to performance. Property prices now reflect the value local schools are perceived to have, and a high-performing school "wins," even if that same school ranks among the highest in cases of teen depression.

How are we scoring these schools?

Who decided that all children learn the same way and should be taught the same way? During our four homeschooling years, it was evident that the children were different—they learned differently. Shouldn't education be about providing a venue to highlight and hone their individual talents and gifts rather than robotizing education, streamlining them all to be measured the same, pushing them into one system, like products generated on an assembly line? We claim to value diversity on other levels—in business, breakfast cereals, consumer products, and apps on our phones, so why should our children be mass-educated in public education?

What happened to freedom of choice?

Where are my choices?

I read about how kids are being prescribed and getting hooked on ADHD drugs, one of the most prolific medications in the United States. In the panic to compete, if the doctors don't prescribe the drugs, students (or parents) procure them illegally. Have we created a system in which they are destined to get lost? Driving it full throttle, afraid they won't get jobs otherwise, one day? Make money, or be lost. Or worse, fail as a capitalist. Isn't this true?

I recall a conversation I had once with a mother, arguing as to how to find the fun and individual achievement in sailing versus competitive sailing.

"It's the way, though," she had said, shrugging.

Is it the way though, or have we simply made it the way?

Lately, I am attending and watching my son's first-grade class. Even at this young age, technology and big money is moving in, taking the power away from teachers, the information. Our children are learning to be workers, not critical thinkers. Business, so-called success, and money are the end goals.

What has happened to the intellectuals, the ones who question the system? The thinkers? The artists? Is this education, or is it perpetuation? People talk casually about climate change on the playground, without engaging, without knowing much, if anything, about it. What the hell has happened to our ability to think for ourselves? We no longer take responsibility, content instead to give power to others who claim to have the answers. "Don't worry your heads about it," they say. "We're the experts. Let us handle it. We know what we're doing."

Yes, they do. They are the ones profiting from it. Profiting from our ignorance.

I can no longer bear to be at the school grounds. I watched the PE teacher stand there, with a recording device that tells the kids what to do while he watches. The children line up on marked lines, darting from one to the next, are told to be quiet and do as they are instructed, while, nearby, parents smile encouragingly. I look at the schoolyard and its marked areas for competitive games—basketball, baseball, a plastic gym on rubber mats, all with so many rules. I see a huge, wide open, grassed area, devoid of trees, rocks, or other contemplative nooks where the quiet children might find respite from those children who are loud and aggressive, those who win the attention of teachers.

I watch children line up, fight to be first. This feels wrong to me. I have to leave a classroom at one point as I watch my six-year-old son, along with others, sit in their chairs staring at their individual iPads, something we as parents, I was told, should be happy about. They spend thirty minutes learning how to log in with passwords. Working individually instead of as a group, the children stare at screens filled with silly cartoons asking questions that require the children to push buttons to answer. As all this goes on, the teacher sits back and sips her coffee.

"Why do this?" I ask the teacher.

"This way we can track their learning, the information, and report it to the state." She continues to sip her coffee.

Information? That's all we care about? When a teacher sits with a student, it's not just information that is exchanged and shared—the nurturing and language are also shared. It is about being human, not a machine simply exchanging information.

I can't stand watching my son learn this way. I have to do something, but I don't yet know what that is. Why don't other people see what I see? My gut tells me this is all wrong, but I can't explain what I see and what I feel.

Ricci and I find something else to argue about.

"Ricci, I want to move. I don't want our kids at this school. Let's move to the countryside, move toward our dreams."

"Sorry, Barbara, but you said it yourself—we're broke." He shuts the door.

I am losing everything, including my voice. Or maybe I just don't realize how long it has been gone.

Lucy sits with José inside his cottage, plucking notes, while I sit outside and watch a squirrel collect bay nuts from a big laurel tree. Music notes pop around me like bubbles, lingering and floating before disappearing.

There is some joy here. A comfort. I look at Lucy who is growing so fast. Blond hair, long. I remember, long ago, sitting next to my guitar teacher, licking my painfully cracked lips while playing *Greensleeves*. I had just returned with my parents from the Grand Canyon, where the Hopi live, where I'd sat in the car, rubbing my fingers on a worry stone or sticking my head out the window to feel the wind flow through my hair. My guitar teacher, seeing my cracked lips, had paused my lesson to buy me Blistex. It's the odd kindnesses we remember, the kindness shown when we need it most.

Other childhood images come to mind. Sitting alone in my room, a *Herbie the Love Bug* poster on one wall, dolls scattered about. The pollywogs down the street. The sounds of neighborhood kids playing tag, or hide-and-go-seek.

My brother's stereo. My brother, as he left. Listening to Bread sing "If a picture paints a thousand words," late at night, as I thought of my brother. Mom was right. He had always protected me when we were growing up. And then the music was gone. My brother was gone. There was no one left who would protect me.

"Your father is making a big mistake," my grandfather had said. His Irish temper, some claimed. My grandfather was trying to protect my mom, his daughter, to make sure she was safe with my dad.

The yelling at labor union halls. "Gentlemen, please put your beers under your chairs when the news teams come in." The men had been drinking, discussing, worrying, still optimistic that Reagan, the leader of our country, would see reason and make a deal.

I sat and watched it all.

Ricci stands above me, yelling at me. Yesterday, I couldn't figure out how to make a rabbit shelter with a hammer, nails, and wood. The rabbits are digging a hole in the yard. I dreamed last night that the house fell into the rabbit hole.

I feel worried all the time about what to do. I'm tired of the yelling. I feel so alone, with my thoughts and worries.

I'm going to get my family back on track, I think.

"I'm going to get my job back, Barbie," Dad had said.

"Dad, you got fired."

"Barbie, I stood for what I believed in."

Dreams.

When are they delusional, and when should we fight for them?

October 2013

The junior dictionary is removing words like "acorn" and supplanting them with words like "broadband." Kyle refuses to go to school now. He's always had trouble with transition. On his first day of school he squeezed my hand three times, his signal that he didn't want to go. I have to drag him sometimes in the morning, football-hold him at times, once in his pajamas.

I attend my daughter's sixth-grade class to help lead a book club. They are required to read *The True Confessions of Charlotte Doyle*, a fantastic adventure story about sailing the high seas, mutiny and more—my sort of thing. But instead of excitement, I was confronted by lethargic kids wanting only to weather the assignment. They knew the answers to the questions, but there was no vigor, no passion, no excitement, no imagination. Weren't they inspired? Didn't they feel something? Anything?

"Have you ever sailed?" I asked.

"I've been on cruise ships, and sat in hot tubs," one said.

"These kids are half-dead," I told the teacher afterward. "They need adventure!"

The teacher didn't disagree. She was doing her best, I could see, a good teacher in a broken system. We are killing our children's spirit. Killing them with luxury, fears of maintaining safety, and padding them with comfort.

"This is wrong." I tell Ricci. "I want to go back to homeschooling."

"Not going to happen, Barbara."

"Then I want to change schools. Let's move to Bali and go to the Green School or something."

"Not going to happen."

"I have no say in my children's education? I am their mother, Ricci!"

"You said it yourself: we're in debt."

"Then sell the house! I want out, and I want a say in my children's education. If I don't, then I'm going to do something about it."

I don't have a say in anything, apparently. I want to sell the house, but he won't. I want to live in a smaller house with less responsibility, but he doesn't. He tells me to get a job, but when I have a job, he doesn't like it.

I've been his support but he hasn't been mine. I have to do something. I need to write. My first stop, though—I need to return to school, to graduate school. However, we don't have the money.

But that didn't stop me before. I decide I will find a way.

No excuses.

November 2013

It's a midwinter day in San Francisco. The air is cool and clear. I need to connect with my old writing mentor, Bryna Stevens. I need comfort, and her little studio piled with journals, half-written projects, books, and music sheets would nourish me. I missed the writers' group from San Francisco, the same group where twenty years earlier I'd shared my mediocre, disconnected stories. I watched authors Tamim Ansary and Joe Quirk launch their writing careers. When would I ever finish my short stories, and when would I ever sell them? I am losing hope. I am still exhausted from the summer sailing program. I feel I have no control of anything in my life.

I envision Bryna as I drive across the bridge into San Francisco—her dangling cable-car earrings, her swinging crocheted purse with the pencil invariably sticking out at the bottom, through the threads. I haven't talked to her in years, and I haven't called to warn her I was coming. She must be pushing ninety, I think with a start.

I recall the tune she would play on the battered old wooden piano at Simple Pleasures Cafe. She always smiled when she did, always prefacing it with "Have you heard this one?" It was always the same tune.

I thought back to dancing with her at a party in Pacific Heights with thirty-somethings.

"Is she your grandmother?" they'd ask.

"Nope."

It's easy to be a rebel by simply having an intergenerational friendship. She never let anything stop her from doing what she wanted, even if societal norms dictated otherwise. I miss those days, and I am hoping Bryna will lightheartedly joke about my current life state, to loosen the tension and help me bring it all together.

I park my car along a quiet street near her studio, not far from Ocean Beach and the Simple Pleasures Cafe. Fresh Pacific Ocean air is distinct. It cuts straight to your lungs, expanding them and everything you are. I walk toward her building, one designed as affordable housing for the elderly, and recently released prisoners. (I never did figure that combination out. The city houses its most vulnerable among its most anguished citizens?)

Music greets me, coming from somewhere, but I'm not sure where. It fills the salty air. Symphonic maybe, or piano? It is beautiful, expansive, elevating my soul. It surrounds me. I slow my pace, trying to identify the source of the music—an open window, a nearby church, perhaps? I see nothing. I pause and look up, at the big blue cloudless sky. The music was emanating from overhead.

"Oh, no." I whisper, and walk faster. I was suddenly reminded of the black and white photograph I had taken twenty years before, on a day much like this one, clear, quiet and warm. She had said she would play the piano in heaven and we had both laughed before I snapped the photo. I had never shown it to her because her eyes had looked oddly dead in it.

At the door, I scan the list of residents, looking for her name. It's not there. Don't panic, I tell myself. I take a deep breath. Maybe she moved.

There are people in the lobby. I knock. A heavyset black woman opens the door, lifting her eyeglasses, suspiciously, to get a better look at me. She has a big purple bow around her wild frizzy hair. Teeth are missing.

"Excuse me, do you know Bryna Stevens? I'm looking for her."

"What do you want with Bryna Stevens, honey?" Her tone was less than friendly.

"I'm an old friend, come to say hello."

She puts her hands on her thick hips and cocks her head.

"Honey, what kinda friend are you? Bryna Stevens's been dead for years."

My legs nearly give out, and I lean against the wall.

"What happened?"

She shrugged.

Only later would I learn that Bryna had been found dead, naked, on the floor, possibly about to shower in advance of a celebration being held with the other tenants. They had not ruled out rape. She was nearly ninety years old. Nobody came for her. No family. No friends. No one had told me.

I search online for obituaries when I get back home. Nothing. Everything in her apartment, I was told, had been thrown away, including her journals, books, pictures, everything. Her piano was donated to charity. All traces of Bryna Stevens, the author, musician, and amazing woman who wore mini San Francisco cable-car earrings, had abruptly vanished from the earth.

I could have done something. I could have been there for her. I could have stayed in touch. Instead, I let myself become wrapped up in my own life, running a sailing organization, homeschooling, and worrying about my marriage.

The only trace of Bryna's existence I can find are her published children's books. I get online and start to order them. I have no idea where the money will come from to pay for them, but I need these books. I am the only one alive, as far as I know, who cares about this amazing woman, a woman who had touched my life.

I order books secondhand, books scattered around the country, starting at $2.30 apiece.

Guilt is mounting. Who and what else has passed me by?

What kind of friend am I? What kind of person am I?

Who am I?

Ricci continues to find reasons to be angry with me. Spoons are wrong side up in the dishwasher. I don't stack shoes correctly. I should stop teaching my nature classes and get a real job. (He doesn't have a job either.) We're stuck again. I want out of this albatross of a house. I desperately want to simplify my life.

Kyle gets more and more stubborn as the days pass, and it's proving all but impossible these days to get him out to do the simplest things.

The End

Lucy, increasingly despondent, spends too much time alone, in her bedroom. Everything is falling apart, including the house, which is covered in dry rot. We are living off fumes, steadily increasing our debt.

I go to the bakery to write, that forgotten bakery with the cobwebs in the corners, the one where I'd met José, where I can buy a chocolate donut for $1.25 and be reminded of my grandfather, who didn't let money stand in the way of pursuing his dreams. It helps me sift through my thoughts. I want to write about Bryna, but am forced to admit I don't know much about her at all, even after all those years we spent hanging out together. We had talked writing.

Her death needs to mean something. She was a big person. She should be recognized in a big way. She should exit with a flourish, a sweeping bow.

I don't know what to write about.

José and Joe are inside, when I arrive. I am quiet and don't talk much. I overhear Joe talking about the sixties generation and some of what he saw.

"There were a lot of lost kids." Joe said.

I listen, marveling at the interesting relationship José has with Joe. José, a rebel musician who would look at home with Janis Joplin or Jimi Hendrix, and Joe, a grandfatherly looking straight-laced sort of guy who resembles someone who should be coaching Little League baseball. (Later, I find out he has.) They have a relationship not unlike that which I'd had with Bryna. No one could figure us out either.

"José," I say, "what's it like to play music in front of thousands of people?"

He leans back in his chair, contemplating my question.

"It's no different than playing for a few people. It's just feeling, that's all."

Feeling. I think about that. I still can't think of anything to write about Bryna. I feel like a terrible friend.

One by one, Bryna Stevens's books arrive in the mail, secondhand, from libraries, schools, and families. Some have torn pages or scribbles. Others have library cards inside. Evidence of a life.

I sift through the pages looking for any information on Bryna. Maybe I can find a reference to her son, or other family or friends.

I leaf through *Handel and the Famous Sword Swallower of Halle*, Bryna's telling of how the future composer George Frederic Handel strove to study music over his father's objections. The author's note says, of Handel, "There are no diaries or letters to refer to."

That is also true of Bryna, I think, no diaries or letters that I can refer to. I know nothing else about her.

In *Frank Thompson: Her Civil War Story*, Bryna wrote that she found Emma's story "appealing, because it told me how one young woman struggled to find her way in a male-dominated society, as many women are doing now."

I think about that, a male-dominated society.

Dedicated to the rebel in all of us.

Bryna was a rebel, I reasoned, always with a smile on her face, doing what she wanted. I think back to my houseful of young thirty-somethings, when people saw her dance and were surprised to learn she was my friend and not my grandmother. We were rebels.

Things that people have done are more exciting than anything anyone could make up.

I think of my mother-in-law, how she favored true stories about real people over fiction because she found them more interesting.

If only I had a good story, I think.

I open Bryna's *Witches, Great Mysteries, Opposing Viewpoints* and read: "One thing all mysteries have in common is that there is no ready answer."

I like the sound of this idea, of mysteries. I think about the music I heard coming from the sky, that mystery for which there I had no ready answer. I pick up *Borrowed Feathers and Other Fables*, which had been edited by Bryna.

We are the giants of the sea, cried the Great Fishes. All creatures are afraid of us. But you, Little Fishes, are helpless. You cannot defend yourselves.

Bryna had left this world like a little fish. That wasn't right. There should have been fanfare with her passing, her death marked by a big story, not one lost in the shuffle of a meaningless world.

The lady with the purple bow in her frizzy hair had told me that the city of San Francisco had dumped all her stuff and given only the piano to charity, the sole item they felt had any value.

"They took care of her body," the woman replied, when I asked.

Dumped by the very city she loved, whose cable cars she modeled on her ears.

I was not a good friend. My marriage is unraveling and I watch my kids, miserable, in a school I do not feel good about. I am going against my very values of how to raise my kids. Kyle has begun to physically lash out, to hit me, when I don't give him what he wants. In addition to not being a good friend, I feel I'm failing as a mother, unable to raise my kids the way I want to, and in an environment I feel good about. I'm stuck. I have no voice in any decision.

Seeking comfort, I try to write, but my words still feel mediocre and disconnected.

I'm growing weary and thin. I need something.

December 2013

I'm a rebel. I'm doing it. I'm not going to listen to anyone but me.

I went to all my previous junior colleges—Chabot, Ohlone, Santa Rosa, City College in San Francisco, and San Francisco State, dragging Kyle around with me most of the time as I stood in long lines, ordering transcripts and sending them to Dominican University. He was good about it, despite his low temperament for transition. I filled out all the needed paperwork, wrote a letter of intention, paid tuition (Mom is lending the funds to me for the moment) and I am now a registered graduate student in the Department of Humanities.

I'm doing it, even if we're not sure how we will pay the mortgage and property taxes in the coming months. I have no idea how I'll pay for upcoming tuition. Call me irresponsible or call me determined. I'm doing it. It's one night a week, for God's sake. I'm a rebel.

And I'm scared shitless.

Bryna's words from *Frank Thompson: Her Civil War Story* give me encouragement: "I found Emma's story appealing because it told me how one young woman struggled to find her way in a male-dominated society, as many women are doing now."

She had dedicated that book "to the rebel in all of us."

I'm a rebel.

In my first graduate class at Dominican University, Environmental Ethics, I encounter these two quotes from a volume entitled *The Great New Wilderness Debate*.

"Wilderness helps us to put our 'civilized' lives in perspective; it simplifies living; reacquaints us with pain, fear, and solitude; provides us with a necessary sense of challenge; and helps us discover what is really important and essential to our existence."*

"The beauty of the world consists wholly of sweet mutual consents, either within itself or with the supreme being. As to the corporeal world, though there are many other sorts of consents, yet the sweetness and most charming beauty of it is its resemblance of spiritual beauties."**

February 2014

We drive up to Anja's house, up north, along the coast. Dante, my father-in-law, at this stage, had passed after struggling with cancer for fifteen years. It was sad for all of us. I always loved visiting them—mushroom hunting, seaside walks, and bread making. The energy is different now. I can feel it.

We sit at the beautiful crystal glass Cassina table. Anja has arduously sewn a thick tablecloth to protect it from the children damaging it. She understands how to care for things. I admire her for that.

While she's making dinner, I tell her I've started graduate school. She looks at me.

"Why would you do that? Aren't you busy with the kids? I thought you had financial difficulties."

"Yes, but it's just one night a week. I think it'll be good for me.

---

* *The Great New Wilderness Debate: An Expansive Collection of Writing Defining Wilderness from John Muir to Gary Snyder* is a collection of previously published essays on the environment, compiled by editors J. Baird Callicott and Michael P. Nelson, and published by the University of Georgia Press in June 1998.

** *The Great New Wilderness Debate,* excerpted from the 18th century theologian Jonathan Edwards' *The Images or Shadows of Divine Things.*

I'll be able to teach at a higher level once I graduate. My parents are helping me out."

She doesn't answer or look up at me, just keeps stirring the potatoes. We sit down to eat. As usual the food, lighting, and setting are exquisite. She knows how to present life so perfectly. Everything is always done so beautifully.

We begin to eat. I start the conversation again.

"Lucy and I are excited. Jane Goodall is coming to the university to talk about her new book on plants, about the power of plants."

"Who is Jane Goodall?"

"Jane Goodall—I'm sure you've heard of her. She's worked her whole life with chimpanzees, trying to protect them, and advocates environmentalism. It's been her life's work."

Anja pauses and sets down her fork and knife.

"I don't get these people, these do-gooders. I mean, look at Mother Teresa. After an entire life of work, what did she ever really accomplish?"

My jaw drops. Thank goodness for the protective cushioned tablecloth. Did she just shoot down Mother Teresa? My mind spins with questions.

I look at my husband for support. He is either carefully choosing the right words to bridge a divide that has just been created or trying to decide which side of the divide he prefers to be on, his mother's or his wife's.

"Uh, Mother, I think Mother Teresa did a few good things."

"I just don't get it, these do-gooders," she insists.

I think about my grandfather and great-uncle who left their families to fight for strangers in other countries during World War II. They risked death to do something they believed was right and just. This woman sitting across the table from me came to our country, from Germany, to enjoy the very freedom and richness they fought so hard to protect.

My mind is spinning. This woman ridiculed Hershey's chocolate, the same woman who, as a little girl, was given her very first taste of chocolate—Hershey's—by an American soldier who had risked his life over there. How much, I wonder now, has she given back to our country while enjoying all the good things it has to offer? What is the meaning of this family's life, besides possessing fine Arabia dishes, good German porcelain, and Italian linen? It is not lost on me that the very reason she is here to enjoy this moment in the U.S. is because of supposedly misguided do-gooders like my grandfather and great-uncle. However, that fact appears lost on her.

I look past Anja, through the large glass door to the glistening sunset over a wide expansive ocean. An atomic bomb of enlightenment donates, bursting apart a bubble I have been living inside my entire adult life of what the "good life" consists of—what I have been taught to pursue—to smithereens.

The horror of the realization is that I am no better than Anja. I enjoy the good life, with fine food and atmosphere, when the ocean outside the window I sit opposite is being horribly, possibly irrevocably abused. I'm not sacrificing for the next generation. What kind of mother am I to sit on the sidelines, blithely saying, "Pass the potatoes," while her children's world is being devastated? What sort of mother am I to enjoy the good without putting in the hard work for a better future?

"I'm really worried about the ocean, you know," I say, changing the subject. "Ocean acidification is real. I hear the salmon stocks are low again this year. Do you realize scientists say we've lost ninety percent of the salmon population?"

Have I said something else wrong? Instead of replying, Anja gets up from the table and marches away. Why isn't this a conversation to share?

The profound layers of illusion in my life surface in all their ugliness, as I watch the waves crash against the cliffs and the sun drop beyond the horizon. I look around the room at all the treasured *objets d'art* I had once admired. It all looks ugly now. Nothing matters if we don't get what's important right, I think.

The next day we go to the beach. There is a newfound tension between Anja and me. Ricci plays with the kids by the water's edge, where they make sand castles. I sit with Anja and watch the crashing waves move closer and closer to the fragile sand castle onshore, a feeling of foreboding settling over me.

"He's got a job. You should be happy." Anja said. The winter sun is doing its best to take some of the chill out of the air.

"It's a consulting job. He hasn't been hired yet." Ricci doesn't even want the job, I know, complaining about it repeatedly. He is taking the job so we can support the big house his parents had given us that I didn't even want to live in. I don't want him to take the job.

"I think I'll go back into teaching," I say. "I like teaching."

"Teaching?" She is quiet for a moment as she repositions herself on the sand. "Isn't teaching, you know, just women's work?"

I look at her. "It's what?"

"You know, just traditional work for women. I mean, what about the work you did with the household catalogs? You were paid well. It gave you money, a good position," she says, sitting up taller.

Why is it I can't say anything and get this family's support for it? Couldn't she at least have said, "Go for it, Barbara! You'd make a great teacher." That's what my Auntie Ann would have said.

I think back to the catalog work, standing amid assembly lines at the print houses back east, feeling like I was in the belly of a beast, an economy driving wants and desires. I would color-correct the images of cozy homes designed to inspire and sell products. It left me feeling so empty. It was work to create and sell illusions, nothing more. And after a long day, Ricci would tell me my job wasn't valuable, even if I was the one paying the mortgage while he was struggling with his business.

"Your job doesn't have values," he repeatedly said. He was right, but without it who would pay the bills? I had missed years with my daughter. He was good at pointing out the problems, but wasn't coming up with solutions.

I watch as a large wave swallows the sand castle, and bite my lip as it disappears before my eyes.

It's a disaster.

We have a tenant living with us to help with the kids in exchange for a reduced rent. I really need help. Between maintaining the house and yard and kids, I can't keep up. There's no money for sitters. My clothes look like rags and my hair like Medusa's. Kyle is out of control and it's only gotten worse since Dante died. Ricci yells all the time. I tell him I can't hold on to everything anymore.

And if that's not enough, I'm in graduate school, even if it is just one night a week. I don't care how unreasonable or irresponsible it seems. I'm not giving that up. It may be the one thread that stitches everything back together, as crazy as that sounds.

My Environmental Ethics class has been intense as I re-enter the larger, outer world and learn the disaster our planet now faces—climate change, acidifying oceans, and more. It makes every problem in my own life a non-problem. Isn't there a Zen saying, that the way to solve one problem is to deal with a bigger one? My God, how are we living our lives?

Every day I look around at people all living in la-la land, going around doing their daily business without a thought for the bigger picture. Grocery shopping, getting kids to soccer games, planning family vacations to Mexico—nobody is awake to our new reality. I think of my children and what we are leaving them. It is OUR responsibility to stop this mass consumerism and competition with one another. We are killing ourselves, and we are out of control.

I am given a class assignment to write an essay describing a wilderness experience. I ask if I can write about my voyage on the ocean. I mean, the ocean is part of the wilderness, right? I think the teacher was expecting one set on land, and I had to push her, pointing out that the ocean comprises seventy percent of our planet's surface. It is as wild as it gets! As I write these papers, I learn more and more of the horror we face—coral reefs dying, the dangers of overfishing, and more. When is enough enough?

I'm struggling to do all the domestic work at home. Ricci works full-time at a job he doesn't like, leaving me to wonder how long it will last. I am fully responsible for the kids as well, and I feel like I am treading water, never getting ahead, barely staying afloat. The house is always a disaster, so I get up in the middle of the night to do my homework. I am convinced the garage is still breeding stuff because I am not buying anything and yet the piles grow. I try to shield the children when Ricci gets upset. We're in a rut, I keep saying.

Kyle's rage has gotten out of control, and it's exhausting me. He's only seven years old and yet he refuses to go to school and flies into tantrums, kicking and biting me, when I insist. Ricci has occasionally stepped in, but the other day he walked by when I had pinned a flailing Kyle down so he wouldn't hurt me, and I asked for help, all he said was, "You're the mother—you handle it."

I receive no support with anything. I plead with him.

"Ricci, I have no community, no support here. This house is too big for me to handle, no grandparents to lend a hand, we have no money, and I do not like the children's school. Please," I beg, "I want to move somewhere simpler. At least I'd like to get our son help. I need help!"

"We handle this by ourselves," he says crossly, and waves me away.

We? He's not helping me.

The clusters of spiders grow in the corners. I just watch them weave now.

I'm failing on all levels and growing despondent.

I bury myself in my books.

I take Kyle to the bakery to get a donut. A simple, round, $1.25 chocolate donut somehow comforts me. And I like quiet places, where people whisper and think.

José and Joe are inside, talking, sipping coffee, and eating blueberry muffins. I try to say hello and chitchat but Kyle keeps pulling me away.

"Come on, Mom, I wanna go now."

I am exhausted, thinking about the problems and big life decisions I must face.

José looks at me. His words are soft, gentle.

"It's going to be okay."

I absorb his words eagerly, like a dry sponge inhales a drop of moisture.

"I'd like to believe that. I really would."

But what is there to believe?

I still listen to his music online. It also reassures me that somehow it's all going to be okay.

I am thick into reading about John Muir, how people considered him crazed when he first spoke in defense of the wilderness, when José walks into the bakery and sits in his usual chair, after ordering his usual blueberry muffin and coffee.

"Hey" I say. He seems lost in thought. "Where's your partner in crime?"

"Joe's with family." He points up to the speakers. Steve Winwood's music is playing. "Higher Love."

"Are you okay?" I say. Something seems to be bothering him.

"Oh, stuff, you know. Divorce and that."

I am not sure it's a good idea for me right now to talk about negative things. He talks about being old, his career, and though he doesn't say it in so many words, he seems to be feeling regret about the good days being gone and how maybe he's just an old guitarist sitting in a bakery filled with cobwebs. Maybe he is, if he thinks he is.

I listen, thinking he's an artist who has followed his passion. He's played with the best in the world and his music is stunning. How can he possibly feel down on life? Surely, if he isn't riding high and happy then there has to be a problem with the world.

I wanted to say, "Dude, you've still got it! If you're going down, there's no fucking hope for little people like me. And I'm not going down. So, that means you've gotta go way up!" But I don't say that. I just listen, and feel a strange rumbling, a little seed cracking in my belly.

We no longer sleep together.
I need to hear my own voice, beyond his.
"Ricci, please, stop talking so much at me," I would say, between his words perpetually listing what I was doing wrong and what I should be doing. "Please, Ricci, I can't hear myself think."
I need quiet.
After each of his admonishments, it takes me days to recover. Am I too sensitive?
Be strong, Barbara, be strong. Don't be so sensitive. I remind myself of his mother's advice to me. But his voice goes around and around in my head. It's taking a toll on my health. My nerves are frayed. I feel weak. When I speak up in my defense, my words only spur his. All I can do is walk away, which is what I've finally done. I now sleep in a separate room.
"Where are you going?" he demands. "You can't even finish a conversation."
"I need quiet," I say, and disappear into my room. I listen to José's music. It calms me.

Ricci appears in my room and wakes me up. He stands near the window. Red light pulsates on his face. Police are removing a homeless person who has camped out behind our fence, something that has never happened before. Ricci looks at me. The air is still. He's not angry, or irritated, but he is upset. I listen.
"I had a dream," he says. "I had a dream that a bald man with your voice told me all the things that I've done to hurt you all these years.

I woke up and shivered, feeling the hurt myself." He looks at me. "I am so sorry, Barbara."

Am I dreaming?

No, this is real.

"Anything you want, Barbara."

"I want to simplify. Ricci, I want out of this house. It's too big. Let's move to Fairfax. It has community. It's a relaxed community."

Ricci nods and walks out of the room without another word. I think maybe I should pinch myself. Something is happening. Something beyond my understanding.

Something.

I take Lucy to her guitar lesson. We knock on the cottage door and enter. José emerges from the shadows and steps out to greet us. He isn't wearing his customary bandanna. He is completely bald. I smile and shake my head.

I am beginning to believe, to have faith, to feel hope. The universe has a plan, I think, as I listen to Lucy and José play "The House of the Rising Sun." Notes pop around me. I can almost see them drifting through the air, translucent, iridescent bubbles floating, surrounding me.

After the lesson, I pull out money to give him. He seems reluctant to take it, as if it doesn't matter whether I pay him or not.

"Are you okay?" I ask.

"Just things," he says.

I don't know what to say. "Keep perspective," I offer. I don't know what I mean or why I've said it. It just comes out.

"Yeah," he says.

March 2014

Today, March 8th, is my 46th birthday. Things are worse than ever. Ricci is increasingly angry. He's working, but he hates it, all to keep a house from rotting, a house I don't want. Kyle is still hitting me, hard, and it's getting worse. His rages are sparked when I say no to candy or try to ready him for school in the mornings. I still have to hold him down to keep him from hurting me.

We have plans to go to dinner with Cathy and Frank, to celebrate our birthdays together. Cathy has a gift certificate to a nice restaurant she is sharing with us. Earlier in the day, Uncle Bob's old friend, Arianne Paul, calls to say she's come to town to look at the tall ships, The *Hawaiian Chieftain* and *Lady Washington*, which have docked at a port in Sausalito. After ten years I still owe Arianne a drink, to thank her for having taken our German *au pair* sailing. I dash out of the house to meet her.

"I'll be back in two hours, Ricci!" There was still plenty of time before dinner. Ricci, angry, tells me not to go.

"It's my birthday, Ricci. Can I please do something I want on my birthday?"

I meet up with Arianne and we have a great time looking at the beautiful, tall ships, taking pictures with the pirate-looking crew, igniting stories of history and adventure, a real maritime treasure. We sit and have a drink together and talk about Uncle Bob. She had admired him, not just for his racing skills but his integrity.

"I'm not going to dinner," Ricci announces, when I get back.

"*What?*"

He does this.

"Ricci, it's my birthday and Cathy's birthday. We've been invited. We've committed."

"Nope." He shuts his door to the office.

What to do? I call Cathy and Frank and apologize.

"We have to cancel. Ricci isn't feeling well." They are not happy about this. I am practiced at doing this, making excuses so we don't look bad. It's wearing thin now.

I am relieved to hear that Jane's daughter Meg is going to run the organization this year. I had encouraged her to do so, to move from New York to California and take over the organization. To my amazement, she packed up her apartment and drove cross-country to take the helm. I offer to initially handle the communications, part-time work, and then pass the baton so I can get on with life.

Jane and I attend the Boating and Waterways conference in Oakland. I am on my guard because although I see the good in her, she still makes jabs about Ricci, and I still stick up for him, not wanting to allow her to drag our family name into the mud. What Ricci did for the organization was exceptional. The organization would have long been dead without him. Then I go home and face his anger while he complains about me to me. I have to defend myself.

We'll get through this, I insist. I have to believe. Be strong, Barbara. Be strong. Don't be sensitive.

A flyer is passed out at the conference. The 11th Hour Racing program of the Schmidt Family Foundation is offering a sizable grant. I grab the paper without even thinking.

"This one is mine." I say to Jane.

Why am I so confident? I have never written a grant proposal before. But I feel something compelling me to do this. Jane eyes me.

My thoughts whirl. An idea is taking shape. I think of Carlos Grana, the film director, the final person in the organization whom I've wanted to find a way to give back to. So many people had given so much to the organization and left, frustrated or angry because they either weren't sufficiently recognized or burned themselves out doing stuff nobody else wanted to do. I hadn't wanted Carlos to be one of them.

In the organization, I had also found my heritage, one to be proud of, after so many years spent believing I had a rotten family. If I could recognize Carlos properly, I was convinced any lingering debt I owed to the organization would have been paid, and I could truly be free of it. With Meg taking over now, our family name would be cleared and we could go back to being a family, and live our dreams.

I Skype Carlos.

"Carlos, I have an idea for a film." Kids sailing, and science, a short film. It is inspired by the 1930s English series of books, *Swallows and Amazons,* by Arthur Ramsone. I describe a film about sailing kids discovering the tiny copepod, animal plankton that live in the ocean. I thought this little one-eyed creature, combined with the children's enthusiasm for it, might help people understand the magical beauty of, and responsibility we have to, the oceans. It's not just the oceans that are imperiled, I have learned, but the planet's oxygen too. Most of our planet's oxygen is produced by the oceans, oceans that are now acidifying, dangerously.

"If we get the funding, you will have absolute creative control, and you get your day rate," I tell Carlos. I pause. "I am the producer."

He smiles. I smile back. A line has been drawn, one that unites points in the universe. I can feel it, even if I have no reason to believe it. Notably, I have never produced a film before. I admire what Carlos, a young 40-something, incredibly good-looking Peruvian Latin guy who speaks three languages, is doing, having given up a very successful international language business to pursue his dream of being a film director, in Los Angeles. He wanted to make movies. With no experience whatsoever. None. But that hasn't deterred him. I see that drive, that passion, in his emerging film work online.

He likes women, capturing their poetry—visual poetry, their depth, below the surface. Not just women but landscapes too. He illustrates how the body mirrors the textures of the earth, the gentle curves, deep caverns, the seductive innocence and power, the urge for domination combined with the fear of being dominated.

It takes guts to pursue crazy dreams. And I want to pursue this one, with him.

I sit on the edge of my chair, my body shaking with anger. How can they do this?

I am at the Ocean Film Festival, in San Francisco, watching a film called *Sand Wars,* by Denis Delastrac. We are raping our planet! I watch footage of vast amounts of sand being scooped from bays and beaches to build fancy skyscrapers, and more, around the world for the rich, and to lure others to the rich lifestyle. What are we doing to ourselves? I think of my pollywogs. We no longer cover just runoff ditches with concrete—we're covering our entire planet!

I can't stop thinking about this film.

Ricci signs us up for a basket-making class up north, near his mother's home. We stay with her and learn how to weave a Native American basket. He's trying, trying to stitch more than just a basket. We sit together in silence, under fluorescent lights, in a room with strangers. We are given instructions on how to weave long pine needles into a coiled pattern.

It is our first night and his mother takes a bad fall and breaks her arm. It is a horrible accident and I feel badly for her. I go back the next day to finish the basket on my own, alongside strangers, under the glare of fluorescent lights. I feel so alone.

Where is my community?

The basket, when I finish it, is beautiful, and more than that. It connects me to the indigenous cultures and reminds me to respect the work and art of something so delicate and small. I'll give it to someone, like the Ohlone women have done, I think.

I know it's important to be here for Anja, but I need someone here for me too.

April 2014

"Why isn't he answering his phone?"

It is Easter Sunday. Ricci left for the weekend and I don't know where he is. I try my best to hide the colored eggs in the garden and create some sense of joy. I look at the kids. There are expectations—egg hunts, brunch, and celebration. I am determined to make the best of it for them.

I am alone. Again.

"Jane has invited us to the ranch where she keeps her horse," I tell the kids. "We'll go ride a horse for Easter." I sense a subtle uneasiness in them.

I hide eggs in the garden, but the spirit isn't there. I try calling Ricci again. No answer. Damn it, it's Easter Sunday, for God's sake! But I can't get mad, not in front of the children.

"Let's get ready to go, kids." I say. My daughter is enthusiastic. She loves horses.

"I'm not going," my son announces.

"Horses, Kyle. We'll do an Easter egg hunt too."

"Nope, not going."

I can't disappoint my daughter again. She has missed so many good times because of her brother's defiance.

"Kyle, you have to come." I am growing impatient.

"Nope." He positions himself into that all too familiar willful, stubborn angle and walks over to my computer to play video games.

"Kyle, you can't stay here by yourself and you are NOT playing video games."

I don't have the fight in me. I text Ricci again. I am unraveling. I find myself with no husband, a defiant son, and a daughter I'm anxious not to disappoint, on Easter Sunday, and God knows I don't want to be late for Jane, considering the fragility at times of our relationship, and especially after she has arranged something so nice. I'll get him a babysitter, I think, but it's Easter Sunday. Who would be available?

Just then, our tenant, Brenda, drives in. She's my only hope.

"It's Easter Sunday!" she says, glaring at me.

"I know, but this is important for my daughter. And Kyle." She does not look happy. "Please?"

She doesn't actually say no, so I take that as a yes. I hustle Lucy into the car and we speed away. I need to get out. I need to see Jane, although I don't know precisely why. It's my gut feeling. Not for the horses, but for some other reason I can't put my finger on.

I call Ricci again. Still no answer. Damn him! It's his kids, for God's sake. I have no help, no money, a huge house that's falling apart, my nerves are a wreck, and a tenant who likely wants nothing more than to kill me at this moment. And who can fault her for it? And I have a husband who has disappeared.

I turn to Lucy. "We'll get through this. I promise. You dad is just going through something."

Lucy and I drive the hour to the stables without talking. Too many other voices are spinning through my head. We play the radio instead and I try to find hidden meanings in lyrics, words, and tunes, anything to soothe me and help make sense of everything.

We find Jane at the stables. Lucy joins an egg hunt with the country kids, but finds no joy in it. It is driven by nothing more than a sense of duty, of polite obligation, and so I find no joy in it either.

Jane harnesses the horses. I watch her talk to her horse and give it tough love, jerking its head up whenever it tries to eat grass, followed by a pat of affection. There is a stirring in the air, a sense of balance. I am here for a reason, I think, and so I watch every move and listen to every word, seeking clues.

"Let's get the carriage out," Jane suggests.

Lucy and I help her pull out an old carriage and hook it up to the horse. She takes Lucy around the arena, a small space with no walls. The air is warm and I sit on spring grass, smelling its earthy perfume. A turkey vulture swoops in the distance, circling, mimicking Lucy

The End

and Jane as they continue to circle the arena. Then it is my turn to get in the carriage with Jane.

I strap on a helmet and step into the rickety carriage, sitting hip to hip with Jane. I have a heightened sense of anticipation I can't rationalize, and think back to the day I stepped into a small, rickety boat and how it changed my life. I am fully present in the moment, as if it is trying to communicate to me in another language. My job is to decipher the message.

Jane cracks the whip and we trot around the arena.

"Remember, you're in charge. Always stay in charge," she says, holding the reins. I watch the gallant horse, bound to us, obediently following orders. I can feel the horse in this moment, its broken spirit, doing as it is told, over and over again, with no heart, no joy, no passion.

"Sometimes you let the horse go where he wants." Jane's words pierce my reverie. "Let him feel that for a moment, and then pull him back, so he remembers who is in charge."

This horse has surely circled this ring a hundred times, I thought. How many times has it been jerked into obedience, away from what it wants to do, where it wants to go? I am this horse, jerked, tethered, perpetually bound to someone else's chosen path instead of my own.

"Would you like to try? Remember, the horse can feel you through the reins. That is how you control it, how you get it to do what you want it to do," she says, as she hands me the reins.

It works both ways. I can feel the horse as well, through the reins. It is like we are one, the reins an umbilical cord that ties us together. We trot around and around, the horse and me.

"Now, let him go just a little, and then jerk him back," she says.

I do as I am told but my spirit does something else. Following its lead, the horse shakes off its harness and my spirit jumps onto it and rides, bareback. Together, we race out of the arena like a mustang and a wild child. I can see it in my mind's eye, the whole moment as it plays out. I am naked, raw and free. The horse and I both look back, it with a neigh and me with a war cry that reverberates across the land, shaking free of anyone who has tried to control us. I can taste freedom. It is time for me to leave the arena.

The horse and I look each other in the eye for a long moment before we leave. I feel the horse urging me on.

Lucy and I return home to find Ricci there. Kyle is outside, playing. It is as if nothing had happened.

"Where have you been?" I ask.

"I was camping. Sitting on a hill," he says.

"It's Easter Sunday, Ricci. We were waiting for you. I tried calling, texting you all weekend. No answer. I had a little girl who wanted to see horses today and a little boy who threw a fit."

"I had a spiritual experience."

I pause. "You had a spiritual experience. Well, I'm happy for you, Ricci. But while you feel entitled to do whatever you want, like you always do, I'm here, running madly, trying to maintain a family. Believe me, I'm the one having out-of-body experiences."

Ricci says nothing.

The next morning our tenant is in the kitchen, making breakfast. I would prefer not to face her, but I know I have to.

"Brenda, I know it was a lot to ask of you yesterday. Thank you for watching my son."

She is silent for a moment, before turning to face me.

"Your son needs a lot of help. He acted like a spoiled child. Then your husband comes home and doesn't even reprimand him. Instead, he kisses and hugs him, and tells him everything will be okay. What the hell?"

"I know."

I did know.

"I'll tell you, it *was* a lot to fucking ask me on Easter Sunday. He needed a good spanking! That son of yours…" She stiffens and puts her bread and butter down on the counter, giving me her full attention and demanding mine.

"This place is a disaster! I walk out of my bedroom and what do I see but, like, a forest, flora *blooming*! Laundry, mounds of it, sprouting everywhere! This place is a wreck. Dishes in the sink. The place is disgusting!"

I am strangely calm. I lean against the counter, fascinated, as if enthralled by an actor onstage espousing truths we all need to hear. Her words are quite poetic. I marvel at how she calls my dirty laundry "flora," as I would have a chosen far less complimentary description. Her choice of words are quite kind, when you think about it.

"It's like a fucking petri dish here!"

Okay, perhaps that wasn't quite so kind, but still truthful. I continue to be present, in a relaxed state. I nod, even agree. I could add another colorful adjective or two, to help her rant, were I to choose to. I stifle the urge to lift my hands and stroke the air, a conductor before an orchestra, coaxing the highs and lows of the cadences, the intonations. I understand completely.

Once done, her words spent, she is panting, hard. I am mildly surprised she hasn't throw anything. She exerts better control than I do.

"Brenda, I think the time has come for you to find a new place." My words are clear and calm, matter of fact. "Consider this your one month's notice."

"Fine. I'm more than happy to accept that."

Flora, hmm, really? I look around. Describing it as a garbage heap would be complimentary. I have school work and a paper to write about ocean literacy and sailing. And that is what I am going to do. Let the laundry bloom and be wild and free. I intend to do the same.

"All I've ever wanted was for you to live your lives and be happy," Mom says.

My brother, sister, and I are with Mom and Dad to discuss their plans for the future, what they would like if they become infirmed, and after they die. It is a family meeting to discuss financials, burial arrangements, and how to manage if and when they can no longer take care of themselves.

They invited a planner to join us, to talk numbers, calculations, deeds. We talk about long-term care. We talk about death.

"We want our ashes to be scattered at sea," Mom says. Dad sits quietly to one side as she talks. He doesn't look scared or discomfited. He looks like a man who will go freely when his time comes.

"That's how I want to go." Dad's words, years earlier, return to me. We had been sitting in his Oldsmobile at a drive-in movie theater long ago, eating popcorn, and watching an old western film about a Native American chief. Dad had always loved the mountains. He was a mountain man displaced in modern suburbs. In the film, the chief knew his time was coming, and so, without fanfare, he climbed into in a small canoe and headed out to sea. He accepted death nobly. My dad admired that.

"I don't want you crying and all that nonsense," Mom insists, looking at us. "No sadness."

I watch my dad watch my mom, nodding, supporting her words. After so many years they were still together, despite all the challenges, the arguments, the financial worries. This love has emerged from years of suffering.

The ocean. The bay. The water. It has been my sanctuary for the last ten years. A friend. How could I ever face the water, and my mother's scattered ashes, when I know I'm not happy? Even my sanctuary would serve as a reminder of how unhappy I am.

Why am I so unhappy? I have to be happy for them.

I give my mother the Native American basket I made. I have to be happy, but I can't be happy living in my house. There is something I have to do. I just don't know what it is.

The stress continues to ramp up higher: kids, schoolwork, financial worries, middle-of-the-night writing, Ricci yelling, a disastrous house, Kyle hitting me, cobwebs weaving, dust settling into layers, carpets collecting soil, feeling out of control. My one respite is listening to Neto's music, over and over again. And the grant. I want the grant money. The film. That feeling deep inside keeps telling me not to worry, that the film project is a good idea, even if I've never made a film before, even a little dinky one about a sailing organization most people have never heard of.

The day comes for the grant announcement. There is no announcement. I keep checking my email all day.

I become despondent. Forget it! Why even email to ask about it? Just forget it. Stupid idea, Barbara. Stupid. Why do you do these things?

Oh, what the hell? I decide to be bold. I email to ask who got the grant and wait for the grant manager to confirm my idea is stupid.

The next day I receive an email.

Congratulations. We look forward to your proposal to determine the final round.

Could this be a mistake? A joke on me?

I wait anxiously for the proposal papers to be emailed. They don't come. I wait. I wait longer, a week, two weeks. I call. I email. I begin to wonder.

Stupid idea, Barbara. A waste of time.

I call one last time. I talk to Kate. It is not a warm conversation. Am I attacking her? Well, she is late in getting the proposal documents to me, but I am not accusing her of that. I suggest they might have gone into my spam filter.

"I sent them yesterday. You didn't get them?"

I hadn't. I look everywhere. Is she lying to me? I don't want to sound like I am harassing her. I wait some more.

I've decided I need a lesson, a guitar lesson. I will do it after Lucy's lesson. I need to learn the next song in my music book, where I left off when I was a child. I am embarrassed but I ask José, and am surprised and relieved when he agrees.

I tell Ricci, who is not happy about it. Then again, nothing seems to make him happy anymore. I think of the times I played my guitar at Christmas. His mother would look at me without a word, as if the notes irritated her. Or perhaps my playing suggested there was something I knew that she didn't. I could never understand this. The guitar is so beautiful. Even the piddling songs I play over and over again make me smile. I need a lesson and I don't know why. I need to pick up where I left off when I was thirteen years old.

"You're in love with him," Ricci accuses.

"What? Jesus! Why do you say this?"

"I read your journal."

"You? You read my writing? Ricci, I'm a writer. I get inspired by something and then I write about characters, inspired by people. I wrote about a woman who takes clown lessons and ends up having sex with a man cross-dressed on top of the Empire State Building. It doesn't mean I'm having an affair. I have an imagination."

He continues to yell. I can't hear my thoughts. The more he shouts, the more I withdraw. I desperately want quiet. I NEED the quiet. It is mentally distorting me, not being able to hear the quiet.

I get up in the middle of the night to find the quiet and revel in it, alone. Sometimes I am outside, playing tennis with Kyle, and I stop as the wind blows, feeling that freedom, that same peace I find on a sailboat, on the Bay. It soothes me. I close my eyes and feel that something else. I remember lying on the bow, staring at the expansive sky, with a white sail above me, listening to its fullness and moving with the rhythmic water.

I often hum *Greensleeves* over and over again, the last guitar song I learned to play. I learned recently that King Henry VIII allegedly had the music written for Anne Boleyn, in an attempt to seduce her. The same Anne Boleyn whose head he later had chopped off when she failed to give him a son. All she'd managed to produce was a daughter, Elizabeth. Yes, the same Elizabeth who would later become one of the most famous and revered queens in history.

Why do we still honor such a king, and why should his portrait hang in museums? Do we value power and domination over truth and compassion?

I need a guitar lesson. I need to learn a new song.

I drop Lucy off for her lesson with José and head off to run an errand. A feeling comes over me, a dreamlike feeling, of being in a groove, when the elements around you are all in balance. It's seductive.

I return to José's cottage before the lesson ends and find Ricci there, sitting in his car. I feel his suspicion and a sense of dread washes over me. He is making me feel guilty for doing something I am not doing, have no intention of doing, and have never done.

How did he know where to find us, where José lived? He looks at me suspiciously, like he has no reason to trust me, like he knows me better than I do, that he can see in me something I refuse to see, or have suppressed, making me doubt myself and my intentions.

"My God, Ricci, please, don't embarrass me! I'm here for a guitar lesson."

We stand outside while Lucy finishes. I hear them plucking the strings, and even the simplest notes lure me to quiet thoughts. Ricci is stiff and watchful of me, as if my mere enjoyment of the notes is evidence that I am an unfaithful wife. When I introduce him to José, it is awkward. Lucy gathers her things and stands there as I take my guitar, feeling silly. I sit down in the student's chair. Ricci watches. It's a simple, goddamn lesson and I will not walk away from it. I open my guitar book under his watchful eyes.

"I've had this book since I was my daughter's age," I say to José, and point to the dates from 1981. The book is open to "Mezzo Tedescom," a German piece, dating back to the Renaissance period.

José examines the piece.

"It's been a while since I read music," he admits, and plucks the first few notes. Ricci watches for a few minutes, then rises and leaves, shutting the door. I feel as if I have witnessed the end of one thing and the beginning of another. I feel overwhelming sadness. I want Ricci to understand why I need this.

I turn back to José.

"I'm sorry. I'm mistaken." I turn the page. "This is what I want to learn, 'Dove Son Quei Fieri Occhi,'" which translates to "Where Are Your Fiery Eyes?" It is by an anonymous Italian composer.

José studies the notes and begins to play, slowly at first, note by note. At first, I just stare at the page in front of me. I feel myself melting back into that thirteen-year-old child. Joseph Blea, chapped lips, chapped soul. Healing. I lick my lips. A sadness starts in my eyes and travels to my throat, where it gets stuck for a moment, before journeying deeper, down into my heart, supplanting a numbness I've been carrying for so long that it hurts now to feel again.

Slowly my fingers form the chords on the frets. I pluck the strings with my right hand, arpeggio style—index finger, middle finger, annular finger.

I M A, A M I, I M A, A M I, I M I. I A M.

The years of pain, my father, my mother, my grandfather, my marriage, my country—locked vibrations in my flesh and bones, slowly release.

I M A, A M I, I M A, A M I, I M I. I A M.

The hurt from Ricci. Don't be so sensitive. Be strong. The anger. The suspicion and lack of trust. Me always doubting myself. Me protecting myself against words thrust at me, over and over again.

"You have to memorize it," he says.

I M A, A M I, I M A, I A M.

The light dims. Shadows grow more vivid on the walls and it is getting harder to see the notes. All I can do is listen.

I M A, A M I, I M A, I ... A M I. I AM.

When we stop. I am quiet, pensive. I give him an awkward smile.

"Thank you, José. It's probably a good thing I didn't continue with guitar lessons because I really suck, don't I? The world doesn't need one more bad guitarist." I want to lighten the mood, but I am not sure how I am coming across. I don't want him to feel awkward.

"Just practice and memorize. It has to go deep, like it's part of you."

Ricci is sitting on the couch, stroking the cat, when I get home. He looks at me accusingly, like I'm guilty of doing something wrong.

"It was just a guitar lesson, Ricci. That's it."

I am driving to Phoenix Lake to teach my children's nature program when a blast of light flares inside me, a fiery image consuming every bit of my mind. I have to pull over and stop. What just happened?

I am surely going mad. Why me, I want to ask, why me?

What am I talking about?

I sit on the banks of the lake with my young nature students, Phoenix Lake, where I took a walk the day my great-uncle died. Everything around me feels different, unlike before. Everything seems more alive, speaking to me through various forms of music—the wind in the trees, the sparkling of the water, the dropping of leaves.

Little Kayla sits quietly next to me, as she often does, when a puff of wind ripples across the water and passes through us. *Through us.* Little Kayla looks at me with wide eyes.

"Did you feel that?"

"Yes," I say. "Yes, I felt that." It went right through me.

I go home and head straight into the bathroom. I sit in front of the mirror, staring at myself. My eyes look frightening to me, like they are ablaze. I feel different. Something inside me burns.

Ricci knocks on the door.

"Are you okay in there?"

I don't know. I don't know, I want to say. But I don't.

"Yes, I'm okay."

I need to talk to my friend Marilyn. The next day I head to her house and pass by the house of another friend, Mandee, who plans to spend the summer in Europe. On impulse, I call her.

"Mandee, I would like to housesit for you while you're in Europe."

"Well, that's weird," she says. "We were just discussing what we'd do with the house. Let's talk next week."

I arrive at Marilyn's house.

"Marilyn, something is happening to me. I need space for a while. I need quiet. I need to write." I sound crazy. I feel crazy. I go into her bathroom and look at myself in the mirror. My eyes still look wild. I shift my head to the side and see the face of a panther with blazing eyes staring back at me, and I draw back, startled.

What is happening to me?

May 2014

Everything is unraveling faster than ever. I wake up in the middle of the night to find the quiet, and write. I feel things in a way I've never felt them before, the sounds around me, the vibrancy of light and colors. Everything feels alive.

We're nearly through the school year. I'm exhausted, watching my daughter weighed down with so much homework, to the point where I went to the school office. I had to watch my words, I knew. I was a thorn, but honestly, I just wanted to ask the hard questions no one else seems to be asking.

An eighth grader bounced in, talking excitedly about an upcoming trip to Six Flags Amusement Park in Vallejo, and triggering my memory of taking Lucy to a dolphin demonstration the year before, during our homeschooling days.

After the girl left, I asked the office staff whether the kids were educated about the dolphin shows there. My question was met with quizzical looks.

"The dolphins. People shouldn't go to dolphin shows. It's horrible for these animals. It's totally disrespectful to them, and our oceans."

They looked at me like I was a crazy woman. Maybe I am, but it's the life everywhere I'm recognizing, and how we don't value life.

"You guys don't know about how these animals are treated?"

"You'd have to talk to the principal."

I couldn't believe it. One of the most highly rated educational schools and they're not onboard with what good people are trying to do for the next generation? Entire communities of people are trying to educate the public about how to respect these magnificent creatures. Films are made about how they are brutally killed in Japan. Ric O'Barry, who captured and trained the dolphins used in *Flipper*, who is arguably responsible for the entire global dolphin entertainment operations, is spending his last years doing what he can to stop the dolphin hunts in Japan and other countries. The general apathy reflects our society's attitude toward nature and life. How many are willing to change their lives, their attitudes and careers, in order to address these very issues? Not enough. Not nearly enough.

I write a letter to the principal. He admits to knowing nothing about the treatment of dolphins; neither has he ever heard of the film *The Cove*, despite the fact it had been an Academy Award-winning documentary that spurred an international effort to stop dolphin hunts.

Is it education, or merely the perpetuation of a system of entertainment, competition, and self-indulgence in the California Distinguished Schools? If this is the model leading our educational institutions, then how are we leading? If this is our ideal education, then who really is insane?

"Ricci, I need quiet. I'm going to housesit for Mandee in Fairfax this summer," I tell him.

We take off our wedding rings.

I didn't mean it to be forever. I'm just lost in this turbulence all around me. I can't find a course. And he's not listening to me. I feel like we are on that race with the Corinthian Club again, where I was skipper and shouting out orders, and Ricci wasn't hearing, wasn't listening. That day didn't end happily.

I want to move. He has said he would move, but instead he brings in new furniture and changes the house around. His words say one thing but his actions say another. Mayday, mayday, I want to cry. Help me!

But no one is listening.

June 2014

Fig trees, roses, and lavender. The smells of the earth, the sound of wind through branches instead of halyards, the insects that crawl on you when you repose on a broken lawn chair amid three dogs running amok. This was my day, the day I felt my skin wrapping around a rejuvenating spirit. Like anything in nature, however, I had to first sit quietly, like a seed, before coming vital, stretching, growing, feeling alive again.

The End

I had told Ricci I needed quiet, that I was going to housesit for a friend, in Fairfax. I am not planning to leave, I said. I just need to recalibrate, to write. It's pulling me and I must respond. He's angry. When is he not, these days? Maybe this will be good for him as well. Maybe he needs to feel something too.

Mandee's home might be called a disaster by some. Its junk drawers set a new standard for junk drawers. They are wild and beautiful, like an abstract painting, or jazz music—pure anarchy. Half-opened packages are strewn in cupboards. There are three open packages of the same noodle product, along with an assortment of half-used sticky notes, pens, checkbooks, used batteries, leek seeds, crystals, and a broken old-fashioned mini toy car, stamp pads, and pictures of families and friends, some torn, some scribbled on. The mantel is littered with picture frames, many with broken backs leaning on those still standing tall, and lots of loose pictures, of Mexicans, Germans, with smiles, serious faces, silly faces, faded faces.

I love every item. I always wanted a junk drawer. I decide I now hate having everything lined up, perfectly labeled and orderly. Life is messy, so why shouldn't a junk drawer be messy too? It's an honest reflection that you can face, laugh at, and explore.

There's an oval mirror at the entrance, cracked to the point where you have to bend down low to see your full image—a perfect way, I think, to display humility and be reminded to ask hard questions each and every day. Children's drawings are taped to the walls as if by a child, layered, crooked and at random. I absorb it all. I don't bother to straighten anything on my first day. What is important is to declutter my mind.

I look out the kitchen window as I sift my thoughts. Shadows, multiple shadows of varying shades of gray shift, mingle, merge, and separate into individual abstract shapes. I stare at them, as if they're speaking to me. They speak to me each morning.

This is my world now, for the summer. I could not be happier. Mandee has made me feel welcome with an empty drawer for my clothes, and hangers on the back door to hang my coat. Heartfelt instructions greet me: "Make yourself at home and don't worry about anything. Take care of yourself."

She loves this home. I recall her telling me about the former owner, who died here. He and his wife owned it since the beginning, and they built the lush garden that Mandee's husband continues to nurture, with its trellis of green grapes punctuated by apricot and lemon trees. The house inside has old-fashioned décor, rich crimson walls with lattice windows. Fresh air flows uninhibited, without screens, inviting moths, spiders, and bees to enter, if they so choose. I open my eyes one morning to meet the stare of a black spider that has joined me, on my pillow. We stare at each other for a moment. I carefully pick up the pillow and set it on the floor to permit him to run away freely.

I see him from time to time. We understand one another. We have an agreement: no webs spun in corners in exchange for no squished spiders.

When I first arrive on Sunday, I find the door locked.

"I can crawl through the window, Mom," Kyle offers, surprising me. He succeeds and unlocks the door. There appears to be someone living in the house. A quick call to Mandee reveals that the son of a friend of hers needed a place for a few days. He was in transition. We arrange to meet, this young man, his German mother, and me.

I feel an immediate kinship with his mother; we are instantly like old friends. She came to the United States in the 1970s, when she was young, much like Ricci's family did. She is sweet and kind. I can tell right away. Her son Bo, who is in his thirties, is a musician, a guitarist. We talk about his father, David Hess, who has recently died. He was a musician and songwriter for Elvis Presley, Pat Boone and others. "Shake it up" and "Sand Castles" are among some of his more well-known songs.

I sense something special in Bo, an intensity, a passion. He has wild eyes and has been unsettled in life, but I can also see he is kind and has high standards. He cringes when TV commercials come on.

"I can't stand commercials," he will say, visibly, almost physically upset by them.

"Why doesn't Bo live with me for the whole summer at Mandee's?" I suggest. He could take care of the yard, which would leave me more time to write.

There is hesitation. I am encouraging. There are two bedrooms and it'd be good to have some company. Finally, his mother concedes. Mandee expresses concern about my need for space, but I reassure her—all of them—that it would all be great. Aside from gardening help and more writing time, I'd get to hear some guitar music. That's a plus for me, I say.

Just a few days after I arrive at Mandee's, I learn that Neto is scheduled to play in Oakland, so Bo, Captain Richard Gillette and I pile into my car to watch the performance amid a packed crowd at the Paramount Theater.

When the lights dim, Neto steps onstage, out of the shadow, mysteriously, just as he had done in his studio that first day. He strapped on his white guitar and I could feel the energy shift across the theater as he began to play, generating electricity that pulsated through the air with no more than six strings, ten fingers, and one spirit.

I think back to the article previously published in the *London Times* that said, "…as soon as he touched his custom-guitar, sending a shower of harmonics into the silence, he rendered all musings about categorisation redundant."

Can this man be the same one I met in the donut shop?

He begins to jam and I can feel that energy flutter up my spine. I looked over to Bo, whose eyes are closed as he disappears into that electric world, trancelike. The apocalyptic sounds of José's guitar rips across the stage, through the audience, and bounces off the walls. I hear Captain Richard mutter, "Oh yeah," as I watch in awe.

As we leave the show, people talk about Neto.

"That man with the white guitar—jeez, did you hear him?"

But nobody seems to know his name.

Bo and I spend time on the front porch, chatting, those first few weeks. He tells me about his travels and I reveal the marital challenges I am having, and how nice it is to have a little quiet time to work things out. During the day I write fiction, stories that I had been working on for more than a year now. At times I gaze out the window, into the garden, and watch Bo, in his tank top, shovel earth and prune and water the plants. He appears remarkably connected to the garden. He is worried about a pot-bound pomegranate tree I had brought. It seemed to physically pain him that the tree might be suffering. I watch him with curiosity.

Later, he sits on the porch, singing and playing his guitar with so much passion and talent bubbling up from his soul.

"Strumming across these days, I'll see you around the sun," he sings. I like to listen.

During the summer days I help Rob Harrington run his outdoor nature program at China Camp, in San Rafael, playing in the water, making mandalas in the sand complete with pickleweed, broken shells, sand glass, and rocks, and listening to six-year-old Quincy cry, "Look!" every time she finds a nature treasure the size of an ant. These are details we fail to see as grownups, despite their surrounding us each day. Children are our angels. They remind grownups about honesty, generosity, and how to see this beautiful world we've been given. Rob is a gifted Waldorf teacher, and a friend, and possibly a saint too. He always carries a smile and gentle kindness, along with an overwhelming dose of adventure.

We sit during low tide and watch a symphony of tiny snails carry their spires across the mud, making music as they do so. We kayak on the water, like natives. Rob's twenty-year-old daughter joins us. She grew up on the beaches of Santa Barbara where Rob ran his camp for twenty years. Here, she seems so free, unencumbered by what others think. She does headstands when she feels like it. She plays her ukulele, drawing others to sing. She's comfortable with herself and carries the likes of an old soul. She wants to sail.

I sit on the sand, doing macramé with Quincy, while the other children run and splash, until some of them spy what we are doing and want to join in, to make macramé bracelets too. I try to rush Quincy along in her progress so I can get them started. I am showing her how to do the weaving when she attempts to stop me, to show me a shell and thread.

"Not now, Quincy. Let's finish this first," I say.

Rob squats down next to her.

"Quincy, what is it you were trying to say?"

She eagerly explains her vision of the little macramé bracelet we're making, how she wants the shell and thread to loop through the center before weaving in another bead and shell, and so on.

Rob smiles at her and then at me, and it dawns on me how I had attempted to shut her down. Our sitting together has nothing to do with a finished pretty macramé bracelet and everything to do with allowing Quincy to use her voice, her ideas, and be recognized for them. I had reduced it to merely being a macramé bracelet to wear and show off to friends.

Quincy delightedly adds her shell and thread and we finish the bracelet. Without hesitation, Quincy gifts it to me by tying it to my wrist, and runs off to the beach. I hold up my wrist to admire it, the uneven clumsiness of it making it more precious, a reminder of how she had been given the freedom to express herself.

This is education. This is teaching. This is learning.

Bo walks in through the garden gate and passes me as I sit staring at a crack in the concrete path, backpack slung over his right shoulder and carrying his skateboard.

"They're really beautiful, aren't they?" he says, and points to a mass of white roses. "There's music tonight in town," he adds.

"Sounds like fun."

When we enter the club where a DJ blares trans music, I feel a bit out of place. It's been years since I've been in a club. I focus on the people around me, dressed to be eye-catching, hoping to be noticed, smoking cigarettes with practiced flair.

People still smoke?

The drinks they order reveal things about them, much like one's astrological sign. The security guy takes his job so seriously. The bartender deftly passes out elixirs to those hoping to soothe their turmoil and get lucky.

"Next week I'm going to The Fenix," Bo says. "Maybe they'll like what I play." Fenix is a small jazz club. "I only have eighteen hundred dollars to get me through the summer."

I give him a rueful grin. "Well, that's better than me. I've only got eight hundred, and I've two kids to worry about." I shrug. "I'll do it, though. I know I can. "

The bouncer approaches.

"If you stay, you need to pay the ten-dollar cover."

Ten dollars?

We finish our drinks and head out, ending up at a small bar, where we chat, as friends.

Abruptly, Bo blurts, "My dad is dead."

There is anger, perhaps resentment, in those words. Maybe tinged with regret.

"Bo, your dad's not truly dead unless you say he's dead. He's still alive in you."

He looks away.

"It's like my uncle," I continue. "I carry his spirit with me, always. That's what it's all about. It's not about making money, or fame, or any of those things."

His gaze swings back to me.

"Yeah, maybe you're right."

"You have a musical heritage, Bo. Go for it."

"Yeah, I'm just waiting to take on the world."

"There is no waiting. You just have to do it."

"I was in jail."

"What for?" When he hesitates, I joke, "Let me guess. You robbed a bank?"

"I got into a fight with some business people in suits. They had more money for lawyers, more money than me. I spent six months inside a cell." He shakes his head. "It's absolutely miserable to be locked up in a tiny space, where you can't move."

"Well, now I understand what you mean when you say you have a low tolerance for some people. Have you written any songs about it?"

"That's all I did during those six months."

"Good. Then it wasn't all in vain. Use it."

He places his hand on my back, but it's a line I have no desire to cross. I get to my feet.

"I'm going to head back. I want to get up early to write. You go ahead and stay. I want to be alone."

July 2014

Lucy is far away, in Japan, her first time out of the country. Kyle is asleep, near me. Bo is outside drinking beer. He's been acting strangely lately, more so than normal, more disoriented. It's making me nervous.

Things pain him so easily—TV advertisements, the pomegranate tree so desperate to be repotted, his understandable anxiety about making a living. He's highly sensitive. I tell myself that these are all telltale signs that he feels deeply about the right things. He has a deep aversion to what is untrue and ugly in our world. We tend to shun people who are sensitive. Perhaps the reminders make us uncomfortable. I think of my mother-in-law. "Don't be sensitive," she would repeatedly say to me.

Bo plays the guitar and sings all day. He has a driving passion to share his soul and give to others, but he struggles because he has trouble working in this world we've created, one where individual power is valued over the power of community. I see how deeply good he is, both in character and as a musician. If he didn't have to worry about the expenses of rent, insurance, and all the complexities we've created for society in addition to the true necessities, we'd all be dancing and listening to his music. We're missing out.

More often than not, we abuse the gentle souls and worship the bullies. No wonder there are such rampant bully issues at schools. The children learn from us what is prized, and we have the formula wrong. The givers, the teachers, the artists, even the destitute—they are the ones we should look to as our guides.

We have been taught to value greed.

Bo and I sit on the porch together in the evening, under the stars.

"I really want to help you," I say, "but I just can't do it right now. I will help you though. You just have to wait a little."

A tree talked to me and told me to run for my life or I would be pummeled to death. I listened, and I ran.

Bo's odd behavior is intensifying. He wakes up in the middle of the night and turns on water. He is drinking more and more beer. A restlessness within him is building. He leaves glasses and plates around the house, and I find myself cleaning up after him, more and more. This was not my plan.

I call his mom and we meet.

"What's up with Bo?" I ask, and tell her what's been happening.

"Bo is mentally ill," she admits, reluctantly. "He takes medication for it, so it's controlled. But the doctors say he's psychotic."

Now I realize why everyone was hesitant about my having offered to let him live with me.

"Is he dangerous?"

"No, never. Well, there was that one fight."

The one that landed him in jail, clearly. I'm still having trouble reconciling this with the Bo I've come to know.

"It's funny," I say. "I watch him and I feel he such a good guy, a misunderstood guy. I don't get it."

"Barbara, it's been hard for years. There are no services for the mentally ill, unless you're rich, and we're not rich. He has a hard time working and taking care of himself in our society. He is a good guy. It's just he can't pull himself together."

"He's an amazing musician. I've heard his songs and watched him play."

"Yeah, but that's not enough. He has to learn how to make a living and get on in this world."

I sigh. "We put so much on ourselves to be independent, don't we? I mean, we all have different capacities for living and giving, don't we?" I put my hand on hers. "What can I do?" I don't want to give up on Bo.

"Keep him busy. That's one way. Don't let him get too much into his head."

My brilliant plan to occupy him is to have him plant a big vegetable garden. That should keep him busy.

We buy lavender, tomato plants, green beans, and squash. The planting starts innocently enough. Bo shovels intensely. He is strong. His brow beads with sweat as his muscles flex and his breath grows heavier.

"How about the tomato plants there?" I suggest.

I watch him continue to dig, muscles flexing, releasing the occasional grunt, and inexplicably I feel apprehension, the seeds of fear sprouting in my belly, for no reason I can put my finger on. What's the matter with me?

I shake it off and begin setting plants into the earth. Bo has his back to me as he stands, pausing in his labors. My eyes move from the freshly turned earth to the shovel in his hand and I envision me in that earth, Bo tossing shovelfuls of dirt to bury me. Sharp tools litter the ground around us. Bo stands there, lost in contemplation. He turns and our eyes meet. His are wild-looking. I swallow hard.

"Bo," I say, gently, "it's getting late. Why don't we wrap up and continue tomorrow?"

"Yes."

I walk toward the front door, assailed by visions of gardening tools plunging into my body and me being buried in the earth. Blood and pain. Bo heads toward the back door instead, and I hear it slam behind him.

The tree above me moves, dreamlike, faster and faster. I watch, fascinated, as the branches sway back and forth violently, panicked.

Run for your life!

I take a deep breath and exhale with a shaky laugh. Barbara, you have very overactive imagination. Calm down.

I tear my gaze from the tree and look back at the house. It is dusk, and the light is fading. The house looks dark, oppressively dark, evilly dark. I chide myself again for being foolish and glance up at the sky. A cloud drifts, revealing a brilliant full moon.

I open my mouth to call out to Bo to come look at the vivid moon when the true import of this revelation hits me. Forget all the werewolf stuff of legend—the presence of the full moon is believed by some to agitate those with mental disorders.

Psychotic, Bo's mother had said.

I step cautiously into the house, where Bo is busily slicing polenta into disks. His eyes are still wild.

"Sit down and have some polenta," he says. He is staring intently at me, the knife in his hand.

"Oh, wow!" I exclaim, backing up. "I forgot to feed the rabbits! I'll be right back, okay? Keep dinner warm for me."

The rabbits are at my house, in San Rafael. I move toward the door and reach for my car keys. He walks toward me, but I run to my car, lock the door, and drive away.

What just happened?

My nerves are rattled. I think about how the tree talked to me. I pull over, on a side street, to collect my thoughts. I am breathing heavily.

Am I going crazy?

I am tempted to end everything right then and there. Maybe I have gone mad. I've left my home, and everything is a disaster. I want to cry and think of ways I can end the pain. The bridge. A garage. A freak accident. But what looms up, above all this desire for a quick resolution, is an overwhelming feeling that there was still something left undone, something I still have to do.

What is it?

I pull away from the curb and head to my house in San Rafael, thinking about Bo. I find myself wondering about Bo's father. All I knew was that he had been a songwriter for Elvis Presley and was a well-known figure. I turn on the computer and search for David Hess. What I read makes my jaw drop to the floor.

David Hess was not just a songwriter but also an actor with a cult following for his films in the 1970s. I watch a part of one, *The Last House on the Left*, in which a group of friends go to a concert—just like we had when we first met, I think—only to have David Hess's character rape and mutilate a young woman before burying her for dead. *The Last House on the Left*. I think about that for a moment. Mandee's house, where I'm staying, where Bo is staying, is the last house on the left, in her town. A chill goes down my spine. Had Bo made the connection? What was it I had said to Bo? Your father lives through you.

My God.

The next day I return to Mandee's house. I ask Bo to come outside. He looks even more disheveled than he did yesterday. I give him a hundred dollars and tell him to leave. He doesn't argue.

As he is leaving, I ask, "Bo, what were you thinking last night?"

He pauses, drops his gaze, and then looks away. His voice, when he speaks, is subdued.

"Indecent thoughts."

"Bo, you're a good guy. I see that. One day I want to help you. One day. Just not right now."

He leaves. Still uncertain, I call the police. An officer comes by, a funny short man in uniform. He introduces himself and fumbles for his notepad, which he can't find.

"Ever have one of those days when you think you're going crazy?" he says, stirring the air with his finger, next to his temple.

I think of Bo, of the full moon, of the tree that arguably saved my life. I nod.

A neighbor walks by and I introduce myself, explaining that I'm housesitting for Mandee for the summer.

"Do you live around here?" I ask.

"Yes, right there," she says, and points.

I ask if she wouldn't mind helping to keep an eye on the place and report anyone she sees besides me on the property.

"Of course," she says, with a friendly smile. "I'd be happy to."

"What's your name?" I ask.

"My name's Tree."

I stifle the urge to laugh hysterically. She might think I'm crazy…

I stand there looking at myself in the mirror. Not the half-cracked one, where I have to bend down, but the full-sized mirror in Mandee's room, adorned with images of saints and fortune-cookie prophecies.

"Your life is about to change, Barbara." My reflection stares back at me, equally optimistic.

I got the grant.

We got the grant!

The grant manager of Schmidt Family Foundation calls to congratulate me.

"All eyes will be watching," she warns.

Not a problem, I think. I have sailed the seas aboard *Summer Solstice* in the black of night, surrounded by glowing sea eyeballs and whispering voices. I could handle the scrutiny of a few human eyes and voices.

I take a deep breath and exhale hard.

This global foundation was trusting ME and my big idea!

My big idea, under "the little sailing organization that could." A huge global foundation is trusting me.

ME!

Holy shit!

They are trusting little me and my stupid idea.

Jesus Christ!

I think back to elementary school when one kid in particular was fond of chanting in front of everyone how I was in the dumb class while he was in the gifted class. I'm trying hard not to let my head go there.

I call Carlos. I had needed an accomplice and he had signed up, so he was stuck now. We had originally planned to film in the fall, but we realize now that this is just not possible. We have three weeks.

THREE WEEKS!

To pull together an entire film filled with kids, captains, instructors, crew and more?

Three weeks. That's twenty-one days.

Carlos will get his day rate, which will be my gift of thanks to him for all the work he's done for our little organization, and then I am DONE with this organization and can finally get on with my life and pull my family back together again.

I've given back what I said I would give back. I've got it all figured out now.

No excuses.

Mandee is returning, so I'll have to get my own apartment so I can dive into this project with no distractions. I can't possibly get it all done if I return to the chaos that is our house. I can't return to the rot, the dirty carpets, the overflowing garage. I need absolute focus for this film.

I hope Ricci understands.

August 2014

I've slept in my clothes for three nights straight.

I'm writing announcements, trying to rally twelve kids, still unsure where they will come from, organizing boats, Captain Richard Gillette, sailing instructors, and scientists, and rushing around in a frenzy, figuring out everything that needs to be done.

Joan, my retired neighbor is moving out of her four-bedroom house. Full circle, she says. She and her husband are moving to a small apartment in San Francisco, where they lived before they had four children to raise.

After forty years, they are emptying their house filled with books, crafts, dishes, furniture. I watch her, day after day, week after week, lug stuff into the garbage bins. It can't be easy discarding your life. Her husband has trouble walking and so she must manage all by herself. I offer to help her one day, despite running around with kids, schedules, film prepping, and rallying. Amid all the hectic activity, I find myself drawn to her as she moves between her house and the garbage bins out front, stacking things higher and higher.

Her kitchen is filled with all the conveniences one could ask for. Cupboards are filled with wine glasses and coffee cups. She has entertained a lot over the years. I can see it's hard for her, but not in the way I imagined.

She pulls out a spatula.

"It's amazing to think that I spent hours trying to find just the right spatula for a cake I made one time. One time! I used this once in thirty years and haven't used it since." She puts it in the "get rid of" box.

Inside her cupboard sit appliances still in their original boxes from the 1960s.

"Do you want these?" she asks. "Look, the tag is still on this." It was an egg poacher. "Funny. I didn't even know I had it until I started gutting the place."

It follows the spatula into the "get rid of" box.

Over the course of days I watch her garbage fill up with valuables. Sometimes I sneak over and peek into the garbage can. Treasures. Artwork. Unfinished manuscripts. I spy an original portrait of a woman looking pensive. I take it.

"Joan," I say, holding it up, "how can you throw this away?" Someone—the artist—had spent valuable time creating it.

"It's just rubbish. I can't spend the last years of my life thinking about all this stuff that means nothing.

"Look at all my CDs," she says, sweeping an arm at them. "You can just download it all from the computer now. I'm spending my time schlepping stuff around, worrying about what to do with it all, when I could be living my life."

She was donating the bulk of her belongings to charity. We move it all into my garage, filling half the empty space. "It's just for a few days," I assure Ricci. A charity will come pick it up. He isn't happy about it. Maybe because it is competing for space with all the stuff we have growing in our garage.

Lamps, linens, shoes, belts, furniture—she was done with all of it. I sifted through it and spotted some things that would prove useful, now that my own likely move was becoming more imminent.

The next day Joan takes me to lunch to thank me for my help. I like Joan a lot, and have always admired her. She is someone who has always been committed to community work, politics, education, and family. A good neighbor, always. Well educated and kind. She is grounded. Real. Honest. Her husband was a doctor. We start talking.

"I'm housesitting in Fairfax," I tell her, "and I had a bit of run-in with a friend's son who is mentally ill. Good guy though. It's amazing to me how little we understand about mental illness."

Joan shook her head, regretfully.

"You know, Ronald Reagan released them into the streets, back in the eighties. It was a horrible thing to do. They lost a lot of services. It created a lot fear too."

I sit up. Was this the universe speaking to me again?

"Really? Reagan?"

"I remember going to Congresswoman Barbara Boxer's party shortly after Reagan became president. She had a list the length of an Olympic swimming pool of the environmental organizations that Reagan had virtually shut down by pulling funding."

My veggie burger sits, forgotten, on my plate.

"It was sad. Very sad. We lost a lot at that time, a lot of what we had tried to build in the seventies. Everything was lost, just like that. A lot of us, too many, just gave up."

Later, when I go home, I look it up and discovered she is right. The website Grist.org quotes David Alberswerth of the Wilderness Society as saying, "The Reagan administration adopted an extraordinarily aggressive policy of issuing leases for oil, gas, and coal development on tens of millions of acres of national lands—more than any other administration in history, including the current one."

I read more about the consequences of when Reagan pulled federal support for the mentally ill. A 2005 PBS Frontline story called "The New Asylums" reported that over 500,000 individuals suffering from mental illness were locked up in American prisons and jails. Some have even been placed in solitary confinement. This feels wrong. What have we become as a country? Locking up the most vulnerable, those in most need, and labeling them as criminals? When they are released from prison, there are no safeguards, no support system, nothing, to help them back on their feet or get them the help they need.

The next day I pull a lamp and some bedding from Joan's charity pile in my garage. Who knows, I think. I am ready to risk everything to finish this film project and I need absolute focus.

What that might mean for Ricci and me I don't know. But I could not do it in this house, not with spiders lurking in corners, dust collecting, wood rotting and white carpets spoiling. What that makes me I'm not sure. A bad mother? A horrible wife? Maybe. I was willing to take the risk for a bigger vision and remind my children how beautiful the world is, even for the one-eyed tiny copepods invisible to the naked eye.

In sailing we have a term "lee helm," which is when a boat turns away from the wind, making it difficult, even dangerous, to maneuver as there is a risk of losing control. The leeward side is the side away from the wind. I was taking the helm and making a hard tack.

"Helm's alee," I say to myself. It's time to live life, and more than that, take responsibility for it. All of it. I pray Ricci will hear me this time.

"It'd be better if you were with me," I say. I want his support.

But he doesn't hear what I say.

I'm staying at Jenn's place, in Sausalito, a week before moving to my own place. Carlos comes by to talk about the details of the film. We start next week.

"What happened to you and Ricci?" he asks.

I sag into my chair.

"I feel like I'm on the wrong team. I love Ricci, but he's against this. I can't shake this feeling that I have to do this film project. I can't return to that big house. I've wanted us out of there for years. I'm not doing what I'm supposed to in life. I know it in my heart that's all. I need absolute support and he isn't willing to give it. He doesn't listen to anything I say."

"And the kids? How are they doing?"

I glance over at Kyle. He is staring at the TV. I feel like a horrible mother. Just a year ago, when we were homeschooling and feeling free, setting our own terms for our lives, the kids weren't permitted to watch TV or listen to any media. Now, when Kyle watches TV, it's often my only respite, the only peace I have.

"They're doing okay. They'll be okay. It's going to be hard, I know, but I have to do it. I just can't do it living in that house, and I have no voice in my kids' education or where we live. I don't know what else to say."

Carlos contemplates my words.

"I guess there are lots of different ways of living life." He leans forward and looks at me intently. "Listen, I'm giving everything to this project. *Everything.*"

I meet his gaze, my expression serious.

"I'm there right with you, Carlos. I am putting everything I am into this. It means everything to me."

"Good, so we're on the same page."

"Yes."

I am free-falling off the Golden Gate Bridge. I'm on a close haul and feel the growing turbulence all around me. I have brought all this on. It's my fault. Everyone can point their finger at me, when the time comes.

After Carlos leaves, I walk to the docks to sit alongside *Magic Bear*. But *Magic Bear* isn't here. I look out at the expanse of water. She's out there, somewhere. I sit on the docks, listening to it splash against the timbers. A pulsating jellyfish passes by and I inhale the heavy scent of salt and wet wood. I stare at the dark water, filled with microscopic life. Everything is alive, even if we can't see it.

He got me here, my great-uncle. I feel as if he's telling me I'm on my own now. He got me to this place and time. Now it's up to me to take the helm, to navigate. How I wish I could sit with him. A tuna fish sandwich and a highball are all I ask for in this moment.

> *A long-haired hippy came to the door with some petition to save the world. I told him to get a haircut and get a real job.*
>   *Uncle Bob, that was so mean of you! Here's a guy trying to save the world and you knock him down?*
> *Yeah, Barbie, I guess you're right.*
>
> *Stop helping me, goddamn it! I can do it myself. Stop bothering me.*
>   *Uncle Bob, that is so mean. You be nice to the nurse. She's only trying to do her job.*
> *Yeah, Barbie, maybe you're right.*

Barbie, why are you going all the way to China? You can find adventure right here in the San Francisco Bay.
I like adventure, Uncle. That's who I am!

I look out to the San Francisco Bay, toward Angel Island.
You can find adventure right here.
"Yeah, Uncle, I guess you were right," I say out loud. It was true. I had barely traveled outside of the Bay Area at any point in the past ten years and yet I had discovered so much that I didn't know about the Bay—China Camp, Angel Islands, Petaluma River, the Delta. I'm now connected to an entire community of salty characters, part of my heritage, as well as to an international community of sailors. And, most importantly, I have discovered what it means to feel free and take the helm in one of hardest places in the world to sail.

When you take the helm, you have to feel it, Barbie. Feel it.

I feel it. But it hurts. It hurts like hell, Uncle Bob.

Ricci is stacking my things in the garage. The kids are with him. I'm alone at the moment, feeling a shift happening in my life. Tomorrow we begin filming. All the roads have led me here and it feels like a big wave is coming at me.

I don't know why I feel this. It's just a short film, a little film about a nonprofit sailing organization that most people in the sailing world couldn't care less about, a little sailing organization that has been on the brink of collapse for over ten years. A little film that I'm doing, as a renegade, because of one simple idea that refuses to leave me—to support Carlos in his dream by devising a project for us and giving him an honest day rate to do it.

That was it. But it's becoming more than that. I'm thinking about those pollywogs. I'm thinking about that blue star at Santa Barbara University. I'm reclaiming my childhood dreams and reminding my children that the world merits our awe and wonder. And how important it is to fight for all of it, if you have to, even if that means breaking all the rules.

I think about the trees in Fairfax and the voices from the ocean. I hear Bryna's music in the sky. The mother goat that had spoken to me. And the music by Neto with the message, "Take care of my father."

I am going mad.

I manage to shower before the filming begins on Monday. I don't even have time to brush my hair and can't remember whether I brushed my teeth. I am rushing, packing, making lists, prepping my children for the day, and dealing with phone calls. The plan is to film for a week, on San Pablo Bay.

We found twelve perfect children sailors with international roots—Japanese, Swedish, Italian, African, German, and more, all ready to take the helm of little sailboats and talk big for the ocean. It just happened that way.

Carlos and I have no script, nothing specifically planned except to have the kids do science experiments with Jane's daughter Meg, and sail on the water. The final Friday we will sail on a big boat, the *Derek M. Baylis*, with Captain Richard Gillette and scientist Ann Holmes with the Romberg Tiburon Center, which is part of San Francisco State University, in an effort to find tiny one-eyed copepods in the San Francisco Bay.

"We'll shoot everything and then string the pearls together," Carlos says.

We are all mad.

There is one little girl in particular, Mikeyla. She is the only African American, and is quiet, almost withdrawn. Her community helped pay for her to join us, but Mikeyla is reluctant to participate and stands, watching, at a distance, as we take the children through various safety drills. She doesn't want to be filmed either. I felt bad about the situation and consider letting her go home. Yet when the children finally get into the boats to sail, I approach her.

"Do you want to go sailing, Mikeyla?"

She hasn't participated in any of the safety drills, or set foot on a boat before, which logically makes her ineligible to sail. It would be a risk.

To my surprise, she nods her head. Well, if she wants to sail, I'm certainly not going to disappoint her.

"Who would you like to sail with?"

She points to me. I hesitate. I hadn't planned on sailing.

"Okay, let's do it."

I take the helm on a little Pico sailboat and get us out to the open water. I glance at her. She looks scared. I explain what I am doing with the tiller and sails, but she doesn't appear to be paying attention. I grow concerned that I am devoting all my time to her and abandoning my duties to Carlos and the other children.

"Do you want to take the tiller, Mikeyla?" There is a good chance we might capsize if I let her do so, especially as she has never sailed before, but I find myself anxious to engage her in what we're doing.

We carefully switch positions, and when she takes the helm, a huge dimpled smile lights up her face. I watch, astonished, as she tacks, she heels, with absolute control. She is a captain in the making! I laugh with delight. Should the film come to nothing, just fade and disappear, I will always treasure this moment with the delighted, dimpled Mikeyla. It's the quiet ones, those who watch and listen, who know the secrets.

During the week, we hand the kids a questionnaire to take home and ask various people in their community three questions:

Where is San Pablo Bay?

Can you name at least one source of oxygen?

What is the fastest member of the animal kingdom?

We don't expect many, if any, to know the answer to the third question, but we are shocked by their other answers. People just five miles from it have no idea where San Pablo Bay is. Most don't have a clue that the majority of our oxygen comes from the ocean, up to as much as possibly 80%, instead assuming it derives only from plants and trees. And the peregrine falcon and jaguar are the popular, if incorrect answers to what is the fastest animal in the world. None of the kids have ever heard of the one-eyed copepod. One guesses it's a type of cereal. No one knows it to be the fastest animal in the world.

"We're land-based," explains one of the kids. "We don't even think about the ocean."

We are liberating the mighty copepod, I tell them, the fastest and arguably most abundant animal in the world, a link to the world of plankton in our oceans. Plankton, I explain to them, comprises all the small organisms, from jellyfish to the microscopic, those invisible to the eye, and serve as a major food source for fish and wales.

It's the small things in life that matter, I say, smiling, and they laugh. I am thinking about my pollywogs.

My apartment is small, cozy, and my objects surround me, objects that have stories to tell—my stories. Photographs of my uncle with his beloved boat, *Magic,* my grandmother's quilt, my guitar and sheets of music. My children's artwork—not a hundred pieces, just two.

Last night we played a Chinese horoscope game with a simple deck of cards, a game I had played with my grandmother. There are pictures of my grandfather and uncles, three of them, as children, sitting in a wicker cart being pulled by a billy goat. My grandfather had spoken to me about billy goats.

Another treasured possession, my homage to my great-uncle, is Diane Beeston's photography book. The cover is emblazoned with white sails crossing the bay, like spirits. And, there's the bell. A man who had bought my Great-Uncle Bob's boat, a Bristol 29, *Lark,* after his death, invited me to his house to view all the items he had removed from the boat, in case I wanted anything. I took the bell, nothing else. There had been a journal. I wish now I had taken it. What would it have said, I wonder.

I read a poem written by my grandmother.

> *Dreams are warm and softly lighted, the inner reflection of our souls…*
> *and what a day it'll be when our dreams shake hands with reality.*

I submerge myself in old letters and photos.
My Great-Uncle Don wrote an essay that I read again and again.

> *So, you're considering, have been considering for a long time, getting afloat on a boat of your own … The boat is the means. The means for what? The means to submerge your carefully concealed lust for power through your engagement with the forces of nature … a wooden yacht, built, not manufactured, serves no purpose useful to society but requires art … such may be the last refuge of the individual in a world overwhelmed by organization.*

I spend my days at The Good Earth, an organic grocery store, where a long table sits next to the Rachel Carson Café. Town regulars sit together, eat lunch, talk about the past, the present, politics, art, and everything in between. Some come to work, people doing good work with their lives—nonprofits, writing, being creative. I don't have internet at my home. I don't want it. I don't want the excuse to waste my life with information. How much information do I need? It becomes diluted, meaningless, in the actions of my day-to-day life. What matters is what's in front of me: the people—my community, my friends, my family. I can't take on the whole world but I can take on what speaks to me. I've been missing out on my own life. The one life I have. The one life I can share with others.

The music sifts through my realm of reality now. My original goal with this film project was simply to help Carlos pursue his dream. Now, suddenly, unexpectedly, I find myself learning about my past.

I'm in my own apartment, without my husband and children, but I do not intend this to be forever. My husband reluctantly agreed to watch them, to take care of the house.

Meanwhile, I'm producing a film, one that I wrote and we shot last week, with those twelve children, a sailing instructor and counselor, a Jefferson award-winning captain and community activist, a 65-foot marine research vessel, sailboats, and scientists. Soon I shall sit in a theater and watch my film, full screen, and ideally influence some individuals in what they can do for our children. My children. Our world. Their world. It's about hope. I'm thinking big here, not small, and I hope others see that.

I sit outside, on the balcony, amid the chatter of cicadas. I feel a war coming on, a future clash of ideals. It's a feeling I had once before, in China, as I sat on a porch listening to cicadas twenty years ago. I feel the need to stand at a podium, like I did in China, but scream loudly, with no apologies.

I want to be infinite with my feelings, my generosity and spirit. These are my newfound mantras. I hope I can maintain them.

I feel a wave coming. A big one. But I can't see it.

I can only feel it.

September 2014

The days are spinning and I can't keep up. Every day Carlos and I talk about music, images, stock photography, social media needs and all the other requirements for the film we are creating. I feel like a renegade with the sailing organization. Nobody was telling me no, but was it because this whole project had taken everyone by surprise? Like a runaway horse, there is a sense of awe in watching it run free and wild. I keep listening to José's music. It keeps me going and I don't know why.

Meanwhile Ricci has the children, and the guilt is tremendous for me. I have to get through this. I must. Then he will understand. I want to believe that. I am taking a stand for the future of our children's world. It's his world too. I am screaming.

Another crazy day. Meg, Carlos, Emma and I were shooting, using radio-controlled camera drones, at the Marin Yacht Club. At one point, one of the drones dive-bombed into the water and Carlos launched himself into the water to retrieve it. He emerged, triumphantly raising it in the air, like Rambo, the blades nicking his throat slightly.

Then I get a call from Jody.

The *Derek M. Baylis* is in Sausalito, she says, making ready for a voyage south, to Santa Cruz. If we hurry, we can get a few hours on it and film the last of what we needed, which was just one more major shot of the *Derek*.

"Carlos! *Baylis* is in Sausalito. What do we do?" The Picos were lined up along the docks, sails flapping in the wind. Dave, the harbor master, will be fit to be tied if we leave them like this, but what choice do we have? There's no time to put them away. We'll just have to deal with him later. Carlos agrees.

"Let's go!" We jump in our cars and drive like hell the twenty-something minutes to Sausalito.

Sure enough, there she was, Tom Wylie's Wyliecat, the *Baylis*, a single majestic sail, a 65-foot-long white beauty. Tom Wylie, the boat's environmentally conscious designer and a salty relic of the San Francisco Bay, had recently become known as the "John Muir of the Sea," thanks to a write-up about six months earlier in the Sierra Club's magazine about his building boats that are kinder on the seas.

The End

We grab our equipment and run to the boat.

"I'll be onshore with Richard, operating the drone," Carlos says. "You guys need to tack back and forth, in front of us. Keep your phone. We'll communicate that way."

"Roger that."

Captain Dan Zane eases the boat out of the slip.

"We're gonna make Tom look good, everyone. Let's raise them all!"

The wind is blowing up to twenty-two knots, with gusts at thirty knots, maybe more, so to raise all the sails is a bit crazy, considering how close we are to the channel and other traffic. But we obey, without delay, and without question. I stand in the companionway, phone in hand, while barefoot sailors dash back and forth in a perfectly choreographed and well-rehearsed dance. The crew, clad all in white, know exactly what to do and how to do it, without the need for spoken commands.

The boat heels hard as we tack around Hurricane Gulch, just off the tip of Sausalito.

"In the water! Ease the main!" come the cries, as the boom dips below the surface and a rush of salt water washes over the side.

I text Carlos with the heads up.

We're coming.

"We're dipping!"

We heel again, so far that the clew, the lower corner, of the main sail, sweeps the water. Inside the cabin I stand and brace myself, arms and legs akimbo, to maintain my balance so I can continue to text Carlos. He messages me.

Drone prepared. Ease toward us. No. No radio signal.

We try again. And again. Every time it's the same—whenever we tack or jibe past Carlos, who's trying to take the shot, I get the same message.

No radio signal.

No radio signal means the camera drone can't fly. And if it can't fly, it can't film. And we really need this shot.

Nope. Sorry, no shot, apologies. It's a wrap.

What! There was no way in bloody hell I was going to demoralize this crew. I look at them. I imagine all those sailors across oceans long ago who worked so hard to achieve something only to have to give up their dream, their voyage a failure, to be told by their captain that their efforts had been wasted. A voyage across the world to find the chalice only to return home to beleaguered, broken lives, broken dreams.

Okay, melodramatic, I know, but I can't bear seeing the disappointment in their eyes. I maintain a poker face. No more broken dreams, damn it!

"What now?" they ask, awaiting their next order. All eyes are on me.

"Sail toward Carlos."

I text back.

Take the shot. Pretend, if you have to, for God-fucking sakes!

My text reads like a captain's order.

The wind is blowing thirty knots and we're still all sails up, which is absurd in these conditions. But the crew is doing it. I am pretzeled inside the cabin, braced between a table and wall, my butt wedged up against the sink. Everyone is full tilt in their positions when we hear the strange loud buzz of a large insect piercing the wind.

We all turn our heads and watch as a large mechanical mosquito with a single large eye rises into view and pursues us. The crew stares, momentarily mesmerized.

"Turn around!" I bark in my best captain's voice. Time, I know, is of the essence. "Act normal!"

They obey, snapping back into action, as if no longer being hunted.

We get it.

We get the shot!

October 2014

I can barely keep up. Carlos likens this project to a blazing train and says we're hustling at full speed to lay the tracks down in front of it before it overtakes us and disaster happens. Instead of flattening ourselves against the tunnel wall, hoping to dodge the train as I had done once, as a teenager, we were now running in front, trying to outpace it.

I had arranged to film scientists with the kids on Saturday at the Romberg Tiburon Center. But Romberg calls me Wednesday and informs me that I need insurance papers, a security guard, along with all the parents, completed permission forms, and more before they can allow the children onsite.

The End

What?

I have only Thursday and Friday to pull all this together before we film on Saturday! I spent hours on the phone with the insurance company. It's unbelievably complicated. We're just a little sailing organization trying to construct a good message to put out there, to save our oceans, and all these people look at are all the worst-case scenario things that *might* happen. The perpetual state of fear we live in is crazy.

It's now Thursday night and I get a call that more time is needed to sort out the insurance issues. We can't film at Romberg. I sag in my seat. What now? The film will be meaningless.

Carlos and I sat in my car last night, in San Francisco, until eleven o'clock, talking about the project. I had been trying to reach Dr. Sylvia Earle, one of the premier oceanographers in the world. Her own film, *Mission Blue*, had just been released. Although local, she was proving tough to reach. At eighty years old, she's been meeting with world leaders to establish Hope Spots, protected areas in the ocean to promote their healing. She hasn't replied to any of my emails.

I tell Carlos this.

"Then we go tomorrow," he suggests. "We just show up, in person, at her office."

"Okay, nine o'clock, right when the office opens. I'll pick you up at eight."

"We need a narrator for this film. Peter Coyote, Leonardo DiCaprio—somebody big."

I know the voice we need. "Kimball Livingston," I say.

"Who?"

"He's our Neptune. He's a sail writer. International. He was also the announcer when we hosted the America's Cup here."

"You have his contact info?"

"Yes. He's the one!" I say, excitedly. "He's the one."

Carlos looks at me, approvingly, like I know what I'm doing. I haven't a clue. I know nothing—zilch, nada. I maintained my poker face. I was getting pretty good at it.

I call Kimball on Thursday.

"Kimball, we have no money and no film to show you, for you to write to, but we need a writer and we need a narrator. Would you do it?"

There is a pause and I feel my gut tighten.
A voice rises from the sea, a trident surely in hand.
"Yes."
Yes!
Neptune has been reborn.

"It feels like history has just been made," one parent says, as we leave our interview with Dr. Sylvia Earle, the world's leading oceanographer, "Her Deepness," as she is affectionately known in the media.
The winds of the universe have indeed shifted. I feel it too.

Carlos and I drive, as agreed, to downtown San Francisco the following morning. We are tense, nervous, and don't talk except to say, "Turn left here," or "make a right there," until we reach the parking garage.
As we walk down Pine Street to the nonprofit office of Mission Blue, I can feel myself cutting through a layer of the universe. I don't know how else to describe it. It is like sailing upwind, in the groove, when the balance of wind and water is all around you. We walk quickly, but assuredly, with one intention, to interview Dr. Sylvia Earle.
We press the elevator's button for the 20th floor. Nothing happens. The doors won't close. We look at each other. I step out and explain our difficulty to a lobby security guard.
"Oh, let me help you," he says, and swipes his magnetic card past a reader and pushes the button. To our relief, the doors close and we start to ascend.
On the 20th floor, we approach three older ladies, working away, outside her office.
"Hi, we would like to interview Sylvia Earle for our film," I say, Carlos standing right behind me, with his camera, ready to go.
"How did you get up here?" one of the women demands. "This is a secure building. You can't come up here without an appointment."
"We've sent several emails and left several messages," I explain. "The security guard let us up."
"Sylvia's message about the ocean is the same message we're delivering to children," Carlos adds. "Please."
One woman picks up the phone, speaks quietly for a moment, and then hangs up. She jots something down on a piece of paper and turns

The End

to face us. "You're lucky. Sylvia's usually never in town. She's agreed to give you twenty minutes tomorrow. Follow up using this email and phone number."

I take the piece of paper, my hand shaking ever so slightly at the realization of our good fortune. I could feel the weight of responsibility between my fingers, like I'd been given gold in a time of extreme poverty.

I spend all day Friday on the phone, rallying the children's families, various scientists, and captains to figure out carpooling options and schedules. I call DOER, the Department of Energy Resources, which says yes to the twelve children and say they will call their insurance company, no problem. They make it so simple, so easy.

Carlos has already been on the premises to set up when we arrive at DOER. Their large warehouse is a wonderland of chambers and deep-sea vehicles. I am reminded of the day I first sat in my grandfather's plane as a little girl, eager to experience the joys of flight. It hadn't happened, not on that day. Looking around, I find myself wishing that maybe one day I would find myself sitting inside a submarine as it navigates the murky deep.

The children are gathered at the door. I grin as I open it to permit them inside.

"Children, if you think Willy Wonka's chocolate factory has wonders, wait until you see inside this place. This is where dreams really are made!"

The children's scheduled twenty-minute interview with the world's greatest oceanographer stretches to an hour.

"Know your place in the universe," Dr. Earle advises.

The high stakes of this film have skyrocketed. "No excuses," I can hear Mark O'Brien say. "It's all connected," film director Mike Leigh had said to me, all those years ago.

I wake early in the mornings—3 a.m., 4 a.m., unable to sleep. I write. I make tea but forget to drink it. I make lentils. They sit, congealing, as I lie on the sofa and ponder life, people, the past, the future. I watch the sky go from dark to light. A red-orange light emerges from behind the hills outside my window, hills that form the backdrop to an immense sky filled with stars and the occasional murder of crows. Sometimes a singular hawk perches on top of the redwood and watches the crows swoop and soar as they try to knock it off its perch. It maintains its place, dignity intact. Watching it gives me strength.

The sky turns a brighter red now, as the sun threatens to chase away the lingering darkness. Soft clouds fill the sky with cotton candy appeal. A sweetness heralding the new day. And it is a new day, one that I can create. One that I can choose how it will be. For now, I choose to finish this thing I have, that I need to do.

November 2014

Carlos had turned over all of his project earnings to pay the film editors, while mine had gone to pay for the studio where we recorded Kimball Livingston narrating the film. We are broke, but determined to keep making it happen, somehow. And we do.

I get text messages from Carlos in the middle of the night. He works around the clock. I am up too, even if sometimes I just sit alone on my sofa, staring at my reflection in the sliding glass door. My mind spins incessantly. Sometimes I break into tears. I left my family. My children. I miss them, but, I keep reminding myself, I'm trying to do something big, something that others aren't doing. Do people not see what I'm trying to do? It's certainly not for fame or money.

Eventually, I have no choice. I start asking around for money, something I've never felt comfortable doing, to help underwrite the film. My friends give suggestions. We are seated around a table at Good Earth. "What about this place?" someone says. "The owners are loaded and the're good people."

I call the number listed for Good Earth and leave a message. The next day, Al, the owner, calls back. He is silent for a moment, following my pitch, my description of the film.

"How much do you need?"

"Another five thousand, that's it."

"I'll put in a fifth of that, one thousand," he offers. "I'm on my way in now. Meet me there and I'll say hi when I get there."

I like Al straight away. He makes small talk with Joann, an animal rights activist, about how crazy all the hubbub is over the San Francisco

Giants. We agree that it's crazy how people can be so fanatical about a ball and bat and yet ignore the fact that our environment is a disaster, with its acidifying oceans and melting polar ice caps.

He excuses himself to say hello to Congressman Jared Huffman, who had stopped by. Shortly afterward, he returns.

"Why don't you come meet Jared?" he suggests. "He does a lot of work connected to the environment." I am caught off guard but grab the opportunity to connect. We talk briefly. Cameras snap.

"Do you know James Redford, Robert Redford's son? He made a documentary last year. He lives the area."

As we say goodbye, he adds, "You're doing good work."

I wish more people felt that way. Friends have disappeared and unfriended me on Facebook. They see someone who moved out to do her own thing, who left her children behind. I'd heard the stories. But I also know I am where I need to be. There is a force catalyzing me across this new plane of existence. I feel its vibrations, as if it were talking to me. I am no longer in control. I have to remind myself to eat. I grab a handful of sunflower seeds from the diminishing bag anytime I begin to feel dizzy. Cooked lentils grow soft and fuzzy, and dishes stacked in the sink begin to stink.

The kids come over.

"Mom, I thought you moved out of the house because you couldn't handle cleaning up after all four of us on top of everything else," Lucy says. "It's worse here, and it's just you now."

She has a point.

Kyle calls me a few days later, to talk to me before going to school. He misses me, and I miss him. I feel sad knowing it feels like I've abandoned my family, but I had to make this film. I need absolute focus. I'm going big picture here, and it's not just about projecting it on a screen.

Meanwhile, Lucy is going into a darker place. She's in her room, alone, whenever I stop by, on the computer. I keep thinking of that goat's kid, crying, as the blood drained out of its mother. There is nothing I can do. Not yet.

It's Kyle's birthday tomorrow and I have nothing for him. I have only a hundred dollars in the bank, and I need money for food and gas for the car. I'm waiting for the balance of my retirement fund, which I cashed out to see me through rent for the month, to arrive. I don't want to ask Ricci for money. I want to do this myself.

Ricci gets on the phone.

"I'm about to enter a relationship with someone."

My mind stops. The world stops.

After twenty years together, and just two months apart, he is entering a relationship with someone else? I'm frozen, unable to move, the classic picture of a deer in headlights. Full stop. I can't even rewind. I'm numb. And yet it's validation of all that I sensed and believed for the last eight years—maybe longer, if I'm honest with myself. He hasn't been there for me. I'm not sure he ever was.

At the same time it's like death, a permanent severing. Ironically, I dreamed about Ricci last night, finding comfort in his arms, a feeling I hadn't had for years.

Maybe it's time to stop holding up the house of cards. Let things fall where they may. Let it be, as John Lennon would say. I'm done fighting. I'm done protecting and defending. I'm done making up stories.

"I'm happy for you, Ricci. I really am." I was too, in a strange way. He sounded happy for the first time in years. I wanted him to be happy, didn't I? It's like I've never known him when he wasn't angry.

I am exhausted, from too little sleep and a perpetual pile of unfinished homework.

"It's amazing, Barbara, like we know each other from past lives."

"Really?"

"I learned how to be loving and kind from you. Now I can take it to a higher level with her."

"Really?"

"I've learned that we help each other rise to higher levels."

"Really? Don't you think it's a little soon, Ricci?"

"That's what everyone says, but I know it's right."

"Really? Well, can you keep it from the kids, for a little while, at least?"

"Sorry, too late."

It's just two days later when I find myself sitting, a film projected above me of the slashing and burning of the Amazon rainforest, Chinese oil companies setting up shop, and talk about the end of American democracy, the fall of capitalism.

I see him, across the room, well dressed, smiling, his arm around some woman. That's when blood began to course like fire through my veins.

"Excuse me," I say to the woman hosting the table I'm seated at. "My husband is here with his girlfriend. I have to go."

I walked to my parked car and hear my Great-Uncle Bob's words.

Barbie, he never showed you respect.

Ricci texts me from the fundraiser.

Where are you? You said you wanted to meet her.

I had said that. I thought I could handle it. But I no longer felt numb.

I head to the house to reclaim what was mine. There's an unfamiliar pink laptop, unfamiliar ruffled bedding, pink shoes tucked beneath the bed. Another woman's clothes hang in the closet, next to my wedding dress. I collect my treasures, including my most prized possession, my Uncle Bob's silver platter from the St. Francis Yacht Club, engraved with *Magic Bear 1963*, First Place. That very trophy that had started our sailing adventure had brought me to this place in time.

One last time I stand in the living room, light shining down through the windows overhead, highlighting the familiar spiderwebs in every corner. I close my eyes.

Why did you leave this home, Barbara? Think hard. You are making one of the most important decisions in your life.

He never respected you, Barbie.

"Goodbye," I say, to a life that was never truly mine.

I pick up our daughter from school, seeing pain in her face that cuts me to the quick.

"Hi, sweetheart, are you okay?"

"Mom, I'm learning to smile and pretend I'm happy."

I knew then that she'd met her. He'd brought her home, of course. I had seen that already.

"I'm not supposed to talk about it," she says, angrily.

"It's going to be okay, sweetheart. I promise."

I've created a disaster. My family. My film project. My life.

"He's done what?" my mom demands, her Irish temper audible when I tell her Ricci has brought another woman into our house, into our bedroom. "Divorce papers haven't even been filed! You're still legally married! Barbie, you had better get a lawyer." She sucks in air. "Could he sue you for child abandonment and get full custody? Be careful, Barbie, please be careful. He's a rat."

I take a deep breath.

"Mom, I am not going to live my life in fear. I don't want to, and I won't. And, I don't want to talk about what the worst is that you think might happen, not now, not later. This project is magic and I have to finish it. He refused to support either me or it. I can't control him. I'm done making excuses for him. Maybe something good will come out of this for us." Maybe, I think, we'll get our family back together and be stronger for it.

I am determined to believe this. She thinks I'm crazy. Maybe I am. One thing at a time. I just have to get through this project. I can't think beyond it. We have only weeks left until we have to deliver it.

The next day I head to the Good Earth. A portrait of Rachel Carson hangs nearby, from the wall of the cafe that bears her name, its eyes on me. Don't let the fact that she's been dead for fifty years fool you. Her spirit is alive, and it's pushing me.

The regulars here have served as my therapists and support group. Mere strangers weeks ago, they are now my allies, my friends, my confidants.

There's Joanne, the matriarch, who sits always at the end of the table. People move aside to let her sit when she comes. She spreads her rebellious ideas on kindness and charity across social media.

Then there's Tom, the surfer, who appears to live up in the woods, in a tent, I'm not quite sure. He is one of these guys who is always happy. If you tried to corner him with convention, he'd wiggle out, grab his surfboard, board a plane, and hit the waves in Peru. He's as free a spirit as they come.

Bill is one I can't always listen to but who inevitably speaks truth. He'll tell me to cover my ears when it's time. He's kind. His life partner died and now he's single and busy learning new tricks. Literally. He knows I don't want to hear about sex right now. God, no.

"Did you know you can go to seminars and learn about anal sex and they do it right there in front of you?" he asks before describing it in detail, his eyes wide as he discovers a whole new world after years of marriage. I cover my ears and sing "La, la, la, la" to drown him out. The world has changed and I'm not sure I want to change with it all.

David is teaching me about sacredness, right down to the sacred power of a slice of pizza. He wears thick glasses, walks with a limp, looks to be over seventy, though it's hard to tell, and when his eyes aren't deep into a book, they are closed in reverence for the plate set before him, sometimes five minutes or more. I watch him. He's grateful for the food, life and anything else before him. He served in Vietnam and has a large scar across his cheek. He recently went through a painful divorce, which I think has scarred him even more deeply.

My favorite, and the most mysterious, is someone I call Macbeth. He wanders around town, stroking his beard, deep in thought about life, existentialism, music, and likely quantum physics—who knows? He sees poetry everywhere, even in the most unlikely places. He doesn't talk to me, but he listens.

"I can't believe him!" I say of Ricci. "He has a girlfriend!"

"What a rat," someone says. Heads nod.

"A dog."

"A snake."

I sip my green chai and email Carlos. I'm behind and need to catch up. I'm not letting go of this film. I won't let emotions get the best of me right now.

Someone has just offered us imagery of the one-eyed copepod, high-level imagery from this incredible scientist, from Plymouth, in England. Carlos needs it fast.

Music. I have to find music and order it. I have to source more money. Too many needs as Carlos fires one request after another at me.

Jane keeps prodding me with questions.

I will not let this project get away from me. I won't.

But yes, I pause to search Facebook to learn about the girlfriend. I'm human. She's with my kids, for God's sake. We investigate dog walkers, after all. It's my parental duty.

And there she is, in full splendor. I read what Ricci has written.

"A spiritual goddess?" I choke. "A high priestess? The goddess of joy? What the hell?" I stop and look around at my Good Earth therapists. "What in heaven…?" I joke, and laugh at my weak attempt at humor. "Holy shit! I have a husband who is irresponsible, controlling, and perpetually critical, and now he has a 'goddess' on his side? Jesus, I'm really going to need a lawyer, aren't I?"

I look around, hoping for sympathetic smiles but see only pitying expressions. I continue to read.

"Oh, here comes the real dig. She's a former Hollywood actor. No, it's worse. She coaches people to be Hollywood actors, *and* she's German! I do not need another Hollywood actor in my life!" I say, thinking of Reagan standing on that podium, calling my father a federal criminal.

"Barbara, you are a much higher goddess," Joanne says.

I pull up her website. She claims to be a healer? She teaches female empowerment? Who the hell is she healing? Wait just a minute. What about the fact that I worked to empower myself and my husband couldn't handle it? My husband, destined to become a great spiritual leader? Oh, wouldn't that be a laugh after all those years of anger toward me. I look around in amazement, not realizing at first that I'd spoken these thoughts out loud.

Macbeth, who never speaks to me, but only listens, eyes me hard now, as he strokes his beard.

"It's possible."

I look at Rachel's portrait.

Get back to work. The ocean needs you.

I have to finish this project. It has been the source of my oxygen. I'll deal with the emotions and everything else later. I'm a mere human. Then it hits me.

I don't have anything figured out. The impact of this insight is jarring. I know zilch. Nada. Niente. There was a reason I'd been put in the dumb classes in elementary school. They knew it, even if I hadn't. I was as stupid as could be. Who have I been kidding all these years, thinking I could do something important?

The universe is laughing at me.

The End

I pick up the kids from school and drive them to my apartment. It's late and there's school tomorrow. Kyle asks to use the computer to play games as I park the car.

"No, Kyle, it's bedtime," I say.

"Give it to me," he demands, and hits me. I leap out of the car.

"No, Kyle!" He gets out. Enraged, he moves toward me and strikes me with his fists.

Lucy gets back in the car. "Mom, I'm scared."

"Me too." I jump back into the car and lock the doors. Kyle shrieks in fury and kicks the hood. Moving to my window, he hits it so hard I fear he'll shatter it. I stare at him, stunned and appalled.

I call Ricci. "Ricci, Kyle has gone ballistic. I need your help. Your son is in a rage. He needs the both of us to work this out. Can you please come?"

"No, Barbara, I can't." His tone is measured, spiteful. "You left. You take charge. Use your producer skills to solve the problem."

"Ricci, this is about our son, not you and me anymore. Our son needs help."

He hangs up.

I don't know what to do. Who do I call? I have no community, no family. I could call the police, but what good would that do?

I am scared for my son.

I am scared *of* my son.

I am scared for me and my daughter.

I am scared for the world.

Not knowing what else to do, I hand him my laptop and he stops. We go inside.

I am drained. I'm convinced I'm a horrific mother and that everyone shares this opinion. I stare out the window at the redwood trees. They're talking to me in some strange language. I can feel it. Or maybe I just yearn for the quiet.

I've been spending my weekend nights in San Francisco, aboard John Paul's boat, *Summer Solstice*, the same boat that had taken me on my first ocean voyage down the California coast, where I had first heard the whispers and seen the glowing "eyeballs" in the water watch me during my first night at the helm in the Pacific Ocean. She is a comfort to me. John Paul has given me the keys, a sleeping bag, and a few beers if I want them. But I'm not drinking. I have enough problems.

I attend a conference in San Francisco, one that helps participants scour their souls, their intentions, both past and present. We talk about our parents, passing blame, and how we have unjustly donned the role of victim. We talked about how all of life's choices are our responsibility. It has given me much to think about.

I walk, in the dark, along the San Francisco Embarcadero, as words from the day buzz through my mind and the state of my life insinuates itself into my thoughts. I climb onto the boat, hearing the comforting sounds of water splashing against the hull and the wind whistling through the halyards. My head hits the pillow and I am out almost immediately.

At 4 a.m. I sit bolt upright and gasp, "Oh, my God!" My mind explodes.

I have been dreaming about my father, my childhood, and what I had learned about Ronald Reagan these recent months regarding his policies related to environmental issues, education, and mental illness.

My dad wasn't the bad guy! It was Ronald Reagan who was the rat. My dad stood up to a powerful president whose labor, social, and environmental policies have taken down our entire planet. Carter had us on track with sustainable energy, saying the difficult decisions we faced in making the right energy choices was "the moral equivalent of war," the only difference being that such a war would unite "our efforts to build and not destroy." Ignoring all that, Reagan pushed oil back into its primary role in our economy, and we've suffered through thirty-five years of oil wars, devastating spills, and ocean acidification because of his bad policies. Then add to that the recent fracking projects that have increased seismic activity to dangerous levels in previously relatively inert regions.

In the face of all this, my dad had stood up to arguably one of the biggest environmental disasters of a leader in the history of the U.S and possibly beyond. My father had stood his ground. How had I not realized this before?

I gasp in horror as I think back. I had been horrid to my father and mother! Only now, in this moment, do I understand the incredible courage, the sheer guts it took my dad to do what he knew was right, when his entire family and country repeatedly told him he was wrong.

I start to cry, sobbing at what a fool I'd been all these years. After I cry, I start to laugh. I had fallen for it! I think back to all those years of anger, the drugs, the bulldozing through school with holes in my shoes, all the while firm in my conviction that I would never be like him. This newfound truth fills my soul like a welcome wind lifts a sail in all its glory.

My father is my fucking hero! He stood his ground against a powerful president, a disaster of a leader. *That's* my fucking heritage!

Anyone in proximity to my boat surely believes a crazy lady is onboard. I alternate between laughing and crying. I am rewriting my entire life, now taking ultimate responsibility for every decision I have made in life. My marriage to Ricci, I can see now, came about because I didn't believe I came from a good family, and so I had been determined to marry into one, anxious to create one of my own. All the while I never stopped to see that I have the most incredible mother and father alive.

My father stood up to the president of the United States. Damn! All thirteen thousand of those men did. Why? Because they believed in something bigger than themselves. My God, what courage it took in the face of losing everything. And most did lose everything. That takes fucking guts.

Despite the hour, I call Ricci and explain my revelation about my father and how proud I am now of him.

"You have to know yourself," he says flatly. I stiffen. Why is it he never hears what I say?

"Ricci, I'm sharing something that goes deep for me. Do you not hear me?" I explain everything to him again.

"Know yourself, Barbara."

I can't help but wonder suddenly whether Ricci truly knew himself. I recall how, over the summer, he had said to me, "Barbara, I'm tired of looking at the world through your eyes."

I want to scream.

It's now 5 a.m. I can't wait a minute longer. I call my father and my mother picks up the phone. Her voice is worried.

"Is everything okay?"

"Mom, I have to talk to Dad." She passes the phone to him and whispers something.

"Yep?"

"Dad, I want you to know I am so, so sorry for all these years. I was horrible to you. You are my freaking hero! You stood up to the worst president of the United States! You stood your ground. We suffered, but it didn't kill us."

My dad was quiet for a moment.

"You got yourself through college by yourself, didn't you?"

Puzzled, I say yes, I had.

"Well, you got that. You did it yourself."

I did. And I understand what he means. We suffered financially, but we got through it. I suffered, but I got through it. The pain went deep in those years, but in the end it's not the pain that lingers; it's the truth, and the truth shines bright. I can feel it blaze.

"You've got a big spirit, my dear, a big spirit," he says.

As I sit back and relive our call, relive all of the revelations I had been given that morning, a bright light abruptly pierces the portholes. The sky explodes with colors—reds, golds, and pinks, and the water joyfully mirrors the stunning sunrise. I am speechless, looking at it all. A new day, a new world, deserves a dramatic entrance like this.

I climb slowly up into the cockpit, feeling as if the universe is talking to me, welcoming me for the first time. Cormorants and seagulls fly, dipping and soaring madly, singing and squawking, heralding the newness in Paul Revere style.

I look around, eager to share this marvelous moment with another person. I see no one. It's just me, sitting in a cockpit, alone, aboard *Summer Solstice,* in San Francisco, witnessing this spectacle. Perhaps this is what it's like to view the world without a dark veil of anger, without fear, that shaded lens now removed, permitting me to feel and see the full spectrum and splendor of pure universe. Could I describe the magic of this moment? And, if so, who would ever believe me?

I sit there for an hour cradled in awe, seeing the wonder and magic of life and feeling a renewed sense of purpose, knowing I had something to do. Something. I have to stop thinking. It is time to trust my feelings, and let them guide me. I can feel it.

I am at the Cafe Roastery. It is 6:30 in the morning. I love these cafes, so Bohemian, the music they play. Old, intellectual-looking Jack Kerouac and Allen Ginsberg types reading paper books, taking notes, contemplating literature, philosophy, and poetry. They still exist, flesh and blood, not merely names in tattered, dusty, yellowed pages found at secondhand stores. Flyers advertising music events, community yoga, spiritual retreats, and even children advertising dog-walking services decorate the walls. People here talk life, love, and politics.

Carlos and I talked last night, the first time without the spin we've been in. We talked about future projects, Japan, England, Africa, and the world. Helping people, making his dream, and my newfound dream, come true. He is a friend now. There was a softness to his voice. I did not want to get off the phone. Even sitting in silence felt good.

"This is the first time we've really talked, isn't it?" he said.

I had met with Ricci earlier the previous day, when I went to get the kids.

"Ricci, what were you thinking," I say, "bringing a woman into the house like this so fast? How do you think the children feel about it?

"You're always using the children as an excuse," he fired back. "Can't you just be happy for me?"

I couldn't keep up with the rest of his words.

What has happened to my family? I fought so hard for it all these years.

I call Captain Richard, who's been a real support for me.

"Don't make it into anything," he suggests. "Just follow your path."

"It's hard. I've lost my family."

"It'll be okay."

December 2014

We're still rolling with the film and we have just days before delivery. It's keeping me busy, distracted. My life is becoming a series of text messages, mostly from Carlos, on a three-inch screen:

Call when ready.

I do.

Part of next project is to bring editor on board at start so they can advise and prepare from the very base of the project.

Night drive is dangerous. Just leave early Wed morning. Your call.

I text him that we got another $1400 in donations last night.

Wow! Take what you need first. Remainder as you see fit. Yes, come to LA Wed or Thur.

Well done tonight. You are a phenomenal producer.

Save a few hundred dollars for some animation tweaks. I have a very clear idea of film focus now, thanks.

And I hear from Richard Gillette:

We made it—we anchored at Panama—rough couple of days! Ships galore!

Ricci also texts me.

I know this is hard. Thank you for being who you are. I am coming at this from a place of love and compassion.

Help me.

I am in the garage with Ricci, bickering over all of our junk. He insists on keeping the hibachi.
"That's mine. My parents gave that to me."
"Okay, but those wicker baskets your parents gave to both of us. So, how does that work?"

"Well, you took the Cuban artwork without asking. If you're going to make rules, you had better honor them."

"That was mine! I left the one that was yours."

"The porcelain from your grandmother was a wedding gift."

"No," I insist, "that came later, when my mother gave it to us."

"That's not true. What did she give us then? You snuck that out of the house."

"That was my inheritance."

We go inside the house. Suddenly, all the ridiculous things I didn't want have become precious to me. I go for the plastic egg holders that look like purple dancing chickens.

If this guy has become spiritual, I think, why is he so concerned about holding on to material things?

And why do I care about purple dancing chickens?

"The problem with spiritual people is that they're all dirt poor," Ricci states. "I end up paying for everything."

"Great. Just remember it belongs to the kids. Don't squander their inheritance, please, like this house has been squandered." I reflect on his world and then mine. "Funny, all the documentary filmmakers are dirt poor too."

"My girlfriend works with women empowerment, you know. She understands what Lucy might be going through."

"Ha! Women empowerment? What the hell do you think I've been doing? I don't hear you touting what I've accomplished. I'm the one who has just showed our daughter how to empower herself as a woman. And believe me, I know what my own daughter is going through and what your girlfriend brought into our lives."

Again, his lack of respect for me is evident. He wants our daughter to take advice from his girlfriend instead of her mother, his own wife. I can still call myself that—we are, after all, still married.

He holds out a slotted spoon. "You want this too?"

"No, thanks." I suspect he is probably just trying to get rid of it.

He offers me advice as we sort through cluttered kitchen drawers. "You need to brush your teeth."

"Gee, thanks, Ricci, for your concern."

I head back to my car. He trails after me.

"Remember, I gave you that car," he says.

I look at him. "And remember, I gave you the best years of my life." He doesn't respond.

He helps me load the car. He wants my things out of his house. Our house. It's still our house. My name is on it. I still don't know what I want from all this. I get in the car.

"I am proud of you, Barb."

I swallow my tears. "You may have gotten my best years, but you didn't get the best of me."

I sit in the cafe, waiting for my friend Marilyn to join me, feeling despondent, a part of myself still hoping to put my family back together.

Marilyn listens to me pour out my frustrations.

"He's never supported me," I say, bewildered. "Why not? I've always supported him."

She looks me straight in the eye.

"Barbara, let me. I'm here for you. Anything you need."

The word is that Ricci has a new roommate. It's James, Marilyn's brother.

Maybe the house wasn't good enough for the girlfriend, someone says to me.

What?

My best friend, Jenn, had apparently been at the house, as had two other friends of mine, Cathy and Frank, whom I thought of as family. Can I blame them? People go where the good times are, and I'm definitely not fun right now. I'm too busy trying to save an ocean, I want to remind them.

I feel like San Pablo Bay, I grumble, the ugly duckling bay, where no one wants to go. It's just not as fun. Everyone prefers to sail the San Francisco Bay, where the fun is.

I call Jenn, who mentions she's been by the house. It was a party, she says, casually.

"Did you meet her?" I try to keep my voice casual too, referring, of course, to Ricci's girlfriend.

"Yeah, she seems okay," Jenn says brightly, then adds, "But you know, Barbara, you have so much more, so don't worry."

Worry? Whatever happened to loyalty?

"Jenn, I helped you and your child for entire summers while you had issues with your boyfriends, so you could get a grip on life. I was there for you through thick and thin, despite the fact that my own husband didn't want me to be anywhere near you, saying that you, as a single mother, were a danger to our family, and that your daughter would be a bad influence on our daughter. I stuck up for you, over and over again.

"So, now, I leave my house, my home, my husband, and that quintessential perfect life, and not once has anyone asked why Barbara, a sensible person, would leave a big house and her husband unless things were really bad. Has it not occurred to anyone that perhaps she's in pretty bad shape? Has it occurred to you that I might be in emotional hell right now?

"I'm not throwing parties," I continue. "I'm trying to do a 'save the world' project and share an important message about how oceans are being destroyed while my husband screams at me, my son beats the shit out of me, and I'm totally broke. Meanwhile, you and everybody else prefer the party, meeting the new girlfriend, and having a good time. In my house! Help me with this.

"No," I say, abruptly, "don't help. Never ever call me again, Jenn. You go where the good is, and where it's cheap."

I hang up the phone.

I email Cathy and Frank and tell them pretty much the same thing. Didn't I honor Frank by organizing an entire regatta last year? Yep. People only want to go where it's good.

I have no idea who my friends are. Where is humanity? Everyone has deserted me, except Marilyn. Having grown up with a single mother, the oldest daughter of three, she knows the challenges. Carlos, too, has put up with my 4 a.m. calls, and Richard keeps urging me onward.

So, yes, I do have friends. And they are rock solid.

Maybe Ricci was right that day when I asked about doing something for Dante's birthday.

"Barbara, stop thinking about other people all the time. It doesn't help you."

I stare at the redwoods that stand tall outside my window. I sense they are trying to tell me something. But the shouting in my brain that I've been a fool all my life drowns them out.

Jenn telephones me.

"Barbara, let me talk. I am so sorry. I didn't even think of it that way."

She has been really upset the last two days, she says. Good, I think. Maybe she gets it now. I feel no guilt.

"That was exactly what Josie's dad did to me," she continues. "And for years I was a wreck. I just didn't see it now that I'm on the other side. You have every right to be angry. Again, I am so sorry."

"I'm glad, because mothers just do not get respect in our world. I mean, what mother would walk away from a situation, their family, a big house in arguably one of the best places in the world, from a man who will one day inherit generously, without a good reason? No one thinks to ask me this, or even just call to see how I'm doing?

"This planet is crumbling and no one is asking the big questions. I'm sticking my neck out to create a voice for major issues that affect this world.

"Maybe there's a connection between the Earth and mothers. Neither gets respect." I'm on a roll again.

"I mean, I'm not sitting around throwing parties, going dancing, and getting spa treatments, for God's sake. Nobody has given a thought to Kyle and Lucy's welfare during all this, or what this means for them. Ricci's moved way too fast with this. Jesus, my mother's artwork was still hanging on the walls, my wedding dress was still in the closet, my uncle's chest at the foot of the bed when she moved in. It's rotten. Pure rot, Jenn. People don't ask the hard questions and this is where it goes."

"I'm really sorry. Tell me what I can do," she says.

"Keep an eye out for my kids, please. I have to finish this project. I have to finish it and then I'll clean up the mess with my family."

I filed for divorce yesterday. I had been stewing all night.

Marriage is like owning a boat. The best two days are the day you buy it and the day you sell it. I thought of this maxim as I stood in line at the county office, preparing my divorce papers. I was alight, taking control, never to be pushed down again.

"You're being selfish," he told me, earlier that morning. We had talked. Selfish about doing my project? A "save the world" project?

He takes up with a so-called goddess who teaches woman empowerment at the same time she's moving in on my marriage and I'm the one who's selfish? Seriously? Is this a sick joke from the universe?

Or perhaps it's manna from the gods. I'm still undecided.

The line inches forward. While I wait, I consider the word "DIVORCE." I always saw it as such an ugly word, one of failure, of embarrassment. The hard D, like "death," mixed with a V for "vampire," and C for "cadaver," the relationship between those evident. Now, however, while thinking that I was married to a man sleeping with another woman, the word "divorce" slips off my tongue with odd delight, with glee. D for "delight," I think, V for "victory," and C for "cunt." I smile at the grumpy man behind the window. By the time I finish my paperwork, my delight has infected him. He is smiling and happy.

I head to another clerk's office for additional paperwork. I have a fire in my belly. I must be glowing. I ask general questions of the clerk because filing for divorce is like untangling the lines on a sailboat. Who made up these rules? We chuckle over some jokes. She shakes her head.

"I'll tell you, I've seen crazy things. I'm pretty sure people go mentally insane for a while when they divorce."

"They go *what*?"

"Insane. You know, crazy."

"Really?" I think back to my close call with Bo, to the talking trees, the talking goat. My late great-uncle. Am I going insane? I'm not sure. Maybe I've simply tapped into something extraordinary.

I ask Jenn to deliver the papers to Ricci. She's reluctant, but damn, I've done so much for her. This is one thing, at least, that she can do for me.

"You are helping me restore my dignity, Jenn. It restores his as well. I'm surprised he hasn't done this already, or even talked about it."

Jenn delivers the papers to Ricci, and he calls me later.

"I'm surprised, Barbara."

Surprised?

Surprised?

I could barely contain myself.

"Ricci, you are sleeping with someone in MY bed, under MY blankets, alongside MY chest that belonged to my great-uncle at the foot of the bed. MY mother's artwork is still on the walls! And you say you're surprised that I filed for divorce."

I wake up, again, in the middle of the night. I sleep on my sofa, often in my clothes, with a white blanket wrapped tightly around me, mummy-like.

Lightning and thunder perform outside and the rain that accompanies them is hard. I cry again. I miss my family. I remember all of us together, on the bed, trying to sleep as we listened to the rain outside. I would think how safe we all were.

Back then we were still thinking of cruising around the world together on a sailboat. I'd imagine us on the boat, curled up together during a storm, as the rain poured down, overhead, limbs entwined, everyone breathing softly, the feel of the cat's soft fur as it coiled against me.

I feel so alone.

My life is now a complete wreck.

The film is not ready and it must be entered in the next five days to be considered for the ocean film festival I'd earmarked in my grant application. We screened the film at a few schools and communities this past week. People were polite. But they didn't like it. They were right.

The film is absolutely horrible. It's my fault.

I gave Carlos complete creative control, which had backfired. He had pulled together much of his technical skills and went full tilt on his creative ideas, but most of them were just plain bad. Experimental, yes, but they didn't work. By giving him too much freedom and not inserting myself into the process even more than I had, the story I wanted to tell has become lost.

It's bad enough that I've made the gravest mistake in my life, but I dragged a bunch of other people into it—not just my family and those of the other children who appeared in it but also the sailing organization, a major foundation, a science organization, the yacht club, my mother-in-law, sailors, and even the eminent Dr. Sylvia Earle.

Ricci was right. I don't know anything about filmmaking, absolutely nothing. My children will hate me for the rest of their lives. Their mother left them for this? It was nothing but a pipe dream, thinking I could do something big. My mother-in-law was right. I'm a dreamer, a stupid dreamer. I deserve what I get. I am a horrible person. Worse, I am a horrible mother.

Kyle's school is sending me a notice about his delinquent days. What they must think of me. Kyle still flies into rages anytime I separate him from the computer. He refuses to go to school when he's with me, and I've resorted to calling the police on several occasions just to get him moving. He climbs into bed, pulls the covers over this head, and shouts, "I'm not going! I want to be here with you!"

God knows what the police department thinks about a mom who can't control her eight-year-old boy. What makes it even harder is that I'm trying to force him to go to a school I don't want to him to go to, because I don't like it. So, on top of everything else, I'm going against my principles in forcing him to go.

The dishes in my sink reek of rotting food and are disappearing under a veil of fungus. I watch it grow.

On top of it all I'm nearly broke. It's almost Christmas and I have no interest in singing "Jingle Bells" when I already have too many bells rattling my brain. I have university school assignments and deadlines. It's Friday night and I'm alone. All alone.

I'm supposed to drive down to Los Angeles and spend forty-eight hours working with Carlos to see what we can cobble together. Those hours will either give me my life back or pummel me into a deep level of embarrassment and loss, with consequences that will reverberate through the rest of my life, and my family's, all for a stupid idea.

The whole world is crumbling, and I'm about to crumble with it. I'm just another stupid person in it, thinking I could reach for the stars without falling to Earth with a crash.

Here comes the crash.

I wanted to give something to Carlos, a way to help him realize his dreams, against all odds. I wanted to share something with my children, for them always to be aware of and feel awe at the beauty of the world, even for the tiniest creatures that surround us. I think back to my childhood, my jumping over the "Do Not Enter" chain-link fence to see my pollywogs, the only wild nature that still remained back then in my neighborhood. And how I had to do it in secret, in fear of being caught. That is, until the day they poured concrete and buried all those pollywogs. Gone forever. My little childhood friends.

At stake now is not just a little runoff ditch in the hole in the universe that is Fremont, California. No, what's at stake now is an entire planet. I'm just an insignificant being, like a little copepod, believing my dreams would somehow matter.

Without knowing it at the time, the past summer proved to be the last innocent one for my children, and all I want to do is to remind them that the world is big, and still beautiful, and how important it is that we band together to fight for it. I want my children to be on that bow of the boat, with the wind in their hair, feeling and being free. I want them to be free all their lives.

We must stand up for what we want, for what is right.

As a child, I sat and watched as labor union members fought, leaders promoted agendas, and the president of the United States, a Hollywood actor, announced to the world, on TV, that air traffic controllers like my dad were federal criminals because they refused to return to their jobs until better safety procedures, safety procedures that would help them protect all of us, were put in place. There was fear, anger, misinformation, and uncertainty emanating from my country, my home, where I used to think I was safe.

How can I not stand up today and say something? As a child I couldn't. But the legacy of that president who spurred this greed-obsessed generation, who was a leader my father stood up against, lives on, leaving more and more damage in its wake. We have lost our voices while corporations dominate. We have lost our kindness as we compete against one another. We are destroying our planet, leaving our children in the rubble.

It's not a runoff ditch being snuffed out anymore; it's the planet. Reagan is dead and I'm alive. It's a responsibility, one I was ready to shoulder. Clearly, though, I'm not smart enough to make a difference.

Stop dreaming, Barbara. And shut up. You're a wreck.

The End

It's probably a good thing I left Ricci. The kids should be raised by someone other than me.

I sleep on the sofa again, in my clothes, wrapped in my white blanket, and wake up at 4 a.m., thinking of something a child had once said to me.
I text Carlos.

Start with children. The water is alive. We are land-base-minded. We lost the children in the story. They have to tell it.

He texts back. He's awake too.

Yes, but first we start with Sylvia, who said, 'We learn our numbers, we know our letters, but we have to know our place in the universe.'

I like it.

The dark road to Los Angeles is long. I haven't driven this route in over fifteen years. It's hard to see the road. The rain falls and the tears keep coming. Kyle kicked the car radio and broke it during one of his rages, so I'm in my head, where I don't want to be. I'm amazed at the number of trucks. I don't remember so much traffic. It's heavy. It's changed over the years.

Jenn calls me. It's 11 p.m. She never calls me at night. Something must be wrong and she must need help. And here I am, en route to LA.

"Barbara, I want to tell you what an inspiration you are to me. You do things and you include everyone. I realize I'm not taking care of myself. You're helping me."

I'm not sure she's right, that I'm that person, I want to say it's an illusion. Instead, I say, "Thanks, Jenn. You're a good mom. Own that and know your power, just like you tell me."

After we hang up, I think back to a time we had taken her boat out for a sail, just the two of us with our kids. I thought she was extraordinary, managing her boat singlehandedly, anchoring it, and taking charge, a single mom who did not have it easy. No formal education and she's attracted too many two-legged rats who take advantage of her generosity and power. We talked about our dreams of making a difference in our children's lives. We wanted them to be strong. We wanted their lives to be good.

Her call makes me feel good. At least some people have benefited from this film effort, even if I end up left with nothing.

I stop crying. I marvel again at the number of trucks headed up the mountain pass. I've never seen so many before. Traffic is out of control, fuel being consumed by droves of vehicles to supply us with countless *things*. Why do we need so much?

I press the gas pedal, intent on my own need, to get to Los Angeles.

The quiet stillness of the dark morning. The storyline cards are laid out on the floor. A singular light shines at an angle. The monitor that keeps alive my entire world, my hopes, my dreams, is right there too, in a box.

We have two days left before the film must be delivered. These two days will define the rest of my life, I think. Carlos feels the same way.

For now, he is asleep upstairs. I think about our conversation the night before.

We had taken a break and gone to downtown Pasadena. Carlos drove. I could feel his intensity, the drive of purpose. How pushing the gas pedal enables him to imagine moving forward faster in order to reach that something he wanted so badly. That young man's need to find excellence in himself.

He pointed to a pizzeria. I knew he was broke and so I offered to pay, but I could tell he would have preferred to. We ordered a small marguerite and water.

"Why did you ask me to do this project in the first place?" he asks.

I tell him that I have seen people give so much to the sailing organization over the years, like he had, and that it didn't seem right for others to enjoy it without giving back on the same or even any level. I explain how sailing had brought a lot to my life, helped me learn about my heritage, and the friendships I had made because of it.

"Carlos, you were one of the ones who gave and gave, and didn't ask for anything back. It takes guts to follow your dreams and you were doing it. I saw that. So, I grabbed my last chance to give something back to you before I was done with the organization. Now, I feel I can move on with my life," I said.

He looked at me. I could practically hear his brain ticking as I continued.

"The most interesting thing about you, Carlos, is you have this incredible gentleness about you. Not every man takes his dog around and treats her like a queen. Then you can swing the pendulum to the other side of intensity. You basically embrace the full range of the human experience and capacity. You have that. You're going to fly one day."

He kept looking at me with that dark, Latin-eyed intensity.

We stood at the street corner, waiting to cross. I was close to the edge as traffic roared by, enjoying the risk, the danger. A car came peeling around the corner and he pulled me back, out of the way. For a moment, I wasn't bothered by the thought of being hit. Maybe it was a way out of the mess I had created.

Still, what Carlos did felt good, like someone cared enough to watch out for me. I hadn't had that feeling since I was a child. It surprised me, how someone watching out for me made me feel.

We finish editing for the day and stop for dinner. Carlos, a consummate cook, whips up a meal of lentils, egg, and bread. He is as poor as could be, pouring all his energy and resources into his art. It's a good thing he's the one making the food, I think, because all I can do is sit like a limp rag and watch. I am that goat, hanging from a tree, my vibrancy, my very life, draining from me. I hoped I wasn't bleeding all over Carlos. I had dragged him into this, after all.

We talk and he asks about Ricci, listening as I express my frustration, my bewilderment at how everything had turned out.

"Have you guys always been monogamous?" he asks. "Never cheating?"

"No, never," I say, except for one time, long before we were married, right after we'd met, when Ricci went away, on a trip, and I hadn't heard from him for a long time. I explain that everyone kept telling me he wasn't being fair to me, going off to do his own thing, and how I'd met a really nice guy, by chance, and how Ricci had been furious when he got back and found out. "He's never let that go," I add, "despite the fact I've been so loyal, always encouraging him with his ambitions and his dreams." I pick at the lentils on my plate. "You know, Carlos, sometimes I think our entire relationship has been based on guilt and punishment."

Carlos looks appalled at that idea.

Had our relationship merely reflected two thousand years of history?

Carlos washes the dishes, waving me away when I halfheartedly offer to help.

"Just relax," he says.

I feel guilt again. Damn it, I'm not even Catholic!

He puts down the sponge. "Come here," he says, and puts his arms around me in a friendly hug. I just stand there, in this deep soulful hug, his spirit filling my vacant one. Slowly, I feel myself come to life and my arms rise to encircle him. I feel like crying, but I am too worn out to cry. I have no tears left.

"Barbara, you are gorgeous, inside and out. You got that?"

At 3 a.m. I wake up and get dressed. He stands at the front door with me. The worst storm of the season is blasting up and down California. It is a beautiful, intense night and I find myself wanting to stay there forever, but I know I have to leave. I need Carlos to finish this film and I would be a distraction. Or, perhaps more accurately, I would make myself a distraction. Nothing matters but this film.
"It's dangerous. Are you sure you don't want to stay?"

I look at the darkness and the plummeting rain. It will be dangerous driving the eight hours back north to San Francisco. But I no longer care about me. I have poured all of my love for life, freedom, and my children into that film. It is in Carlos's hands now.

It is time for me to leave. The leaves on the trees are telling me so, their soft sounds barely audible above the storm. I can hear them speaking. Almost.

Friday, December 12th, the texts start coming in from Carlos.

5:15pm:	*tight but ok*
6:55pm:	*I hope to upload a low resolution version for you to quickly check around 9pm.*
9:12pm:	*10pm*
10:01 pm:	*Check email. watch movies, call me.*

The End

11:57:   Uploaded the video, trying to pay for the submission. Credit card denied.

Then he sends me a Facebook message at six o'clock the following morning:

Delivered last night, 12am sharp. One screaming body of work. Makes you feel alive.

I am sitting at the cafe, like I do, at six in the morning, when his email comes in, with the link to the new film.

I watch it. It is about twenty minutes long. When it ends, I shield my face with my hands and sob. It's my life, everything that I am about, everything that I had felt since I was twelve years old. Everyone who was a part of it.

There it was—all of it. Redemption for studying oceanography, a tribute to San Francisco State, my late great-uncle's photo of *Magic*, sailing, my children, Neptune, the ocean talking. The copepods, like my pollywogs in the ditch. Even the sailing and science program Ricci and I created together was part of the film. Carlos had done it. He had made it happen.

It was good.

All that was left to add were the credits.

"You were the writer. You get the credit," he writes.

"No! I'm not the writer. I didn't do anything! You wrote the film." We go back and forth.

"It was your idea. You created it, you wrote it."

"I didn't do anything. You did it all!"

Finally, I suggest he credit both of us. His name first.

He makes the changes and sends me the film again. Our names are both there but he has listed my name first and added that I conceived the idea.

It makes me cry again. This had all begun because I had wanted to support Carlos in his dream to be a filmmaker, and here I am, getting so much back. I feel guilty, selfish that I am getting something from what was supposed to be for him. I didn't plan for this to happen. It just did.

I am officially a writer. My dream.

I walk back to the apartment, looking—feeling—for the trees that had been with me during the summer. Back then I was convinced I could feel them. I can only smell them now. I inhale deeply their fragrance, their spirit, and my tears flow.

I miss my children. I miss our life. Though it was never mine to keep.

What is my life? What is right? What is wrong? I sigh. What the hell does any of it matter, I think. We'll all be dead in the end anyway.

That spirit world. It calls me sometimes and I'm listening to it more openly. That in-between place where neither world has you.

I find myself thinking about José.

Take care of my father. I had heard those words in my mind, crystal clear, that day I had been listening to José's music.

I call Carlos. I tell him about this talented guitarist I know. Maybe we could make a movie about him. Carlos is interested. I have to talk to José. His music does something to me. New ideas spin inside my head.

José and I sit face to face at the bakery, over a blueberry muffin and chocolate donut. I tell him I believe he has a story to tell.

"It can't be about me," he protests.

"Okay, you can be the inspiration behind the story."

He smiles, as if contemplating his life differently.

"José, you have led a legacy life, playing with legacy musicians. You have no ego, and as a result your work has been lost to this ego- and money-driven world we live in. You've stayed true to yourself, your music, for four decades without ever selling out. I see what you give, without seeking fame. You don't think about money. I see your kindness. I see your passion."

He is quiet. Neither of us has any idea yet what the story will be about.

"I lost my childhood dream to be an oceanographer and my guitar lessons because of President Ronald Reagan. But despite that, I can say that I've made a film with the world's greatest oceanographer and another with the most powerful guitarist. I believe your music will wake the world to the living, like it did me."

He smiles and nods. That seed in my belly is sprouting.

"Okay."

"I love the ocean," I say. It is out of context, but it's all connected. I pop the last of my chocolate donut in my mouth and lick my fingers.

As we walk out the door he mentions that Sidney Tennucchi, the first person I'd met at Green Gulch, has died of brain cancer. Something tells me Sidney's spirit is behind this project as well. He was an avid surfer and had just published a book, *Poems of Love*, the year before. He loved the ocean.

Like me.

It's quiet here, in this cafe. I am comforted by the guitar music that a dark-haired man strums and sings to. Across from me the likes of an aged Jack Kerouac makes pencil notes in a tattered book and stares up and across the wondrous universe of time and humanity, encountering hard questions that deepen with sips of coffee. His mind is alive and free to sift. I can feel it move.

I miss sitting in the bakery, where I'd see Neto and Joe. It's closed now. Went out of business. I remember those simple words José had said to me. "It'll be okay." I hang onto those words and try to imagine.

I need the quiet. While I'm away from Ricci the memories of pain keep coming, relentlessly, incessantly. For years I thought it was my fault. Everything. I tried so hard. Now I see that my trying so hard was the problem. It *was* hard. And that was not my fault.

We will recalibrate.

I read an article about China preparing to bulldoze mountains, to level them in order to have more space to build upward. How can I worry about cleaning bathrooms and vacuuming when I read such things about the world my children will inherit?

There is a winter chill in the air.

I ask Ricci to take a walk with me, through the woods along Phoenix Lake, the same place I walked the day my uncle died. It's where I taught my nature program, sitting under the trees with the children, feeling the wind through hair. We would watch the dancing water, which was what we called the twinkling lake when the light shone just right.

"I'd like us to stay grounded as we go through this separation, Ricci. I don't want it to get ugly. Let's stay human."

We walked without speaking for a few moments. The earth was moist. I put my hands in my pockets to keep them warm.

"How are things?" I ask.

"Good."

We make small talk.

"I'm picking up a Christmas tree this weekend," he says.

"A Christmas tree?" I blurt, before I could catch myself.

"Yes. You taught me how important rituals are in life."

I look at him, astonished.

"What? But you never got a tree with me, Ricci, no matter how many times I suggested it, even when my parents came for Christmas. And now, all of a sudden, you're getting a tree?"

He shrugs.

I let it go. We discuss the children, school, and money. Then he mentions he had gone dancing the night before.

"Dancing? You go dancing now? You wouldn't even dance with me on our honeymoon."

He shrugs again. "I guess some people just know how to pull it out of you." He changes the subject. "My girlfriend says she can help you with your film work. She used to be in the business and has lots of contacts in Los Angeles and Europe."

What?

And who exactly would be helping whom, I wonder. Is this him controlling me again, or it a genuine offer?

My mind is in overdrive, processing all this. Have I been a fool? Or is he right and I've helped this man rise to a higher level? If so, why am I not the one benefiting from these changes? If I helped him, why am I not getting the goods? Why am I getting the short end of the stick?

Or am I?

We stand on a wooden bridge and look down. The recent rains have spurred the normally quiet creek into a slender raging river. I listen to the water, feeling the energy of it. The mixing. The confusion. Carving deeper edges along the shore, scraping against hard rocks. Carrying fallen leaves, casualties of the autumn season. Smoothing edges over time.

Rage threatens to bubble up from inside me and I don't know how to handle it. I have never experienced rage in my life. Breaking through it is my great-uncle's familiar voice.

The End

It's water under the bridge, Barbara. Let it go.

Damn it, Uncle Bob, get out of my head!

My head aches as roiling blood pulses in my temples. Twenty years, damn it! How do you let that go, let go of all the anger and frustration, when you see how stupid you've been?

I exhale air I hadn't realized I was holding.

Could I let it all go? Maybe I could. Maybe I could be a big enough person and see Ricci as a man who didn't know himself, and now he does. I helped get him there. He admitted it. I didn't know what to do. I need to sort through all of this.

"Well, I have to go now," Ricci says, breaking into my thoughts. He hugs me and walks away. I stare at the river, my mind awhirl with voices and events from the past twenty years.

Water under the bridge, Barbara.

Was it?

It's Christmas Eve. It sneaked up on me. I hadn't so much as heard a Christmas carol I've been so busy with the film, emotional stability, and dealing with Kyle that I can't even think about the warm and fuzzies of Christmas. Lucy has gone to Sara's house and they invited her to stay for Christmas. I said yes. It is best for her. I have no presents for the kids, or for anyone, except a few stocking stuffers.

I open the refrigerator to cabbage, two carrots, and a few potatoes.

"It's okay, Mom. I love cabbage."

I am startled by the stark contrast in how Kyle behaves, at times. Today we have had no rages. He lights candles while I cook us a meal. We don't have a tree, but when I look out my window I see hundreds. These are my Christmas trees this year. They stand tall.

I can too, I decide. At least, I can try. I try not to think of past Christmases spent with Anja and Dante, punctuated by the Finnish dishware, lit candles, and everything so perfect.

Kyle sits at the head of the table and we talk.

"Don't worry, Mom," he says again with a smile. "I love carrots and cabbage."

I watch him. He is genuinely happy, the little prince, cajoling, cracking jokes. We laugh about silly things and lick our fingers, passing them through the candle flames without burning ourselves. When he goes to bed, I kiss him good night and wait until I think he has fallen asleep. I tiptoe past, toward the holiday stockings sitting by the window and fill them with chocolates and little treats.

A voice emerges from the dark. "I knew Santa didn't exist."

2015

January 2015

Feeling empty. Not able to hold onto anything. Complete blackness, depth, like deep in water, unable to breath. Like going through a birth canal, squeezed, asphyxiating. Slipping. Wanting to scream but lungs can't release.

Carlos calls. We talk briefly about the film and hang up.

He calls back seconds later.

"Go be with someone today. Do you have a friend to be with?"

"Tomorrow, yes." I will be with Gianna, to work on the DVD cover. To be with an old friend. She is a friend.

I will rekindle my marriage. Can't he see what I'm doing? Twenty-two years together. It's going to be okay.

I curl up on Gianna's couch. My body collapses. I must have the flu. She brings me tea. Her dog nuzzles beneath my chin. I sleep and she covers me with a blanket. I feel nurtured. How long has it been, I wonder, since someone has taken care of me?

Sleep. I have made plans tomorrow to see Ricci at our house to talk about all our years together, the past. And the future. We'll have a good talk. It'll be okay. I close my eyes.

"She's *here*?" I say in utter disbelief, when I arrive at the house.

Her car is parked in the driveway, establishing her territory, leaving me to park on the street. He did not have the decency to meet with me alone? He could have told me! I consider driving away, but then I remember my new convictions, to look at life straight in the eye.

Even if it's a hurricane.

My birthday plants from three years ago grace the front stoop. I look at the garden I planted. My grandmother's quince tree. My daughter's gourd birdhouse we'd made together. Everything looks tired, disheveled.

He answers the door and steps back to permit me to enter.

"Why didn't you tell me she'd be here?" I ask.

"I didn't want you to get mad."

"Mad? What the hell do you think I am now?"

"She's really sick, Barbara. She has the flu."

I can't believe I am hearing this from him.

"I can't believe I actually considered sleeping with you, thinking I could talk sense into you. I am so fired up on life again, and I was ready to go fuck your brains out. Really! I had hoped we could restart, Ricci, mend our differences and heal our family. Maybe you'd see the good work I was doing. Maybe you'd get inspired. Maybe you were over your fling." The words tumble out with a force of their own.

"You emasculated me, Barbara. I was your whipping boy."

"You were my *what*?" I can't believe my ears. "My whipping boy? What on earth are you talking about? I stood by you the entire time, Ricci, while you did what you wanted, so you could find something that would make you happy."

I broke into tears.

"Damn it!" I cry, as they gush like a firehose. "I loved you, Ricci, and I stood by you. You never supported anything I wanted to do."

"Well, I'm supporting you now, aren't I?"

"And, how's that?" I ask, as I march upstairs to our son's room. I glance down the hall to our bedroom door, where my bed lay, the one I had bought, schlepped home, and put together, where she was languishing. I knew she was listening. I mean, who wouldn't? The conversation was getting good.

"Whipping boy? Emasculated? Where is this all coming from? Can't you just be happy for your wife to have success at something? You never could! Anything I did you would find some reason to knock down."

He doesn't answer.

"Ricci, our dreams! The countryside! Traveling! This damn house was just too overwhelming!"

He shakes his head.

Somehow we end up in an embrace, me crying my eyes out. I need something from him, and I don't know what or why. I tell him how much I love him.

Really?

I ask for my wedding ring, which had been sawed off before the birth of our son. Ricci had kept it.

He refuses.

I ask him to come to the screening with his mom.

"I don't think she'll want to," he says.

"Ricci, it's important to me." And it was. Maybe it'd knock sense into both of them. I hadn't been out looking for new boyfriends. I hadn't done all this for selfish reasons. I have been trying to do my part to save the world, the world in which he—and his children—happen to live in. It's in his interest! But he just can't see that.

I leave and drive to the Golden Gate Bridge. I park high on the cliffs, next to a mountain made of thirty-million-year-old chert, microscopic plankton from an ancient sea. It helps me appreciate the insignificance of my life, how the events of these last months—years—don't matter in the course of the vast universe.

Yet the pain doesn't go away. It eats away the gut, the heart, and everything in between. How do women do this? How have women done this?

I look at the bridge and it occurs to me that I can end all this pain right here and now. I could. I think about the details. Parking the car here. Walking down the path to the western span. I'd look over the ledge and then just hop over the low fence, just like I did as a child by the runoff ditch, to find my pollywogs. I'd float with the copepods. I'd be done with it all. So simple.

I am struck by a vivid memory of my mother, crying on the phone, her head down, the long cord of the wall telephone swinging back and forth, like a pendulum. My aunt had committed suicide. Car fumes. A garage. It was intentional. It followed a divorce.

I remember lying on top of the sofa, the edge above the cushions where only a small child could fit. My secret spot. I watched my mother. I felt more of a curiosity than sadness as I listened to her sobbing, the TV blaring commercials for household cleaning products and frozen dinners.

I would have loved to have had an aunt growing up, I think. That's when it hits me. I could never hurt my mother like that again. And I needed her to see me happy, to think of me as being happy.

How many women end it here though? How many feel a failure, like I do? How many take the blame, justified or not? How many times do we blame mothers for our problems? How long have we shut women down?

I wonder.

I cook lentils and stare into the pot. I talk to my uncle. I start crying again. I feel his words all around me.

"I need you," I weep.

I'm here.

"Why do I have to go through this? Why?"

It's going to be okay.

"It hurts."

I know.

"It's not fair."

No, it's not.

"I love him."

I know.

"I want us to be together again."

Don't.

I listen.

Carlos. Follow Carlos. For now.

I think I'm going crazy.

I put myself together on the outside.

I stand up onstage at the Randall Museum and look out at the audience filled with people who represent my life for the last fifteen years. Ricci is there, with his mother, sitting up high, away from everyone else. Anja has her arms crossed.

In one corner are all the children—Kyle, the kids from the film, Lucy with all her homeschooling buddies, and the families who have been a big part of her education, the education I passionately wanted for her, one filled with rich literature, sharing wonder, art, and dreams.

My mom and dad sit in the lower rows, alongside my sister Chris and her husband. They smile. My dad sits upright, proudly.

Jane sits in the very front row, attentive, listening. I would love to know what is going through her brain. Her daughter Meg is with me, onstage. She is poised and speaking well. I brought her here. Jane had better damn well appreciate that, I think. Although I still have words for her, and I intend to let them out when the time comes, I still need her for the project, for the bookkeeping.

The Randall Museum is full. A speaker from the Schmidt Family Foundation joins us and gives a fantastic speech about efforts and world affairs. My entire life is here. Even my former neighbor's daughter has come to play her fiddle.

Now it's my turn. I have my words to speak, not just about the film but to my husband. I'm not done yet.

Standing in front of an audience when you are about to divulge your soul and reveal twenty minutes of video depicting what and who you are, what you believe in, what you stand for, is the most treacherous yet brilliant feeling. I want Ricci to see what I love. We created the sailing science program together. I want him to see the good we created.

I want him back.

I stand on the podium. Before I talk about the film, I want to express my gratitude.

"People can come up with ideas. They are a dime a dozen. It takes people to make things happen and this project proved that. So many people came together. We would not have been able to help make this project without the support I received. Cathy, Frank, thank you for watching our kids. Ricci, thank you for all your support with the house and watching the kids. You helped us make this." I have other words I would love to add, but I am determined to stay positive.

When I finish, Carlos grabs the microphone, which is not part of the program. He spontaneously calls for the kids, the cast, and gathers everyone onstage and starts directing. The rest of the afternoon goes well, the air filled with an energy mixing delight, pride, exhilaration, happy surprise, and enthusiasm.

After the screening, the audience rises from their seats and mobs us. Hugs and congratulations are passed around among almost everyone.

I look around. Anja has slipped out, disappeared without a word. Ricci comes to me and says, "Barbara, I'm proud of you." He hugs me. It is a passionless hug, the hug of a colleague, an acquaintance. "I brought the dishes, as you asked, and put them in your car."

He's referring to our wedding dishes.

When the last of the audience leaves, the theater is quiet. It is over. I turned my entire life upside down for this moment, to do a brief screening in a modest little theater. Now it is time to head back to my equally quiet, empty apartment and be alone. Ricci has the kids.

When I get back to my apartment, I open the box of the Finnish dishes, the Arabia, my wedding dishes, the first material possessions

I valued, the dishes we used for gatherings and celebrations. My beautiful Arabia.

I lovingly unwrap the newspaper from each plate, cup, and saucer and set them on the table. When the box is empty, I look at the set.

He has given me only half.

I'm determined to put my family back together.

We meet again at Phoenix Lake, the same place where the girls in my nature program discovered ladybugs, banana slugs, and emerging cicadas that sing in trees, and meditated on how a single drop of water in the lake has survived as rain, ice, and vapor, as liquid, solid, and gas, recirculating for millions of years.

Parking is difficult so I join Ricci in his van to sit and talk. An unfamiliar crystal dangles from his mirror. Shells I've never seen before line his dashboard.

We start talking. We need to talk. There is so much to talk about. Twenty years of what went wrong. Twenty years of my life. I want to be together again. I want to go home. I want to be together, with my family. I want to sit on the sofa and watch a film. I want that, just like I always have. He seems calmer, more grounded, and nice, for the first time in years. He seems mindful of that about himself. I feel optimistic.

He tells me about meditation practice, his new life, and how I taught him how to be a loving, kind person, which has enabled him to find that in his life. Maybe, he says, life is about helping one another get to those higher levels. I helped him get to a new level and now he can take that to a new relationship.

All I can do is sit there and listen.

Then he hands me a card featuring an illustration of artwork, the same picture that is on his dashboard. It depicts a beautiful woman, facing front and center, amid a bursting spectrum of colors.

"Take a look at this artwork I'm buying."

I found my voice.

"You're buying artwork? I had to fight you to buy artwork on our honeymoon," I remind him. I turn the card over and see a picture of his girlfriend on it. It is a promotional piece for her.

My blood comes to a simmer and I feel it heating further, bubbling slowly at first. I feel the lava rise and burst forth, exploding like a mountain top. I have never done this before with anyone, never felt this way before with anyone. My rage is akin to my son's. It starts in my gut, then rises into my lungs, up through my throat, unravels my tongue, and fires from my mouth. My voice takes control of me, not me of it.

"Why, Ricci? Why? I am your wife. I spent twenty-two years with you, loving you, running circles around you. You, always feeling you were unhappy, frustrated, always angry about something. And all of that was directed at me. And I dealt with it. Over and over again. Making excuses to people for you."

I couldn't stop the torrent of words.

"Everything I did, you questioned, you criticized. You made me feel like I didn't know what I was doing. And I took it. I took it."

I whack my jacket at him, over and over again, in fury. I grab the shells sitting on his dashboard and fling them, hard. Then I grab the card and throw it at him.

"No respect, Ricci! No respect for me then, and no respect for me now. And then you throw *her* at me? Fuck! Fuck, fuck, *fuck!*"

I take a breath.

"And yet it all comes from love," I say, shaking my head. "I loved you, Ricci. I spent twenty years of my life with you. You're the father of my children. How dare you!"

"You left me, Barb." His voice was calm, even.

"What else was I to do? You kept yelling! I had hoped my absence would knock some sense into you, Ricci. It was all about you. It was always all about you. I haven't had a damn vacation for ten years. I've been overwhelmed, full tilt with the children. We lived in poverty in a huge house. My clothes are rags. My spirit feels shredded. I couldn't even keep up with the collecting spiderwebs that weave at night.

"All these years you didn't think about our home. *Our* home, Ricci. I was going fucking crazy as our home fell apart around us, making me fall apart. Cleaning three fucking bathrooms. Being a fucking indentured slave to a big house that I never even wanted to live in, all so you could figure out your life. Your parents and their way of life kept us locked in. I never wanted to live like that!"

Ricci starts the van and pulls out, heading toward my car.

I'm still yelling, but I'm finding my voice. I'm speaking for myself for the first time in years.

The End

He delivers me to my car. I'm still enraged. I am not done. I have years pouring out of me now. I follow him to our house, in my car, like some enraged stalker. I am a wife who needs to speak to her husband and tell him how she feels after so many years of not speaking. Have I indeed finally found my voice?

As we approach the house, he knows I'm following him and drives past, away, around the corner.

I park in the driveway. The garage door is open. I walk in boldly, pull out a pan, and start making scrambled eggs. I am hungry.

He walks in with a recorder.

"I want you to know I'm recording this."

Wow. I was scaring him? Me? I had never scared anyone in my life before. This is new!

"You'll get money," he says.

"Money? The one thing I've been running away from!" I laugh. "Is that what I am? You can put a monetary value on me? My God."

"I honor you. I respect you."

"Those are just words, Ricci. You don't respect me. I'm not a fool anymore. You cheated me, Ricci. You've been growing up all these years under my time."

"You'll get money," he repeats.

"Money?" I scream. The fuck words stream out, burning everything in their path, like fiery liquid. I couldn't stop. (It's a great word if you really stop to analyze it. *F* for "frank," *U* for "under," *C* for "conquer," and *K* for "kill.")

"Barbara, my mother agrees. You haven't even called my mother to meet up on Tuesday."

I'd said I wanted to reach Ricci's mom to arrange to get together, just to talk.

"I've tried calling her numerous times. Her voicemail doesn't take messages."

He shakes his head. Of course, he doesn't believe me.

"Barbara, I'm going to tell you straight out."

I stare at him hard, waiting.

"It was hard after you left, and it left me thinking about a lot of things, about how I was to you, how I was as a partner, who I was and who I want to be." His voice was calm and thoughtful.

"Barbara, when I met her, it was a connection unlike anything I've ever experienced before. We spent a weekend together and it was the most magical weekend of my life. It was like it was all meant to be. She became everything to me."

We are animals. Pure animals. We go around the world suffering illusions, believing in big ideas, and thinking mightily of ourselves. We strut the streets like we are better than the dogs at the end of the leash. We carelessly, often deliberately, step on spiders. Have we just consumed too much Disney and bad writings, and blasted ourselves to the moon too many times, believing we are something that we're not?

We're not big, when you get right down to it. We are less than animals. We are less than a one-eyed copepod. At least they know their place in the universe. We wage wars and bury ourselves under too much junk, too much stuff. We are nothing more than dirt, once you peel away the outer layers.

I look at this man and feel myself transform into a scorpion. The flick of my hand, with all the sting of a scorpion's tail, is a power I had not known I possessed. It's in these times you learn the depth of your character. It unravels and we surprise ourselves with the baseness of our behavior, our smallness. Our pure evil. Yes, it resides in all of us. And when you realize this truth, you can find your bottom and then there's nowhere to go but up, to rise, like a phoenix.

I snap the keys in my hand at him, my scorpion tail. He ducks with fear and I find pleasure seeing it, his cowardice. And my evilness. This was a new me, a foreign me, and I was finally letting it breathe.

"I hate you. Why did you marry me, Ricci? Why did you want a family?"

And yet I didn't hate him, not as much as I hated myself. My mouth tasted sour. Anger and hate were like poison flowing through my body. I could taste the venom as it collected on the tip of my tongue, ready to be spat out.

But it wasn't him I hated in that moment; it was myself, feeling such horrid emotions. I didn't want to be the person I was in that moment. That I was capable of becoming such a person scared me more.

I storm out of the house, throw myself into my car, and lurch out of the driveway.

Sitting at a red light, I breathe and my heart slows down. An odd calm comes over me and I lean back in my seat.

"Wow, Barbara, you've never done that before. You just beat him up! I've never beaten up anyone before. Won't do it again, but it felt damn good!"

Didn't know I was capable of doing such a thing. Wow.

I pull out my phone.

Anja answers.

"Hi Anja, I've been trying to reach you for the last couple of days about meeting. I understand you've been a bit upset that I haven't connected with you. I've tried calling you several times, but your machine isn't taking messages and says it's full."

She hesitates before admitting, "Yes, my machine isn't working right."

"Anja, you could have called me too, right?"

She pauses again.

"Yes. I guess I could have."

February 2015

"I'm alone," I tell Captain Richard. He's in paradise, in the islands—St. Thomas.

"You're not alone. You are supported. You are loved."

"I acted badly. But, damn, it felt good."

"I get it," he says, "but you brought it on yourself—you put up with it. This allowed you to be right. You knew he didn't support you. It's been killing me, watching you be like this."

"It still hurts. I thought he would come around and see the good we had, and fight for it."

"Take responsibility."

I look out to the Pacific Ocean, that grand ocean with unexplored depths beyond its surface. Vast, yet vulnerable. It gives me hope, solace, and breath. I think back to having sailed down the coast with *Summer Solstice*, the fight it took to make that voyage. And the exhilaration I found at the helm, in the middle of night, as the watching "eyeballs" bobbed around me, as I listened to those voices at sea. Had they really been voices calling me, telling me something I needed to hear?

"You're not complete yet. What would make you complete?" Captain Richard asks.

"I don't know. I don't know."

I'm deep in reading. God, I love having the time to read. How long has it been since I could sit peacefully with my thoughts, to think about the world without having to worry about ticking a litany of check boxes, items that compete for my attention? It's been a race for too long, rushing here and there and feeling like I have to satisfy everyone according to their rules, a way of being that does not permit me to be me.

I sit at the university cafe and read about post-modern literature—perceptions, distorted rights and wrongs, and how we cling fiercely to what we think is right, only to discover it's a made-up way of being right. We align ourselves with stories; they are our channels of being.

I think about frogs that turn into princes, knights on white chargers who swoop in to save the day, and pumpkins that turn into carriages that chauffeur fairy-tale housecleaners to royal balls. These color our perspectives; they become our dreams, what we aspire to. What is this doing to our children? We judge people more often by what they own instead of what they do with their lives.

I think about love. Could we not inspire our children with bigger dreams? Highlight those individuals who strive to work for the betterment of us all? Create new heroes, those who have the guts to say, "No more!" A knight in shining armor who can see the deep good in us all and show us sides we didn't know existed.

I love university life. I'm halfway done with my master's degree in humanities. It's the thread that connects me to the fabric of staying human.

Two young Chinese students, a young man and woman, approach me, giggling. They're up to something.

"Excuse us. We are doing a little survey on love. Can you answer some questions?"

I smile, the all-knowing smile. I'm right where I'm supposed to be. I surrender to the universe.

"Okay." I put my books down.

The young man, who's holding a pen and notebook, asks, "Who should buy dinner when you go out on a date, the man or the woman?"

"The man, for sure," I answer. Isn't that in my interest?

He scribbles down the answer and the girl giggles, covering her mouth. This is just too perfect.

"How long should a couple know one another before getting married?"

I don't know how to answer this one. I shrug.

"I guess it depends. There's no clear-cut answer to that."

Disappointed, the young man says, "Okay, thank you!" and they turn away.

"Wait! That's it?" They turn back. My brain registers multiple questions they should ask. "Okay, I have a question for you." I look at the girl. "What is love?"

She covers her mouth and giggles.

"Love to me is somebody who makes me so happy!" she says, bringing her hands to her heart and batting her eyelashes.

I look at the two of them, so happy and innocent.

"Maybe so," I concede.

"Ahoy thar, Wonder Woman!" Captain Richard's voice on the phone sounds far away.

"Hi, Captain, how are the islands?"

"I'm in Mandal Bay. They want to develop it. I spoke with a senator while he was meeting with developers and I told them to keep it protected for the children. 'You destroy it,' I said, 'and you destroy it for all generations.'"

"That's my captain. Keep 'em in line."

"How are you doing?"

I exhale.

"Captain, it's hard, really hard. It's not fair."

"You are not complete yet. Think about and focus on what will make you complete. You have to take full responsibility for everything and everyone in your life. Got that? You chose him. You knew he didn't support you."

"I know. No, I don't know—I didn't know. But why can't he? Look what I did for him!"

"That's the whole point. Open yourself up to the universe."

I need to escape, to go somewhere, anywhere but here. Jenn has invited me and the kids to spend three days at her boyfriend's house in Tahoe. A big house, she says. Enough for all of us. She's anxious to make it up to me, I can tell. The boyfriend won't be there, she promises. It'll be just us.

I would love to see the kids laughing in the snow. Snow angels. I need to smile. Tahoe, a four-hour drive away, up into the mountains. It sounds perfect.

We arrive in Tahoe. It's necessary to take a gondola up the mountain to the house. I have never been to this part of Tahoe and it doesn't take long to see why.

As we dangle from the gondola, the darkness and stinging cold envelop us. I tighten the thin scarf around my neck. The kids are laughing with delight.

Jenn is quiet. Something is on her mind.

I try not to talk about Ricci. I need to put him aside, although I am still hurting. What woman does such a thing to a family, I wonder for the thousandth time, thinking of his so-called woman-empowering girlfriend.

We arrive and transfer to a large snowcat.

"All this to get to a house?" I say to Jenn, trying to sound good-natured about it. She senses my disbelief, giving me an apologetic half-smile.

We entered the house, an enormous eight-bedroom home that sits idle for most of the year.

"This belongs to your boyfriend?"

"It belongs to his family."

I can understand the lure for her as well as me, the yearning to escape the day-to-day struggle to survive, her worry for her daughter. I get why she keeps him around, even if the boyfriend is unkind to her. You can make convenient excuses to experience financial comfort, for even just a short time.

We settle in, finding comfort in each other's words and in companionable silences over cups of tea. The kids are outside, playing in the snow. When they are happy, we mothers can relax. It doesn't take much.

I'd signed my kids up for a one-day ski class and tread down the path covered by no more than a thin, mushy layer of snow, throwing snowballs at one another until we arrive at the ski lodge. We look at it, surrounded by a paved parking lot, completely void of snow. It's mid-January. Mid-January, and there's no snow. We walk back to the house in silence.

"Sorry, kids," I say. "We'll have to just stick to the saucers, okay?" There was still some residual snow by the house.

Kyle abruptly demands the computer. My spirits sink. Not here, not like this.

"Kyle, no, not here. We're here to play in the snow." I can see the rage building in him. I feel sick.

"Where is it, Mother?" His eight-year-old eyes flash with anger.

"No, Kyle, no computer. We'll do other things." We enter the house, and he dashes around, throwing open drawers and cupboards, like a drug addict desperately seeking his stash. Lucy, watching, throws me a worried look.

"Lucy, go into the other room," I suggest, softly. I don't want her to see her brother this way. I try to calm him down but he just gets angrier.

"Where is it?" he barks.

"Come on, Kyle, don't act this way." I take an involuntary step backward as he comes at me. I know he's going to hit me. I push him away. "Kyle, do not hit me."

Lucy appears in the doorway.

"Give it to me now, Mother," he demands, his voice hoarse.

"Kyle, stop it!"

His fist abruptly strikes me in the gut. I double over, gasping.

"Get Jenn, now!" I choke to Lucy.

Kyle's eyes were rolling as he prepared to charge again, like an enraged bull. My God, where does this anger come from?

"Kyle, you sit down right now!" I gasp. "Sit down and don't move." Jenn rushes into the room and bends over me. "Jenn, I might need a doctor. Let me sit for a minute."

There is so much pain I can't even cry. My out-of-control eight-year-old boy has just punched me. Punched me! Over a video game? Is it the pain I am suffering from, or the shock of my young son hitting me so hard?

Later, Jenn tells me that Kyle wasn't himself. She could see it in his eyes, like he was in a different state of consciousness.

"I know," I say. "It's like he checks out when he enters his rages. It mostly started after Ricci's father died. There is nothing I can do but distance myself from him. But I get this feeling that he's trying to get me to do something."

"Girl, you've got big things to worry about," Jenn says, with a concerned look.

I nod.

We agree to leave the next day.

We head down the mountain aboard the gondola, this time under bright, spring-like skies instead of under cover of darkness. Everywhere we look, scattered everywhere across the slopes, sit huge homes. Nothing moves.

"Where is everyone?" I ask.

"People only come for a few weekends a year," Jenn says. "Look. Five families could live in that one," she adds, pointing to a stunning home, the size of a castle. "Disney owns that one over there," she says, and points to another massive home.

"I don't know," I say. "Doesn't feel right to me, Jenn, when so many people are hungry and struggling to survive."

Jenn agrees. The extravagance is too much. It's just not right, this obscene disparity, not in a world where so many people have nothing and our world is caving in because of greed and extravagance. Manufacturing is struggling, but demand for luxury goods has never been higher despite the problems with the economy. We've been taught to want what we see. In the United States alone, the top one-tenth of one percent has managed to amass sufficient wealth to rival the aggregate of the bottom 90 percent. How is this possible? It's obscene, and yet these same few elite are perceived as good or worthy people. Good? How can people feel right about holding so much of our country's resources for themselves?

Jenn's next words punctuate this obscenity.

"They have to keep them heated all season, otherwise the pipes freeze and break," she says, staring down, out the window.

I think about how many trees have been felled to craft one of those houses, how many stones taken from a quarry, how the furniture got schlepped from cargo ship to truck to truck. How much should we each have versus what we need? Having money is no excuse to exploit so many resources in order to impress others by showing it off.

I think of the planet. No respect. I think back to Bo and how he couldn't watch advertisements. He saw the lies and couldn't stomach them. What if he is simply more connected to the natural world than most of us? More connected to truth and what it stands for? What if those who are mentally ill, those who hear voices, are connected the natural world, the spirit world, in ways that others aren't? The unrelenting roar of greed perhaps drowns out the sounds of that natural world.

Maybe it's the high living who are mentally ill.

I think back to the voices I had heard over the past two years. I had connected to something extraordinary. I believe that.

What if?

On the drive back, the kids and I are quiet. My mind spins.

What does all this mean?

We climb into Carlos's roommate's sharp-looking convertible and roll down the top. Carlos dons his sunglasses like some sexy Latin film director, looking nothing like the poor, plebeian artist he is, with his last sixty-eight dollars in his wallet. I sit next to him, newly single, my kids in the back, as we attempt to zip across the Los Angeles scene, failing miserably, getting stuck in traffic repeatedly. The number of cars on the road is dizzying.

At a stop sign I spy an old lady at a bus stop. She looks all alone in the world. She's lived a long life, no doubt accruing wisdom she would willingly share with the world, if given the opportunity. Yet here she is, alone and looking lonely. Her eyes meet mine. I know what she thinks she sees, a young woman sitting next to a handsome man in sexy sunglasses, in a convertible, without a financial care in the world.

The world is full of illusions. We see the world as we expect it to be, as we want to, and not how it actually is.

I sit in thick traffic, in one of the most moneyed, greedy, illusion-building and polluted-centric places in the world, feeling the essence of my being emerge. In a landscape of car engines, hot pavement, and bumper-to-bumper exhaustion, I have the wind in my hair, music blasting. I am that little girl in her grandpa's airplane, asking, "Grandpa, when do I get to fly?"

For the past six months we put everything of ourselves into this film project, an immense amount of time, tapping the resources of people who had no reason to trust us. So, where has it gotten us? Carlos loses his place next month. He has no car of his own. I'm feeling desperate. Life is an absolute mess. Still, I can't let go of this project, or of school. The music of Neto playing his white guitar keeps me going, even though I have no idea where it is I'm headed. Still, the wind feels good in my hair.

And even as my little world crumbles around me, I can feel myself getting ready for a big bang, a totally new existence. I can feel it. Who would believe me? Why do I believe it?

And what form will this big bang take?

March 2015

The big bang has not yet occurred, unless you count Kyle's ongoing rages, when he explodes and hits me. Sometimes I have to get up and leave the apartment. The entire police department knows us now. They are good guys, trying to help us through a hard time.

The school is not happy, but I'm not happy with them, so it's a mutual discontent. As a mother I have no say in my children's education. Something is desperately wrong with this picture.

I pour it all out in my writing. Fiction, nonfiction, my diary, school papers. I get up at 2 a.m. and look at the crescent moon above the redwoods. I look down at words, thoughts, phrases, ideas that have all been bottled up for years, only now coming out to breathe in oxygen and take on life, releasing me in deep ways. I'll stop and sit outside on my deck, under the night stars and just watch the wind move the trees, the redwoods, oaks, bays, and pines, and ruffle my hair. I feel a rhythm, a language speaking to me. Urging me on. Coaxing me. The rhythm seduces me, and then new words, thoughts, and ideas pour out. I can't stop.

I've been sequestering myself for months, except for Carlos, and the kids when I have them. The quiet is not quiet. It's filled with voices coming at me. Conversations of the last twenty-two years return, sometimes those of Uncle Bob, Grandpa, Grandma, and even Aunt Doris before she committed suicide. I rethink all of the trials I experienced in my relationship with Ricci. I'll talk to myself for hours. I'll stare at myself all day. I'll sit in the bathtub, under the shower, holding myself while the water cascades down my body, washing away my tears.

Water under the bridge.

Uncle Bob's voice returns, again and again.

"It's not fair," I say.

No, it's not.

"It hurts."

I know.

"I want him back."

Don't trust.

I can't shake it. I know it's true that I have to move on. I can feel it. But where? When you hold on to something so hard for so long, and you wrap your love, your dreams, along with your heart and soul, into that grip, your knuckles become rigid and resistant. It's hard to shake life back into them. They feel atrophied. The pain to set them straight with life-giving blood flow hurts like hell. And there is no one to help me without my sounding crazy.

I keep going over and over the past year.

"I hope you're getting help," Cathy said to me after I sent her an angry email in the middle of the night. She had replied, saying she has never seen Ricci so happy.

What?

How dare friends who I brought into our lives, cultivated as family, created regattas for, and wrote about, align themselves so fast with my husband's girlfriend? How can this not create resentment and confusion for my daughter? I had a right to be angry. I am San Pablo Bay and he is San Francisco Bay.

But, on the other hand, there is beauty that rises from the ugly. I've discovered what true friendship means. And I will know how to be that kind of friend for the rest of my life.

I think of my old friend Bryna, found naked and dead in her apartment, in San Francisco, the city that she loved, the city that subsequently dumped her body and her stuff without a second thought, deeming it all valueless. I have to do something for her, I think. Sometimes, when I look at her books about witches and fighting women sitting on my shelf, I feel she is the one doing something for me.

Carlos, José, Joe and I meet at José's cottage to begin two days of initial filming. We aren't sure what direction to take or even where the story will take us. We don't even know the story yet. My friend Sophie, in England, interviewed José for two months, and we still don't know what the story is. He's humble and plays amazingly—so what, she said.

I know there is a story there, somewhere, even if nobody believes me. They just don't understand him and his music. Not yet.

The day is perfect, another of those days where you just sense you're in the right place at the right time. There was a balance, like that point of sail with the wind and currents, where they're working with you, not against you, propelling you forward. Carlos begins filming José and I stand on the porch, watching them. Two men with such passion, Carlos with his camera moving around a guitar shaped like the curves of a woman, and José playing chords, his music opening up the universe.

"José, can you tell me the name of that song you played at the Fairfax Pavilion, the one that's online now? It was a solo." It had captivated me for over a year. I'd listen to it in the middle of the night, over and over again. The song that oftentimes keeps me going.

He thinks a moment.

"Oh, that must be the Redemption Song." Our eyes meet and we connect. It feels like a line has just been drawn across the universe, where mere words soar to a different level. "I would play that song for my son and daughter before they went to bed," he says, and strums a few notes before casually adding, "That performance was in tribute to a filmmaker."

I freeze, feeling a vibration, a tingle, a chill, go straight up my spine. The music that changed my life, a song that I kept listening to over and over again—did it help me make my first film? Was that his daughter who came to me when I was half-asleep and murmured, "Take care of my father?"

Am I going crazy?

I seem to ask myself that question a lot lately, but all I know in this moment is that I need to make a film: *José Neto, The Man Behind the White Guitar*. That's it!

I have no idea what it will be about or how to make it happen—or how to come up with the money. But it has to happen, and I am willing to trust the universe to help me.

I meet up with Marilyn some days later and tell her what José said. She pulls out her iPhone to look up the lyrics of this timeless reggae song and reads them out loud. Her words, of old pirates who must free themselves from their mental slavery, reflect everything I am feeling and what I have been striving for. It's like a message, and even more than that—it is a path for me to follow and a message to shout.

My thoughts flash back to that first encounter I had with José, five years earlier, at the Green Gulch Zen Meditation Center. He had reminded me of a pirate back then. I tell this to Marilyn, my voice excited.

"And redemption? That's what my ocean film was all about—redemption for my lost dream as an oceanographer, being a writer, having a voice. I feel I'm dealing with spirits again, Marilyn."

Despite the leap of faith this requires, she believes me. I am beginning to feel less crazy and more confident in everything I do. But I have to trust this invisible space, like darkness, in front of me and imagine there is a light, like a streetlight, in front of me, guiding me. I think back to sailing down the California coast aboard *Summer Solstice,* feeling as if I might crash into a streetlight. Maybe it's been there all along. Now I will trust. The doors will open when they should, not when I want them to. I just need to follow, when the time is right.

April 2015

We sit in the courtroom together. I watch people take turns, demanding money, making accusations, attorneys supporting their clients, people standing up for their beliefs. Nice people, but, still, they find the worst in each other and make it become a reality.

I hand Ricci two chocolate bars.

"There's a love poem inside." I am being snarky. It's the same chocolate bar I saw his girlfriend give him with handwritten words of love on it. I can't help myself. At first, he doesn't take it, and then he takes one.

"All you had to do was move to Fairfax with me," I say.

"I couldn't do that. And I'm not sure that would have solved all of it anyway."

"You never know. You could have tried."

"You'll love my girlfriend. She's really nice. You guys will be good friends."

Fucker, I want to say. Does he say these things to piss me off, to humiliate me, or does he say things with pure genuine gusto? Doesn't matter. I'm playing the game too.

"I'm going to Spain this summer. I'm staying with Carlos's parents. We're friends, you know." I'm being genuine and he is finding the worst in me.

He nods, an all-knowing nod as if there is more I am not saying.

"We're *friends*," I repeat. Just to dig deeper. I'm being genuine. "Here, have some more chocolate."

"Thanks." He takes what I offer. It's so easy for him. And that's when I start to think about matrimony. What if we have it wrong, this concept of monogamy? I mean, why can't he just take another wife? She could be my wife too. God knows, I need help with the dishes. Help with the kids. We could expand our family, since family is spread so thinly anyway. We could have great sex together. Everyone is doing it every which way, these days.

I feel like I'm a little old-fashioned lady stepping out into this modern world, where the rules have changed dramatically. Actually, there don't seem to be many rules. I mean, if men can marry men and women can marry women, why can't we just keep expanding our relationships? Spread love! Build bigger families! Other cultures have done this, where a man takes many wives. Maybe a woman could take a few husbands too.

I would have been happy to take one—tall, dark, and handsome who would help wash the dishes and fix the toilets. Our house would have been in great shape. There would have been less arguing. Oh, and I could sleep with the other husband too, right? Well, if he's good, why not! It sounds like a win-win situation for everybody involved. More shared income, less stress. Why not?

I'm not being satirical. My questions are honest and sincere. But the more I think about it, the more I realize that such an idea would threaten our entire economy, which is inherently tied to monogamy. People have wrapped their careers around helping people weather divorce at $400 an hour, including therapists, mediators, authors, lawyers, and even wedding consultants. It's an entire industry geared toward ensuring that monogamy remains the standard, and any opposing standard is deemed unworthy in order to substantiate the industry. When we fail at this monogamous expectation, we make the other party the bad guy and our feelings get hurt. Some commit suicide or hurt themselves in other ways. Children suffer.

And it's all fabricated, an illusion, a Disney-like idea bolstered by a book written long ago of how we all should live and of what we must believe.

My artist friend Gianna put this seed into my brain long ago when she was with a divorced guy who had two kids. She assured them, "Heck, you've got the best of both worlds, kids. You've got two families to love you and two houses to live in. You got it better than most kids!"

There's something to this.

Ricci and I meet with two lawyers outside the courtroom and they tell us about mediation, where we can work it out between us instead of paying up the wazoo for opposing lawyers. Mediation is only about $5,000, they say.

Only?

Ricci looks to the ground. I know he hates spending, especially when it relates to me. That's how it's always been. It's not going to get better now.

"You know, we can just drop this paperwork, Ricci. Marriage is just paperwork after all." I'm not serious, but he takes me seriously.

"Yeah, I guess we could do that."

It's so unbelievably easy for him.

May 2015

The film project is moving fast. We launched a little Indiegogo campaign to make DVDs. We didn't raise all the money, but we raised enough, with all of the money coming from my or Carlos's personal supporters, to cover the production of the DVDs, but nothing for our own pockets.

It's been exhausting. The semester is close to wrapping up—papers, assignments, and readings. I've had a diet of nothing but lentils for a full week. One more year, that's it, and then I'm done with school. I can do it. I've done it before.

On the last day of the Indiegogo campaign Jane wrote, "The sailing organization is getting the money from these contributions, right?"

Suspicion again, that somehow I was being dishonest when nothing could have been further from the truth. I feel the hurtful repeated yank of that rein. I need her to do the bookkeeping for the film, but once that is done, I promise myself I will sit down face to face with her and tell her how wrong it was for her to treat Ricci the way she did. She would have dragged his name, our family name, through the mud if the organization had failed. I know that. Nobody is going to hurt my family's name again. It was wrong for Ricci to leave as he did; I know that too. I am still navigating between two wrongs, two egos, and this is where it has all gotten me—alone and dealing with two people who make my life miserable. Despite everything, I still hold out hope that Ricci will snap out of what he's doing so we can get back to our family life.

"Mom, where do sunrises come from?" Kyle sits up in bed, sleepily, and rubs his eyes. A magnificent sunrise is visible from his bedroom window, beyond the redwoods. His voice sounds different, almost dreamlike.

"Well, we live on a big round ball that spins, and the sun is like a lantern in the sky. As we spin, the sun is either in front of us or behind us, so we are either on the light side or the dark side. Mornings are when we come into the light side."

He nodded, thoughtfully.

"I have to decorate my paper doll, mom." He has a school assignment to dress a paper figure like one of his ancestors, for Heritage Day.

"We can go to the library for inspiration. You have a choice of Irish, Italian, or German. What do you think?"

"Maybe Italian."

"You always were fond of Nonno, weren't you? You liked making bread with him, didn't you?" Dante would show Kyle how to knead the dough and roll it. I miss Dante too.

We have breakfast together. Afterward, Kyle sits down on the sofa.

"I don't want to go to school, Mom."

I tense and my mind spins. *Oh, please, not today. Do I need to call the police again? I can't keep going through this.* I take a deep breath

The End

"Kyle, you have to go to school." My voice is soft, but firm. *How did this happen? My child is out of control.*

He looks out to the trees, to the soft morning light, as I had often done these past months. He turns and looks up at me, the expression in his eyes defeated, worn out. I felt the same way.

"Mom, I never spend any time with you or Dad. I go to school every day. It's boring."

He wasn't lashing out. His eyes were still Kyle's. He was speaking quietly, from his heart, not from anger, or from any other place.

I look at him, considering his words and think, do I really have to take him to school today? It's just one day. I feel a twinge of guilt. I have deadlines, so much work to do for the film project and school. But what he says is true. Laughter has been missing from our lives for almost a year. The school will be furious with me, if I let him stay home today, but what's more important? I miss my little boy. But neither did I want to fight with him all day again. It'd be exhausting getting anything done. I look at his pleading eyes and a thought occurs to me.

Could I play hooky too? I take a deep breath.

"Okay," I say, and his eyes light up. "But absolutely no video games," I warn. I glance out the window. "How about going to the beach together?"

He nods enthusiastically.

We drive to China Camp, an old Chinese fishing settlement on the San Pablo Bay, where we had once anchored *Fayaway*, the summer before. Along the way, Kyle records himself on my phone singing and making silly sounds. Sometimes I join in and he laughs with delight, in a way I haven't seen him do in a long time.

My eyes are drawn to the sky. Voluptuous clouds sit to the east and the water dances as we drive along the bay. Kyle has brought balloon swords and belt he'd gotten from a clown the night before, at the farmer's market down the street.

When we reach the beach, he dons the balloon belt and hands me one of the swords. With a glint in his eyes, he raises his sword, lunges and gently pokes me with it, in my side.

"I got you!" he proclaims with glee.

"I'm bleeding!" I cry, trying not to laugh. "Take that!" I say, as I strike his shoulder, severing his arm.

"I'm still alive!"

"Well, so am I!"

"Hold on," he says, straightening up and holding his sword at this side. "We need to bow to each other, with respect."

I am struck by his words.

We bow solemnly and the fight is on! We duck and parry, our balloon swords swishing and flying across the beach, like swashbuckling pirates fighting over our pirate ship anchored offshore, filled with rum and gold. Occasionally we pause to drink some rum and catch our breath. He laughs and I cry. Then I laugh and he cries. We yell and stab and try to slaughter each other, hooting and hollering.

Finally, after an hour of sweat and blood, killing each other over and over, we fall on our backs onto the sand, gaze at the sky above, and laugh ourselves silly, joking about who died the most times. Eventually, we grow quiet.

"What do you think happens when you die, Kyle?"

"First you become a zombie, then you become a skeleton, and then you lose your spirit," he says, without hesitation.

"How do you get your spirit back?" I ask.

"You have to heal," he says.

"How do you heal?" I find myself listening carefully to his words.

"You heal by feeling good. Doing what you love," he says, turning to look directly at me.

We stare at each other a long moment, before I look away to gaze at the clouds above. They appear extraordinarily heavenly this day.

"You're my spirit child, aren't you?"

He giggles.

We get to our feet and he takes my hand, leading me along the ancient rocks that line the water. He is uncommonly gentle, guiding me as he points out various plants along the way— coyote bush and rattlesnake grasses, soap root and pickleweed.

We cross a large slippery rock and he holds my hand as I stumble, taking us both down into the water with a shriek. We lie there on the rocks, laughing our heads off again, as the water drips off our clothes.

Later, when we return to the apartment, I feel myself tensing again, fearing a confrontation about video games. I hadn't turned off the internet and I see him reach for my iPhone. Impulsively, I reach for a book, the one closest to me. It's *The Little Prince*, by Antoine de Saint-Exupery. I begin to read aloud.

Kyle looks at my phone and I brace for battle, knowing this one wouldn't be waged with balloons.

"Looks like the internet isn't on," he says, and puts down the phone and snuggles up against me. I keep reading, stifling a grin.

Once, when I was six years old, I saw a magnificent picture in a book, called True Stories from Nature, about the primeval forest.

Grown-ups never understand anything by themselves, and it is tiresome for children to be always and forever explaining things to them.

After an hour, we reach the last page.

Look up at the sky. Ask yourselves: Is it yes or no? Has the sheep eaten the flower? And you will see how everything changes…

And no grown-up will ever understand that this is a matter of so much importance.

Kyle writes a message inside the back cover of the book, marking our day as pirates.

That afternoon we go to the library and find a book on Italy to help with Kyle's Heritage Day assignment. Kyle sifts through the pages and then points to a black and white sketch of Galileo describing the universe to his students.

"This is how I want to dress my doll."

"Do you know who Galileo is?"

He shook his head.

I recall a story that Ricci once shared from his boyhood. He had a doll he loved, but his father grew exasperated by this and took the doll away from him.

"Boys don't play with dolls," he told Ricci.

And now here is Dante's grandson dressing a paper doll in honor of Dante, inspired by Galileo, who had studied the secrets of the universe in Italy long ago.

I felt like Dante was talking to me in that moment, through my son. An apology, perhaps.

I look down at Kyle. I will treasure this day forever, I think.

"I'm going to Spain, to write and connect with some old friends," I say to Ricci. "I feel like I'm coming full circle: graduate school, writing, and the Spanish language."

"That's how I feel too. I'm going to Italy and Germany this summer, to visit family," he says.

We sit side by side at a cafe, trying to be civil, me still believing we would get back together and heal our family. After all, I watched my parents go through an incredibly tough time, but they managed to stick it out. Maybe after he visits with his family, he'll come back to his senses and we'll put our family back together.

I glance at his computer calendar. The word "Greece" is typed in July. *Greece?*

"You're going to Greece?"

"Yes."

I think back to our trip to Albania, eleven years earlier, sitting at the restaurant, exhausted after saving that young boy from sure death, traveling with Ricci for thousands of miles on hair-raising roads in the Balkans—his trip. And there was Corfu, just beyond the mist. I could see it, hear it calling to me, so close, so close. I had begged him to go, to leave Albania and enjoy ourselves for a few days in Greece. He had refused. I had looked again with longing at the distant misty shore. How close I had come to grabbing my bags right then and there and making the sojourn myself. Perhaps I should have.

"What's in Greece?"

"It's a couple's thing," he says.

When I get home, I Google "Greece and couples" and stare at the results in disbelief.

"A week of Tantra Mantra!" I scream, shaking the walls around me.

The End

How to describe these moments of suspended disbelief, as your exterior freezes and your brain, heart, and guts rewire all at once, rewriting your life story, triggering old memories, loops of spaghetti twisted and tied in your body from your head to your toes—tendons, veins, capillaries, and skin cells. It's a new inner-working, as the old falls apart and spills from your body. You start to grasp and choke, pulling it all back, like tangled lines, stuffing it back inside your body while your head spins wildly. No wonder exorcisms were big business for churches—this is how a demon gets constructed! Women have had to deal with too many men with out-of-control appendages and egos. Tantra sex! Who is this man! Who is she? Who the hell am I to have willingly been with this man?

I stew. Then I stew some more. It begins to bubble. But before the simmer comes to a hard boil, I pause and try to dial down the heat. Am I being too hard on him? After all, the world is different today. Maybe I'm approaching this all wrong. I still love him.

I envision our court date, the way we sat, side by side. Maybe I'm letting my emotions get the best of me. I mean, maybe we could create something together. Maybe I'm thinking small and I need to think big.

I reach for the phone.

"Ricci, I was thinking, why don't we just become a threesome? Maybe a polyamorous relationship could work out for us—I mean, maybe we should think outside the box. I mean, why can't we all take ourselves to that higher level? It'd bring us all closer together. We could change the world!"

There was silence.

"Well?"

"I can't do that."

"Why not? If a man can marry a man nowadays, and a woman can marry a woman, why not just expand it all? Maybe we're being too conventional in our ideas. Let's all feel love together! You said it yourself, I would love her."

"I can't do that." He hesitates almost imperceptibly. "It's not according to the Shakti ways."

"But you guys are going to Corfu, for a week-long session of Tantra mantra. And we're still married. You're living in my house still. It's still my house, with my name on it!"

My innards are spilling out again. Mopping them up the second time is messier business.

"Don't get emotional, Barbara. You're doing what you love to do."

He hangs up.

The week before leaving for Spain I have dinner with my neighbors, Duane and Colleen Elgin, friends of other neighboring filmmakers I had met earlier in the year.

Duane is quiet, with his wife doing most of the talking at first. I sense he is studying me. I remark on my walking out of a twenty-two-year-old monogamous relationship, which sparks conversation about communes from the sixties and seventies and all sorts of interesting living arrangements that they either had experienced or knew people who had. My first instinct is to clap my hands over my ears, not wanting to hear it, but I make myself listen.

Duane talks about his book, *The Living Universe*, the idea of consciousness of the natural world. It strikes a chord and I ask to see it. Then I learn about his background. In the early 1970s, he worked as a senior staff member of a joint Presidential-Congressional Commission on the American Future, looking ahead to the year 2000, as well as with other environmental organizations and think tanks.

I ask him, "Do you think we could arguably say that our planet's current environmental state has a direct link to Ronald Reagan's leadership thirty years ago?"

He looks me straight in the eye and doesn't hesitate.

"Yes."

"Was there another way?"

"Yes."

We have a long conversation about our country. Carter had us going in a good direction. He established the Energy Department during his administration and encouraged businesses to embrace and build alternative energy sources, including solar and wind power. Environmentalists were active on the coasts and in the mountains. Carter gave his 1979 speech encouraging Americans not to judge people by what they have but what they do with their lives. He pushed for us to have independent, sustainable energy and people were rising to it. He even had a solar-powered heating system installed on the roof of the White House.

The End

But everything changed with Reagan. His supporters were OPEC and other fossil fuel business leaders. They shut Carter down and instilled fear in the people about job security, resulting in Reagan's landslide victory. People listened to the lies, and the labor union bust secured Reagan's power, leaving the country heavily influenced by billionaires who are intent on ensuring that their way of doing business is honored.

We talked about what had happened to operating in the best interest of the people. We were suffering the greatest level of poverty since the Great Depression, according to intellectual Noam Chomsky, I said. I talked about how dire the state of our planet is, that we have melting polar ice caps and other risks due to climate change. We're experiencing increasing ocean acidification which threatens the very existence of marine ecosystems, killing reefs and threatening fish populations. The shells of crustaceans like lobsters, crabs, clams, mussels and other creatures are limestone-based, meaning that as carbon dioxide enters the oceans in increasing amounts and increases the acidity of our oceans, such shells cannot form and these creatures, along with all the other fish and mammals in the oceans, will inevitably become extinct.

We agreed that instead of being lauded, Reagan should be considered a federal, even global criminal, and climate change deniers should be held responsible. They knew about climate change back in the 1970s, Duane says. This is not a new revelation. My God.

I walk home, pondering these ideas, with Duane's book in my hand.

I have to see Anja, my mother-in-law. I'm not sure what I will say. I'm not sure what needs to be said. But I know I have to talk to her.

It's a three-hour drive up the California coast, alongside the struggling Pacific Ocean. I stop at Peet's Coffee beforehand, aware that I'll be spending the next three hours in my head, teasing out my life's intricacies, pains, responsibilities, and life choices. It's a dangerous place to be, I know, full of cobwebs and darkness.

I order a chai. It's a robotic conversation. What size? Any pastry? Two-percent milk okay? All said with a practiced smile.

Who is this man behind the counter, I wonder? What are his dreams, his desires? Is he really happy serving up one in an endless litany of chais to me?

I ask him, "What are you feeling today?"

"An apricot scone?" He points at one.

I smile. He's been so programmed.

"No. What do *you* feel like today?"

He hesitates and looks at me. I think he is only seeing me for the first time now.

"Amazing?" It's more of a question than a declaration.

"Good!"

"And you?"

"Great," I say, and give him a broad warm smile. He returns the smile. This time it reaches his eyes.

I drive north, along the ocean, a drive I've made over a hundred times over the last twenty-two years with Ricci to visit his parents. I always loved our trips and time there. Anja's skill with colors and textures has always inspired me. She has such talent.

I have much to say but decide to go with no expectations. I just need to see her. I have concerns for Ricci, for us, for our children. He has changed so much and it scares me.

I think back to my conversation with Ricci after I moved out to concentrate on the film, when I argued that I wasn't leaving him for another man. It was something spiritual longing to escape from inside me, I tried to explain. He remained convinced that men would be all over me, no matter how many times I said that he was the only one for me, and always would be. It was just that I had something big to do. He wouldn't listen. He never listened to what I said.

I arrive at Anja's house. It looks the same as ever, yet it feels empty. Everything is placed perfectly, as always, and light shines through the windows. She hugs me briefly, cursorily, but then she was never one to give warm embraces.

I don't want superficial today though. I want to go deep with Anja this day. I want to tell her I'm sorry I couldn't be there for her over the past year, since Dante's death. I miss Dante. Both of them have been such a part of my life for so many years. I want her to know I care about her, that she still feels like family. I admire her and her story of childhood hardship. I'm a bit envious of the mutual respect she and Dante shared. It was a lasting relationship, until he died last year.

"You've had success with your film, Barbara. You should feel proud," she says, as we sit in armchairs perfectly aligned for such a conversation, not quite facing each other, but angled.

"I feel humbled by it all, I confess. It was far bigger than me. The project went through me, creating many things for others. I was merely a conduit, that's all."

I feel her sadness, alone now, in this big house.

"Does Ricci come up to visit?"

She shakes her head. He is her only son.

"What do you do to stay busy?" I ask.

"I walk with a neighbor each morning. It gets me out."

With that, we decide to walk down the hill, to the beach.

"You suffered such hardship as a child amid the devastation after World War II. I remember your telling me about your mother sending you and your brothers off through the forest to walk all the way to the other side of Germany, alone, just before the Iron Curtain came down. I can't imagine being a mother and having to take a risk like that with my children."

She shrugged. "We had no choice. If an adult had been with us, we'd have been shot by Russian soldiers."

We walk in silence for a few moments.

"I remember playing in the rubble with my brothers. Potato-peel soup in the basement." She chokes back tears. She tries to be strong but those memories are right there with her.

"You can talk about your experiences, Anja, and show others why war and being cruel to others is wrong. You could speak for the world our children are entering now. This environmental situation we're in, they say, could lead to something far worse than World War II."

She waves a hand at me.

"They can't learn what I experienced. It's only talk."

"I think people would listen, Anja."

I feel her hurt, her pain. For the first time I see her in a different way, as a child, a hurt child like I had been, intent on cutting off all those hurt feelings. We both came from bad leaders. We both came from the idea of having been part of bad families. We both needed to prove something in life.

I think of her numerous homes, all perfectly finished, and the way she always needed to be right when we talked. The way she hadn't wanted to listen to me play the guitar. I had been her. Trying to live a good life, one that I believed made me look good. It was a game we all played. The music that filled me deep inside, that resonated. Of course she didn't want the music. She didn't want to feel. "Be strong, Barbara," she had once told me. "Don't be so sensitive."

I think about Hitler and the horrors he wrought. At least his motives were more obvious. What we have learned the last thirty-five years of Reagan's intent, the true outcome his policies were designed to effect, was anything but readily recognizable. And the darkness incubated in all of us without us seeing it, until we were completely blind, or dead, until now, as we face a global disaster and can understand who we have been and why.

I want to hug Anja. I want to shout to the world to look at this beautiful woman as I see her and have the world apologize. She had been nothing more than an innocent child, navigating between so many wrongs, trying to find what was right. Haven't we all been doing that? Be strong, Anja, I want to say. Be completely sensitive, don't be afraid to feel the music and dream big. There's still time! Know your power. Open yourself to the universe!

I want to say this to her, but I can't. Not yet.

"What will you do?"

"The house is too big for me to handle alone," she says.

"Yep, a big house is a lot to handle." There is a pause. She knows what I'm saying.

"I've looked into retirement communities. There's a very good one up north, highly rated, run like an engine, and they've been around for 50 years. You have to get in before you get too sick though. Otherwise you don't have choices. I don't want to be a burden to Ricci."

Burden? Is that what we have all been taught? I think of all she has to share with her grandkids, the wisdom she has to impart. She has the real stories, not the contrived ones. We banish our elders so as not to be "burdened" by them. Why do we see them that way? What have we become?

"I always thought it'd be nice to have a house with a little in-law unit. You could still have your independence and you'd have your family close by. I kept suggesting that to Ricci."

"We did what we thought was right, what everyone thought was right," Anja says, a bit defensively.

The End

I know what she means. How could I be angry? Nobody can judge. It's not the coming of Judgment Day; it's the day when we drop all of our judgments and look for the good in everyone, including ourselves. I want to believe this. I do believe this.

We watch the ocean waves and make small talk as wide-eyed seals pop out of the water and long v-shaped migratory birds sweep across the horizon.

"Cormorants?"

"Hard to tell."

"Do you see that?" Anja squeals, like a young girl.

A whale has emerged, arcing its body clear of the water's surface before diving and disappearing. A gorgeous being. A gift. We both watch in awe.

We stroll back to the house, through the grasses and lupine, breathing the deep salt air. When we arrive at the house, she is in no hurry for me to leave and so I linger. This is important time, for both of us. I smile, recalling her here with Dante.

"I remember all of us sitting on this porch, years ago. Your leg was bare and Dante was stroking it, commenting on how beautiful your skin was. He was so gentle."

"He was always kind that way." She sighs. "I had fifty good years. Fifty. That's better than most." She takes a deep breath and looks at me intently. "You have to move forward in your life. Go follow your dreams."

I wonder whether this is advice she would have wanted herself at some point in her life.

It is time to go. I say goodbye, but I don't mean it to be forever.

Spain. Why is it calling to me?

My school is offering an affordable ten-day writing program in La Mancha, where *Don Quixote*, the tale of a deluded, romantic, self-appointed knight intent on righting the world's wrongs, one of the first important novels ever written, was set. I am virtually broke and have no idea where the money will come from for this trip, but I have to go. My gut tells me I must. (Logic is overrated.)

I really have no expectations for this ten-day retreat. I had been sitting, as usual, in the Fairfax cafe at dawn, writing. Steve would often sit in the corner and play his guitar while his adult son painted on an easel next to him—oh so calm and comforting. I watched them, listening to the singular notes surround me, as they had in Neto's garden. Steve was singing the words "keep moving, moving on" when an email notice from the university popped into my inbox.

"Ten Days in Spain, a Hero's Journey, in La Mancha," was the subject line. It promised I'd get an equivalent number of credits for about the same cost as taking a class for a full semester. That was logical enough to justify it, but it was my gut feeling that this was the way I should be "moving on" that persuaded me to override any doubts about what I should do. The fact that I was nearly totally broke, my retirement funds depleted, my car needing repairs, my kids needing to be watched in my absence, and my soon-to-be ex-husband now with the goddess of joy, on their way to Corfu, to rise as eternal god and goddess, were all secondary.

How did I get here?

I listened to Steve play more notes as he sang "perhaps the sun will shine upon us then," and watched his son stroke the canvas with his brush and colors, creating a new world.

My fingers danced across the keyboard.

Yes, sign me up.

I pack my bags a few days before departure with the sounds of Spanish guitar music, performed by Andrés Segovia, filling my apartment.

Arpeggios. The unmistakable IMA AMI IAM and all the passion that lies between those notes. Music I've always loved, yet allowed to disappear from my life. I'm reclaiming it all and taking it to a whole new level. That depth of music with an edge that cuts straight into my soul and mixes with life's vigor.

I look at myself in the mirror as guitar rhythms surround me. Spain, the birthplace of the guitar. The music—it is pulling me.

Is that why I'm going?

I picture Spanish sailors, searching for gold. I will return to Spain to discover something else, something of far greater value, something truly priceless: my soul.

I look into my eyes. They burn like fire.

"Fuck that meditation shit," I blurt without thinking. "I'm going to live! I'm going to live big! To promise not to hurt anybody. I'm not looking for the beautiful polished beauty shit in life. I want the raw! The ugly! The angry. The real!! That's what I'm fucking going to do! I'm going to fucking live life with wildness and danger and fun!! Fuck that meditation shit! I'm going to scream out to the universe, 'I am alive. I'm flesh and blood!' I'm going to live my life with honesty, with integrity, and make people feel good as I make it happen! Yeah! I'm gonna change the world!"

I'm ready.

I am in Heathrow Airport, with six hours to kill. I haven't been outside the US in over ten years, well before 9/11, my traveling since consisting of years of sailing. I can't believe what I see—the apprehension everywhere. The heightened scrutiny of airport security, bags meticulously checked, even little old ladies being questioned. All of us guilty until proven innocent. There are endless racks of information about what not to bring on the airplane, including dangerous tubes of toothpaste and deodorant. Everyone is a potential criminal. No wonder everyone's nervous. How have we allowed this to happen?

I look at myself in the mirror. I look dreadful. Yeah, I could pass for a criminal. My hair has not been cut in over a year and I have bags under my eyes. My old clothes are drooping off me, and I'm wrestling with the guilt of having left my kids and worrying about delivering a school paper that's due the next day.

There's an entire collection of cosmetic counters lining the duty-free area, alongside perfumeries, clothing shops, message studios, and salons. I think, why not? The last time I bought cosmetics was for my wedding, fifteen years ago. Maybe a little lip rouge would be the pickup I need. Or not.

I make a beeline for the cosmetic shop, find a counter boasting all-natural products (to ease my guilt), and plop into a chair.

The clerk looks at me sympathetically. I'm work. A lot of work. She's kind, and speaks with that English accent we associate with Julie Andrews and Princess Diana.

"Okay, sweetheart, we're going to pretty you up."

I quell the urge to say no black lipstick.

I feel strokes on my cheek. A human hand. Gentle. Thoughtful. She pushes my hair away from my face. I'm being restored. Isn't it funny? People go to fancy spas in exotic countries, and yet I am fulfilled sitting on a plastic stool in an airport terminal.

"Here, now, we'll finish you off with English rose cheeks. Perfect!" she declares, and turns my chair to face the mirror. I'm surprised and pleased. I look almost human again, except for my Medusa hair and saggy clothing.

I like that thought, English rose cheeks. I lick my lips.

Oxygen. I'm breathing again. I've been here before. I know it. It feels inexplicably familiar somehow. Perhaps my bloodline traces back to the Spanish Armada, those unfortunate Spanish naval sailors who were blown off course on their way to surprise attack the English and found themselves instead dashed upon the rocks of western Ireland, I imagine. I mean, I am Black Irish, after all.

The Irish, having no love for their brutal English oppressors, reportedly hid the Spanish soldiers from the English troops who were aggressively hunting them down more than four hundred years ago. The Irish hospitality was such that many of the sailors stayed, and were absorbed into the population, their black hair mingling with the Irish fair complexion to create, it has been suggested, the Black Irish phenomenon.

These could be my ancestors. I've got their blood in my blood, scientifically endowed into my DNA. Or maybe it was the influence of Magellan, or Columbus. Or perhaps it's just that I've driven down Sir Francis Drake Boulevard for so many years that I've got it wired in me now.

Doesn't matter. I feel I've survived a voyage, and it is thrilling to be in Spain, with the Spanish fountains, the language, and the beautiful people who know how to linger at their tables late into the night, peppering the enormous stone-paved plazas, to talk life, love, and politics. It is time to shake the sea salt from my hair, shed the ragged clothes, restore the body, and rediscover civilization, Spanish style.

I soak in the history, the sights of fanciful sweets and fashion here in Madrid. I sit in its Plaza Mayor for hours, watching pigeons circle overhead and people walk the same ground where bulls once fought for their lives and thousands of people were publicly hanged during the Inquisition. I can feel them all. I cross the Plaza de Cibeles and am drawn to a fountain of a woman riding a chariot pulled by two lions. She's Cybele, the Roman goddess of nature and fertility who was honored by a cult in ancient Rome and is considered to be one of Madrid's most important symbols. She is a strong woman. I like her.

I walk by a clothing shop and see a line of customers waiting to make their purchases. I haven't bought new clothing in years. The prospect of standing in line to buy something new makes me giddy. Just the idea of lingering in a long line is enticing! I can't remember the last time I did that. The next thing I know, I find myself holding hangers bearing three shirts and a dress, and I'm standing in line with a broad smile on my face. I'm actually enjoying standing in line! I'm going crazy. No, I've cracked!

Like the rapid stitching of an open wound, I zigzag through streets, time, and emotions. I am hungry, insatiable, desperate to heal. Every store looks intriguing—skirts, shoes, scarves, jewelry! If Ricci can get Tantra Mantra in Corfu, I can reinvent myself and become sexy and exotic in Madrid! But can I? I have such a hard time spending money. I put back my items and leave the store.

I walk into a secondhand shop in Madrid's Bohemian area and find a sheer tiger-striped blouse. I study it. Dare I? No, I can't do it. I feel like a wet rag, a used-up prostitute, old and shriveled. I sift through the rack and spot another shirt, one that is gorgeously fancy. I can't do it. Can I? It wouldn't hurt just to try it on. I won't buy, I promise myself. That would be too extravagant for me.

The store clerk walks up behind me.

"This would be beautiful on you, Señora. Next to the swimming pool. Lounging, si?" he says, giving me a flirtatious smile. He waves his hand as he speaks, long olive fingers spread, the pinky held high.

How long since a man has looked at me like this? Even a gay one? He has given me permission.

I try on the exotic dress. It looks ridiculous, not at all like me.

"Guapa!" he says, shaking his thin hips. He thinks it's lovely on me.

I look in the mirror again, holding my hair up. What does he see? I don't feel sexy, or exotic.

"Where was it made?" I ask.

"Paris."

"Paris, huh?" I let the word roll off my tongue. Paris. I let my hair fall loose around my face and look again. It is sexy. It is certainly exotic. Secondhand too, so it would not be terribly extravagant.

I'm merely flirting with the idea. He says something else that I don't understand, but I pretend he's asking me what I have been doing with my life up until now if not looking sexy and extravagant? I'm a drop-dead gorgeous woman, he proclaims. Men will line up for you, for the chance to spend even one moment in your company. You can change the world!

I think, *move over, glamour girls!*

In reality, he may have just been telling me the price, but he is encouraging, admiring, as he does. I have imagination and I need to hear those words. Now, where on this good earth would I ever wear such a tunic?

It doesn't matter. I will wear it one day. I know it.

"Sunglasses?"

"Oh, yes! A pair of black ones, please. Hollywood style."

I walk along the streets of Barcelona as if an apparition, joining the other ghosts of time. No one sees me; I see everyone. The streets echo past centuries. I will not be remembered. And that does not matter. I like it this way as I watch people and try to recapture what it feels like to be alive again. I'm getting closer to the feeling.

I enter a church. I don't notice its name. It doesn't matter. Outside, a woman begs for alms. Inside, donations are asked in order to maintain the statues. Which has more value? I look about me. Statues, gold, the blood of Jesus—stories that have moved people for two thousand years. These stories have molded our identities, our sexual relationships, marriages, family ideals, wars, executions, power, domination, and presumably our assent to the heavens, descent to hell, or whether we linger in Purgatory in a mixture of hope and despair. Christian mythology has determined the end of the world as we know it—dead oceans, death, and the rise of the antichrist.

But we are buying into the story that this is somehow preordained versus taking responsibility for the fact that we are creating this reality ourselves. It's a crime.

There is no sign of nature inside these walls. Neither are these my gods. A god who is feared? What would the point of that be?

I see art, and the manifestation of great stories and struggles, all centering on a fearsome god who damns souls to hell for all of eternity if they don't do exactly right. This god, this male god, sends his son, who is now venerated.

I look around. Where are the mothers celebrated, with their unconditional love? And where are the daughters? Why do they not have voices staking claim to a story of our world? The story is the biggest crime in humanity for the past two thousand years, driving inquisitions, witch burning, and wars.

It's all about intolerance. What sort of god is this? And who follows such a crazy story without a woman's voice? It is women who give forth life. Could we begin to listen to our own hearts and guts and stop listening to others who think they know best? We know what's right. Perhaps we are gods ourselves. We each have incredible power, but we give it away to others, quick to step down as if someone else always know best.

I think of Captain Richard Gillette back in that moment when I saw a flame light in one boy's eyes as he took the helm: "Give them responsibility. Believe in them and they'll rise to it."

Life in its every manifestation is a gift. Every moment of it. Every breathing creature. The beautiful, the sublime, and especially the ugly. It's all sacred.

I give a coin to the beggar woman outside and decide to walk the parks instead of churches.

I meet up with Eva, my old Spanish friend whom I met years before, in China. We spent a lot of time together in Nanjing. She is now a teacher and a mother. She had looked at me, in Nanjing, and told me that the name Barbara means like the wind. It did something to me when she said that. Today, she is like a guide to me, touring me around the beauty that is Barcelona, as if showing me a treasure more profound than the city's history.

We come to an ornate water fountain. Smiling, she suggests I drink the water, saying it will secure my return to Barcelona one day.

Eventually, we come upon the grand, imposing Basilica of Santa Maria del Mar, Saint Mary of the Sea.

"This is my favorite," Eva says. She tells me it was built during the height of the Catalan's maritime history. I think back to those sailors, of such a powerful time in history. The basilica is breathtaking in its Gothic style.

Merchant tables are lined up outside, in the church's square, and we peruse the wares.

Eva picks up a small, framed picture depicting Mary's Annunciation for me to admire.

"I buy this for you," she says.

Next to it is another framed picture, this one of a woman warrior, armed with a lance. It was such a strange juxtaposition, the two old paintings. They speak to me. I snap a photo and feel that vibration again.

"No, you don't have to buy it," I insist.

Eva overrides my objections.

"No, I buy this for you."

June 2015

Back to simplicity, the beauty of it. This is how our lives are supposed to be. Simplicity had been my and Ricci's mantra after we met at Simple Pleasures Cafe, in San Francisco, over twenty-two years ago. That was before life got so complicated, with harsh edges and distorted wrongs and rights.

Our group leaves Madrid to drive the hour to La Mancha, past a patchwork quilt of fields, crumbling old barns, and visions of Don Quixote galloping across the land, with his lance, on the quest for chivalry.

I think of my friends Marilyn, Nancy, and Jenn as we drive along the Spanish countryside, drinking in the vast gold expanse of wheat fields. Friends are pure gold, priceless, the ones who cheer you on, who support you as you expand yourself, while they expand alongside you. They are mom friends, who understand the sacrifices we make for our kids. I can feel myself breathing again, my lungs expanding to drink in the land. If Madrid is where I stitched the surface of my heart's wound with haircuts, clothes, food, and drink, La Mancha would be where my spirit would grow, so I can be strong again.

The End

My expectation for La Finca, the rustic country house that would be our accommodation, is to be a place where I can sit and talk to a cow. The wisdom of a cow, I think, would be gratifying at this place and time in my life. At the very least, a cow would listen without complaint and teach me to chew my food slowly, thoughtfully. I need soul food. But there is no cow. There is no electricity, either, although that I already knew.

First, I am told, I have to drink the holy water. Now, I've never been a believer in such things. People can mythicize just about anything and conveniently wrap religion around it, as I had been learning. Hadn't the Christian Church done that very thing, poaching popular pagan celebrations, like the December solstice to which they decided to align Christ's birthday, in order to encourage adherence?

So, when I take my first drink of the holy water, I'm indifferent, donning a somewhat arrogant "Isn't that cute?" sort of attitude. But as I sip it, I am abruptly reminded of my own, oftentimes odd visions over the past year. With this in mind, how can I deny the idea that a Muslim man once sat at this very spot, sipped the water, and experienced a vision of the Holy Mother? What do I know? What do I really know?

Drinking the cool refreshing water in such a spirit of contemplation makes me feel good. That's enough. Nearby I spot mulberry trees, and immediately think of the year I, along with my two children, grew large silkworms from dot-sized eggs, observed them as they turned spit into silk, and then watched as they died after a day of sexual frenzy. The paradox of life.

I sense that I am on my way to experiencing a blessed week. La Finca is a dream made of dreams, complete with old wooden doors, wrought iron treasures, tile work, art, and a beautiful dinner set at late evening dusk for us, the awaited writing students and their professor. I am eager to sink into the good-humored ambiance at the table, weighted down with food and wine, and stories told by the family of La Finca, all spoken in English. I felt wholly in tune with the music of language, merriment, and embodiment of literary, intellectual, book-making bliss. But it is not to be. Instead, I am struck inconceivably by a splitting headache and must retire to one of the bedrooms to close my eyes and lie down.

"Maybe it's the holy water cleansing you," the owner David teases, raising an eyebrow to let me know he is only half-joking.

I am bitterly disappointed. I had been anxious to walk around the grounds and drink in all the beauty of these surroundings. Instead, I find myself alone with my thoughts and my misery. I might as well be at home.

Okay, I'll make the most of it, I say to myself. But how do you make the most of a migraine? The apparent gift of a migraine is that everything is amplified—the shuffling of feet, voices, and years' worth of conversations. They all spin dizzily in my head, a loudspeaker directed straight at my neurons.

After some time, I can hear something else. Birdsong. And the wind, as it rustles through leaves. A fly, as it buzzes against the window. I work hard for hours, silencing the inner voices in order to concentrate on the sounds of birds, wind and a lone fly.

Maybe David is right. Maybe I am purging.

The next few days are a constant source of new words, ideas, and the beautiful gift of simplicity, as I begin to listen to what is outside rather than what is inside.

"Listen into the dreaming," the photographer Elisabeth Sunday advises. "To know who you are and where you come from, listen to the natural world." She was the first to teach me to listen, that answers are all around us if we simply listen. I had volunteered as her assistant at a Mother's Day portrait fundraiser event years ago. Her advice resembled that of Captain Richard Gillette's: "Open yourself to the universe." My friend Jenn echoed that when she said, "Barbara, know your power."

I sit by myself on a mountain against an ancient olive tree, amid a grove of olive trees planted in Biblical times, two thousand years ago, by Romans, somewhat ironic considering the many years of adversity I had weathered with a Roman man in my own life. A branch pokes me, so I change positions. This tree has survived hailstorms, pruning, and seasons of intense heat, all the while sitting here quietly, without complaint, with complete acceptance of its life, like a buddha, accepting the trials that come and go. It grows upward, toward the sky, without hesitation, expanding its branches each and every day, its gift to the world. It's a comfort, a friend, and it's hard not to listen to its story and be reminded of its truth, to just be.

I reach out to an olive branch full of blossoms and imagine myself as a tree. How can I deny a valley full of olive branches before me without asking the question whether this might be a sign?

Jesus told us to love one another as we love ourselves. What he didn't tell us was that we needed first to learn how to love ourselves. We're not taught that. How can we love others if we don't love ourselves? We have to forgive ourselves first, before we can forgive others, so we can acknowledge who we have been.

I know I hurt Ricci when I moved out, but I saw no other way. I honestly thought it'd make him see what he had lost and come for me. He'd finally recognize what it was he had had.

"Take responsibility." Captain Gillette's voice comes to me again. "You knew for years he didn't support or listen to you. You asked for this."

An ant tickles my leg as it crosses. It's hard being a tree.

The next day we journey to nearby villages and visit caves where the Moors hid when the Christians came crusading, back in the days when Christianity was considered just another of a number of diverse religious cults. Much evil has been perpetuated under the guise of religious fervor over the centuries, and it still goes on today. I've never wanted to be a part of this intolerance, this fear of others. Why do people feel the urge to kill in order to justify their god? The world's cathedrals sit, filled with obscene amounts of gold and valuable art, purchased with the pennies of the impoverished, desperate to secure a place in heaven and thereby make their suffering mean something. It all speaks to the existence of a great god, and yet where is the reverence for nature? There is much beauty to behold in a small stream or sitting by a tree. I no longer go into cathedrals these days.

David, the owner of La Finca, hands me a book to read, *Not in His Image*, by Jim Lamp Lash. It's a big book and difficult to read. It's dark now here, at midday, where grey clouds hover.

I think about love. Bogie, one of the women in our group here, tells me the Greek language has no fewer than twelve words for love. We only have one. The Japanese, they say, do not have a word for it at all.

What is love? Is our definition of it a myth? Have we all been living a story that has no truth? Where we punish ourselves for it?

I think about the idea of monogamy and the pain of couples tearing themselves apart that I witnessed in the courtroom. Is it just a story too, and if we don't fit into that box, we make it into a story that we use to hurt our children and ourselves? Let's expand families! I say that, enthusiastically, but do I mean it? Do I really feel that way? I reread entries in my journal of how I was convinced, once we'd fallen in love, that we'd be together always. I so want to believe the story. Considering the divorce rate and extramarital love affairs, have we all been so blind? And how have women always forced themselves to fit into the formula, despite the heavy price they may have paid?

I start reading Lash's book. I am struck by when he writes of how, in the year 415 C.E., a Pagan noblewoman named Hypathia often mingled with and spoke to the local townspeople, unlike many of her exalted peers, and how this interaction earned her their regard. And yet this wasn't enough to protect her when a zealot Christian converter whipped the townsfolk into a frenzy, condemning Paganism. He convinced them to attack Hypathia, dragging her from her chariot, literally tearing her limb from limb, until "her body was left in a pile of blood."

Why haven't I ever heard this story, I wonder, and contemplate Paganism. I've often questioned why nature isn't at the foundation of our education. I think about our children's schools. Nature is not part of the curriculum, yet it is the most important relationship to cultivate. I think of my Nature Girls program, teaching in the woods, and just how easy it was to connect to our natural world, our only reality. How sitting and observing a stream of water or a cicada emerging from its exoskeleton can nourish a child's life, creating justifiable awe and wonder.

Within minutes, the skies darken and a tremendous storm passes overhead. Hail pummels the farm, the surrounding fields, the olive trees. Candles are lit and everyone is in awe of the thunderous rumbles that shake the earth.

"In twenty-three years I've never seen a storm like this," Ana says as she comes in. She's an American who moved to Spain over thirty years ago and lives in the nearby town. I have heard her mentioned.

"We can tell ghost stories!" somebody says.

I listen to the thunder and marvel at the beauty of the sublime. Is there a connection? I continue reading, now by candlelight. I'm fascinated by the stories in this book, of the fall of the Roman Empire and how the Catholic Church rose to replace it, what the author referred to as a "fateful handover of power." Why have I not been taught any of this?

Power and domination.

Guilt and punishment.

I think back to reading *When God Was a Woman*, a book by Merlin Stone that tells how the story of Adam and Eve is the biggest sham ever, where woman was deemed the destroyer of paradise, a mere rib of a man. It set the course of our perceived reality, causing wars and destruction.

Why have we never been taught about Paganism? There was a time once when I had met a Wiccan and was enchanted by her beliefs and kindness, but I had never encountered such a belief system since. Why are we so afraid of nature being a guide? Having a tree as our temple? Why are we so intent on robbing the Earth's resources to construct temples when nature has already provided us temples? Are we cursed with narcissism? Or can we extend beyond ourselves and acknowledge our place in the universe and be humbled by it all?

I read more.

> *When the people lack a proper sense of awe, some terrible fate decided by the universe at large will befall them.*

Lao Tzu, *Tao Te Ching*

"That was amazing!" Bogie cries, as she comes down the stairs, wrapped in a dirt-smeared wet blanket, her face alight. "It was so exciting! I'm a dripping mud puddle!"

Bogie has been outside, in a gazebo, writing fantasy short stories, and got caught in the storm. She reminds me of a Hobbit coming back from the land of adventures. She sheds the blanket and cozies up to the fire, facing the flames, water dripping from her onto the stone floor.

I head into the kitchen, where Ana is. Candles still burn, but the storm has subsided. She is an artist and I have been eager to talk to her.

"Why did you move from the United States?" I ask.

"Oh, I left thirty years ago, when Ronald Reagan came to power."

I blink, and my eyes lock onto hers.

"Seriously? I'd love to hear more."

"Well, I could see how all the country's priorities were shifting. The disaster we face today is because of him."

I can't believe what I'm hearing. Or maybe I can. The universe is at work.

"My father was fired by Reagan," I say. "He was one of the air traffic controllers who refused to go back to work until better safety procedures were put in place."

"Really? That's something to be proud of. Integrity is hard to find in America these days."

Where have all these people been for the last thirty-five years of my life, I wonder. After all this time I'm only now meeting people who talk honestly, informatively, about Reagan. Why now?

Ana and I talk for hours about America, and how business and money drive agendas.

I think of that chocolate donut ring. The circle of life. The sweetness. My grandfather loved donuts.

Full circle.

Our class gathers in the shadows outside the spheres of the burning candles. Now that the storm has passed, light shines in, through the open windows, and droplets fall from the roof, plinking as they hit puddles.

Despite everything, I am still feeling down. My husband goes to Greece with a goddess, a goddess of joy, a high priestess, while I'm trying to do things to save the world? Can't he see what I did for him? How much I gave to him and our family? He never listened to me. Why did I not have a say in our lives?

I sit upright.

"Kimberly," I say, to a fellow writer, "would you help me with an idea? I've decided to rise above all this goddess stuff and be a bigger person. Here's my camera. Can you meet me outside in fifteen?"

I dart back to my room and look out the narrow window to the valley spread out below, where Romans, knights, and priests crisscrossed for two millennia. It was time to change history. This is where my spirit would grow.

I pull out the gorgeous secondhand Parisian tunic from Madrid that I've never yet worn. I step into a cream-colored skirt imported from Italy that I had bought along the Plaza Mayor. I slip on sandals from Barcelona and walk out onto the hard clay earth, along a single track, to where Kimberly awaits, feeling the world around me, feeling the world about to waken within me. I feel like I'm right where I belong at this very moment.

"You look beautiful!"

"I'm feeling it." I say, laughing. "I need an olive tree."

"I know where to go."

We chat as we head toward her chosen place.

"So, how did you get so good at writing?" she asks.

"Oh, I'm not good. I'm still learning. But I'm getting better." I look at her and grin. "I learned a secret."

"Spill!"

"You have to have sex with your writing."

She stops and stares at me. "What?"

"Yeah, you have to feel it, writhe with it, taste it, and open yourself up completely. Scream. Cry. Tie it up. Let it tie you up. Whip it; then let it whip you. That's the way you have to put it out there. Be completely vulnerable. Then it's truthful and you feel orgasmically free."

"Now that sounds like fun!" We giggle like school-aged girls.

"Here's the tree," she says.

I look up. It's a beauty.

I take a deep breath. I hate being in front of the camera. But I would expose myself and be vulnerable, just like I try to do with my writing. Or at least I would try.

"You know, women can have multiple orgasms," I say casually, trying to cut the tension inside me.

She laughs and covers her mouth.

"We're damn powerful," I say. "Set us loose and we'll change the world!"

"Yes." She believes me.

"The reason women have been shut down since the beginning of patriarchal religions is because men are afraid of us. We're dangerous!

They set out to stomp out matriarchal societies. And likely the reason for our downfall was that we sisters didn't stick together. But we mothers do, don't we?"

Kimberly snaps photos as I talk.

"So, I've decided to write my own story." I raise my arms in the air and with as much nobility as a girl from Fremont can muster, I claim my new identity.

"I am the Great Mother Goddess. The greatest goddess of all!" In that moment, I suddenly feel stupid, yet brave; ridiculous, yet strong. "I am the Mother Goddess, awakened after years of sleeping, since I was a thirteen-year-old child, returning to this planet to set the story straight and heal it for our children."

"Wow!" Kimberly takes more pictures of me.

"That's good, right?" I stop to ask, feeling a bit sheepish and laughing at how ridiculous I must sound.

"Oh, yeah!" she cries, holding back her laughter.

I raise my arms again.

"I have chosen to rise at this point in time. I am rising above it all, above all other goddesses, and I demand respect."

"Oh, yes, I like it!" The camera clicks repeatedly.

"Yeah, I'm feeling it."

Later that afternoon, I sit on the cliff and read about Plato, Aristotle, Horace, and others. I am drawn to the idea that we create powerful stories that define who we are. Two thousand years ago we created one based on patriarchy. Now, stories of matriarchy give rise, complete with pagan ideologies, ideas that served us well before, stories that have nearly been lost, and those we are trying to reclaim. Native American ideals are resurfacing too, the two philosophies heavily interwoven and connected. We have to acknowledge that we in the modern world may not have it right, considering how our planet is suffering as a result. It's time for a new direction, fast.

"Barbara, know your power," Jenn had said to me.

As I sit next to an olive tree and look at the valley below to the land that housed the story of Don Quixote, a man considered insane for his passionate embrace of chivalry and good works. He carried a dream so large that most could not wrap their arms around it. What does it tell us that this book became the most influential work of literature deriving from the Spanish Golden Age and the entire Spanish literary canon?

I pull out my pen and paper. I channel Don Quixote on his horse as he gallops across the lands with his lance, and I write a new story for the world.

That night I dress in my exotic Parisian Mother Goddess garb, and perform amid the flickering candles the story of *The Mother Returns*:

Some call me Barbara, but my real name is Sophia. Others call me Gaia. I have undergone the act of separation that led me morphing into the very world provisioned in my dreaming. I am the fallen goddess embodying earth, the living planet, the Mother Earth. I have returned to reclaim the Earth after two thousand years. I'm disheartened to see what our planet has become in my absence.

I sit here, over the valley of La Mancha, with olive trees planted by Romans when I was last here. The sky is different, the blues are brilliant, and the parted clouds are gateways to heaven. If you look up tonight, you will see the stars, our ancestors, and who we are. If you listen, you will hear the voices all around you.

I have been sleeping, like you. Now is the time for us all to awaken. It is time to see the work ahead of us. Take each other's hands, as brothers and sisters. We are, all together, powerful. Do not listen to false prophets, but be aware that they will be in your midst, as they will rise in this time of crisis.

I will work hard in my film work, my writings, and my teaching to share the awe and beauty of this planet until we all can rise up and do our part to make it heal, to recognize the incredible gift that is still alive and thriving as long as we acknowledge its majestic beauty and value. We are all in good graces, if we believe that. It's all about believing. And I believe.

The Valentinian Gnostics said,
"The World was born of Sophia's smile."

I plan to start smiling now. It will come slowly, but it will come.

And, hey, why not? You have to start from somewhere. I'm sure some Bible guy felt a little silly the first time he started writing stories about angels, burning bushes that talk, and massive rivers that part with the wave of a staff. Did he also wonder who might believe them?

Apparently, many people have. Many still do.

July 2015

My daughter watches as I get dressed in my Goddess Sophia getup, in an imitation of what my mom had done when I was teenager dating my "cool" Gothic boyfriend, the one with the English accent and black lipstick. Her getup had helped knock some sense into me. Maybe it would do the same for Ricci now, and wake him up sufficiently to save our marriage.

"What are you doing, Mom?"

I raise my arms in the air with as much flair as I can muster.

"My name is Sophia, the Mother Goddess, the greatest goddess of all."

She rolls her eyes.

"Oh my God, help me," she sighs, and falls back on the bed.

"Yes, help us all, my dear."

I leave to meet Ricci at Cafe Aroma. Cafe A-Roma—it sounds a lot like Rome. A sign? I mean, what if we were just experiencing some form of incarnations. What if?

He is there when I arrive, sitting quietly. I enter magnificently—full noble entry, my skirt flowing, head held high in a style similar to how we adolescent girls taught ourselves to walk on the beach, in our bikinis, slowly, shoulders back, boobs out, chin up. I greet him.

"My name is Sophia, I am the Mother Goddess."

He appears unimpressed. Okay, perhaps my delivery lacked sufficient drama. I've never claimed to be an actress. I try it again, a little louder.

"My name is Sophia. I am the Mother Goddess, the greatest goddess of all!" I raise my arms elegantly, for effect. He gives me a somewhat annoyed look.

"Can you please keep it down? And, no, I'm not calling you Sophia."

"That is my spiritual name now." I pause. "You call your girlfriend by her spiritual name, so why not me?"

He looks away. I sit down with a sigh.

"Why do I bother thinking you will listen to me now, when you never bothered to do so when we were married?"

He doesn't answer.

"I have presents from Spain for you." I pull out a small jar of porcini mushroom paté. "This is in memory of our wonderful mushroom hunts together. Remember the times we found the hedgehogs, porcini, and chanterelles in the forests up north? Good times, right?" I set the jar down in front of him, hoping for some emotional stir. There is none. I pull out the next present and set it in front of him.

"Bee pollen, in honor of all the time we spent raising bees, making candles and balms, and enjoying sweet honey. Remember? Good times, right?"

Again, there is no emotion. He looks at me making a fool of myself in my Mother Goddess getup. I'm trying. I'm not ready to say goodbye to my marriage.

I have one card left to play. A bag of Shakti tea, to stimulate eroticism. I look him straight in the eye.

"Enjoy Corfu."

He accepts my gifts with a flat thank you, no emotion, not even a sense of humor.

"My girlfriend recommends our daughter do a coming-of-age ceremony. She says it's an important rite of passage." There is a long pause.

Tick-tock, tick-tock.

Venom rises, leaving an acrid taste on my tongue.

Tick-tock, tick-tock.

I look at his aquiline nose, his earlobes, the stubble on his chin. This is a man that I believed I knew. Perhaps I have been wrong all this time. Perhaps I never did really know him. I had not known myself.

Tick-tock, tick-tock.

I look at his fingers, the knuckles, and the way he holds himself.

Tick-tock, tick-tock.

The venom tastes like cheap wine now. I am sitting again, as a sixteen-year-old girl, facing my parents, a jug of wine on the floor in front of us. My dad is pointing to it.

Is this what you want in your life? Is this who you want to be, to be a part of? You brought this into your life. Face up to it.

"Ricci, why did you marry me? I don't think you ever loved me, or even wanted a family."

Ricci stands up, without a word, without pausing, without even glancing in my direction. I watch as he walks out. With him goes my dark shadow.

I sit, motionless, as it strikes me. I have been deluding myself this entire year.

I am not frantic. I am not panicked. Instead, I feel relief. He's gone. And I recognize how delusional I have been.

The farmer's market is bustling beneath the warm summer sun. I walk slowly through the crowd, breathing deeply, my nose rewarded with the scents of ripe summer fruit, the strawberries, the peaches, the olives. I am at one with it all.

I am my father's daughter. I am a mother.

I have things to do in life. Big things. I do not yet know what those big things are, but I am at peace with that. I will let myself trust. I will let myself feel. Those are the only things I have to navigate by. And they are enough.

August 2015

I look at the pattern on the shower curtain and burst into delighted laughter. Cherubs and the words "Miracles" and "Love" adorn the sheer vinyl, from ceiling to floor. This is not just a shower curtain, I say to myself. It is a message for anyone who is listening. It speaks to me. I am where I am supposed to be.

I have brought Lucy and Kyle to Santa Barbara, along with Lucy's friend Sara, to join Rob at his summer camp on the beach, complete with kayaks, surfboards, and beach time. That was the logic, but there was another lure. My gut was at work again, urging me. I had to go.

We make the six-hour drive through the mountains of central California. The golden-colored landscape, with its curves and crevices, resembles the gentle contours of a body. I am reminded of Carlos's films, the women he has filmed, and how he could capture the body of not just women but also the earth. I think of how, in our society, women are controlled and shut down, how the earth has been controlled by us and is shutting down as well. It's the same mindset, the act of power, domination, and uncontrolled desire. The idea that money controls, attacks, and brings us something we think we need. Does his film work liberate women? Or are we being objectified? Could we simply admire, without judging or taking? Could we learn how to be humble, respectful?

Sara drifts asleep on Lucy's shoulder and wakes up abruptly, giggling.

"I just had a dream," she says. "I dreamed you and Lucy were witches and Kyle was a wizard."

"Witches? We're not mean!" I protest.

"There are good witches too," she says with a smile.

"Oh, good. That's encouraging."

"You had a hole in your stomach," she adds, giggling again.

"A hole in my stomach?" My gut has been an endless source of guidance this past year. All logic, along with my bank balance, has flown out the window, but my spirit is rising high. And that counts for more. Maybe Sara is right, and we are witches and wizards, disguised as ordinary humans. I mean, what if? Because I'm certainly done claiming I've got it all figured out.

I spot a beat-up old pickup truck covered with banners and graffiti, one that would look right at home in a Third World country but is unquestionably a rare sight on a California highway. We pull up alongside it. Delighted, I say, "Get the camera, Lucy!" Not only am I on the right freeway to Santa Barbara, but I am on the right road for my life.

"We are sending goods to the Hopi Reservation" reads a banner surrounded by posters of such luminaries as Gandhi and Mother Teresa. "We can change the world!" reads another. A black man with a broad white smile is driving and laughing as we honk and wave. He honks back.

"That is a happy man, making magic for the world, kids. He's a real hero, like a good witch!" I say. Neto's band's name is Fourth World, a Hopi term about a world that lies beyond the material world. I think back to the Buckeye Gathering, coiling clay for pottery, and the prophesy of the Hopi's blue star.

The next day we join Rob at his summer camp on the Santa Barbara beach, complete with beach towels, packed lunches, macramé, and boogie boards. I say goodbye to the children. I would not be helping Rob on this day. I need to sit on the sidelines and do nothing more than watch children play in the waves. I watch my two children lose themselves in pure, unadulterated laughter.

"Children heal," Rob says.
"Yes, they do. I think they teach us more than we teach them," I say. "Honesty, integrity, and the pure joy of life." My stitched wound is healing, scarring over, the rough spot to mark a painful lesson learned.
Rob smiles.
I head to a nearby cafe to catch up on email.
José has emailed me to say that Deborah Santana has offered us seed money for the film project on him. He writes:

She's a good person. Santa Barbara, all the music I wrote and played with other artists represents what I lived, what I feel and believe honestly being there, and most important what I could learn every day from others in a humble way in life. Will be good to share now whatever I can! Just some thoughts… Enjoy Santa Barbara, beautiful place. I recorded and played lots there. My first album, "Mountains and the Sea," was recorded live at the Our Lady of Mount Carmel church in Montecito, 1986, good memories. Thanks again —talk soon —travel safe.

Nineteen eighty-six was the year I graduated high school. The year I would have gone to Santa Barbara. The same school where had Ricci studied. We had all essentially been in the same place, at the same time, yet our paths had not crossed.
Carlos has also sent me an email. He has a project, he writes, a good one, with respectable pay, one the client says they want done in the same spirit as *Racing with Copepods*. "Are you still in?" he writes. "I will pay you more than I pay myself."
I call him.
"Congratulations! But, Carlos, why do you want to pay me so much?" He's completely broke, even more so than me. He has no car and is currently homeless, couch surfing. He could use the money and he could certainly do the work himself.

"I worry about you and the kids."

I ponder whether it's the project I want to do versus just having a reason to work with him again. He makes me feel safe, even if he is completely poor, recklessly generous, and lives and drives hard, with a Latin ego that can be both damned sexy and annoying. I miss seeing him. He's always honest.

"Carlos, I'm okay," I assure him. "I worry about you too."

My mom has also sent me an email.

Went into Fremont this morning for a couple of hours to check out the Art and Wine Festival. I always like to go get my fortune read just for the fun of it. It kind of hit the mark. She asked me if I had a daughter who was going through a difficult time (didn't even tell her I had a daughter). I told her yes, and she said that my daughter was coming out of a situation that was constraining and did not allow her to grow or be herself, but that in about another 16 months things were going to turn around for the better. She also said I was a healer. Not sure what that means but at least it was upbeat and not negative.

Just thought I'd pass it along. Who knows, some people have insight that goes beyond what most of us experience.

I sit cross-legged on the beach. Bits of sand blow across my bare legs. The roar of the ocean is comforting, like a lullaby, subduing all the conflict I have felt for the last thirty-five years. Like a child, I'm overwhelmed by the loving embrace of the surrounding mountains and sea. I look north, up the coast, to where University of Santa Barbara sits, where a lonely blue sea star once tantalized me, spawning my adolescent dream.

Now I sit, a grown woman, accepting the highest gift of education, seeing beyond the surfaces of life and connecting deep childhood dreams to my current adult world. I watch the waves knock down the children's sand castles that line the shore, and I smile at how it makes them laugh. There are no tears, no cries of dismay. They accept destruction as a part of life. Our children could teach us life lessons if we let them, if we were eager and open to learn.

I get up and shake the loose sand off my legs before running into the surf, sun-kissed, and diving into the Pacific Ocean.

Rob is getting into a kayak, preparing to head out.

"Do you want to come?" he asks. "Kayak surf?"

I've never done that before.

We paddle out, past the surf, cutting through the waves as they crash over us.

"Hold on," he warns.

We get past the breakers and settle into calmer waters. I gaze back to the shore, at the beach filled with children.

"Rob, you do more for the world with these kids than any high-tech business executive or schools ever could. You train these kids in the most important life lessons, how to enjoy our lives and let go of sand castles."

Rob smiles.

"It's been a tough year," I say. Rob is quiet, gazing at the horizon. It has been an even tougher year for him, as his daughter Amber had been killed, hit by a car while riding her bicycle. How little I have to complain about, I think, with a twinge of guilt. It was his first summer without her. Every year she would come and help him run the program.

She had been so enthusiastic last year about learning to sail. We had sat together on the beach while she played the ukulele, surrounded by children, looking longingly at Captain Richard's boat offshore. We had had plans to kayak out to him but had to change them, disappointing her.

"I'll get you sailing next year," I had promised. She would have been a great sailor, tough and soulful.

I feel her presence in this moment, here in the kayak with us. Rob wears a wistful smile.

"Guess what?" I say, changing the subject. "I meet an agent next week. My book might get published. The same agent who was involved with Ram Dass's books. It'd be a dream come true."

"*Be Here Now*," Rob says, and smiles. "That book changed my life thirty years ago." He glances back, shoves the paddle in the water, and gives me a devilish smile. "Ready to catch a wave?"

The End

A huge one comes up behind us. I feel the surge, the power of it, carrying, pushing, and lifting, a force greater than us, with the power to sweep us away.

"Hold on tight!" Rob shouts.

The energy is powerful. I hold on tightly until the wave capsizes us. I plunge into the churning water and hesitate, trying to calculate which way is up, but I feel no fear. I know I'll survive, that I'll reach the surface.

I pierce the surface to find Rob grinning at me. Adrenalin races through my veins and I laugh, delightedly.

"How fun was that? Let's do it again!"

I float lightly in between the waves and think of Ricci. I think of the good times, the births, the laughter, and the dreams. I think of what we had together in those early days, and what we wanted.

Remember, Barbara, he didn't respect you.

"No, Uncle," I argue, silently. "I didn't respect myself. I need no man to make me honest. I am already honest."

I would, I now realize, do it all over again if that's what it would take to feel what I feel this very moment, which might be no more than an insignificant grain of sand on the expansive beach of time. Or, alternatively, it might be as significant as the oceans of the universe and all eternity.

Life is teaching me about magic and miracles, if I dare to dream big and have courage to step into them.

I am not done dreaming yet.

It is my father's seventy-eighth birthday and we are together, my parents, my children, and me, on the shores of Monterey Bay National Marine Sanctuary, when my sister calls and says my parents' burglar alarm has gone off, something that has never happened before.

I hesitate telling them because I need them with me today. I don't want them to leave. I decide to wait until later to tell them, rationalizing that there was nothing they could do about it anyway.

Lucy and I are squeezed into skin-tight black wetsuits, preparing for the final dive of our PADI certification. Kyle wades out, behind us, into the water as far as he can go, watching us.

"Ready?" I ask my daughter. She grins.

We put on our masks and dive into the water. Lucy is beautiful, like a mermaid, her long blond hair flowing about her as she swims.

I follow her through the kelp forest. We rest on the sandy bottom and marvel at the tiniest of life. A fish swims past us. When we emerge and bob on the surface, we see Dr. Sylvia Earle also reach the surface, with her daughter, grandsons, and son-in-law. Sylvia is turning eighty, and she is here with us.

The day is sacred, meant to be. You can hear it in the vast blue water and in the light that shines, if you listen carefully, a subtle symphony. I have learned to listen well.

My daughter takes off her mask. "Did you see the sea hare?" she blurts excitedly. There had been two large slugs, guarding a nest of spaghetti-like eggs, a surreal image from another world.

"Sea stars too, right where they belong. I saw a beautiful blue star," I say. We grin at each other.

Our smiles mark the beginning of a new life.

My mom comes up to me when we return to shore. "Kyle loves you, you know. I see it in him. I watched him follow you out as far as he could go. It was like he was watching out for you."

"I know. I know, Mom. I feel it from him in the strangest ways."

I look at my dad.

"I know it's your birthday, Dad, your day, but I really wanted you here with me today, to see this and be a part of it. This will mean something one day, something bigger than you or me."

I think he understands. I think he feels it too.

We take a picture together with Dr. Earle. My daughter snaps the photo. It has been one of the greatest days in my life. Before they leave, I tell them about my sister's call earlier, that their burglar alarm had gone off.

When they get home, my mom calls me to assure me that the house is fine and it appears to have just been a false alarm.

"It's the strangest thing," my mother says. "We have no idea why it went off, but everything's fine."

September 2015

Grad school has started. The school has notified me that the cost of the trip to Spain was misprinted and they now want to charge me the difference. I would not have made the trip had I known the real cost. I contemplate the possible meaning of this.

I walk the streets, feeling, not thinking, something I have grown more and more accustomed to doing. A man is teaching martial arts under the grove of redwoods, the trees that had whispered to me, where the hawk stood its ground on the treetop, repelling the feisty crows until it decided to fly. My gut is working again and tells me to talk to the man.

"Barbara, for God's sake," I say to myself, "you do not need yet another thing in your life right now!"

But I have learned to ignore that internal censor and, instead, follow my gut. Kyle might love me, as my mother said, but he still hits me when he doesn't get his way. Maybe this martial arts teacher could help me broaden my community and knock sense into my son, teach him respect and a proper form of fighting, and when it is and is not appropriate to employ it.

His name is Clayton and he agrees to meet Kyle. He makes no promises, just takes a "let's see" approach, what some might call the Taoist way.

The following week, when it's time to go, Kyle refuses.

"Fine," I say. "Sit on the sofa all your life and fester. That's your choice."

I go to the park without him, to apologize that Kyle isn't ready for a martial arts class. Since I am there, I ask if I can take a lesson instead. He agrees.

"Women are good at this. You have softness. That's powerful."

Really?

"Now, first stand like so." Clayton stands in what he tells me is *mabu*, the horse stance, his legs spread, squatting slightly, and his arms held wide. I mimic what he is doing.

He touched his gut.

"This is your *dantian*. It's a sphere of power just below the belly button. It's the strongest *qi* you have. Powerful energy. That's your energy, connected to heaven."

To heaven? I like what I am hearing.

Your heart and your brain also have *qi*, but they are fast; they are not true. It's your *dantian*, like a sphere of energy around your gut, a hole—that is where your real intuition lies.

I think about how my gut told me to introduce myself to this man.

"The earth has energy," he continues. "You can feel it rise up, through your feet. Now, raise your arms like this. This is your space, your energy. You're not small. Be big." He stands in *mabu* again, arms wide.

As I copy him, I can feel my energy, like electricity, swirl inside. I am ready to be big with it all.

"You're a fighter," he says.

I think back to Sara's words, that she'd dreamed I was a witch, and how I had a hole in my stomach, as I stand beneath the towering redwoods listening to Clayton, feeling the trees' energy surround me. Bryna's children's books had been about music, witches, and women fighting. I feel her with me. Bryna is watching from the treetops. She got me here, and she has done so for a reason. I just have to figure out what that reason is.

October 2015

I still have a score to settle, and the time has come to speak my piece. I need to talk to Jane, the retired sea captain and founder of the sailing organization Ricci and I had taken over, the one I convinced to return while Odyssean-like boats sailed past. The mother of Meg, the daughter I had convinced to drive cross-country to take on the director's role and stake a claim in her heritage, who made me navigate between two wrongs, Ricci ditching the organization and Jane dragging his name through the mud.

I blame her. I want to tell her how mean and contemptuous it is for her to talk about Ricci the way she has, and to put me in the awkward spot of defending him and my family. It's my name too, after all.

I have come with my rehearsed script, prepared to battle an aging sea captain.

First, though, we sit down to review the final finances of the film. It is business and politics. I had needed her for the project. She offers me coffee. We sit at her round table, next to dark wooden shelves filled with four decades of racing trophies, plaques attesting to her years as Master Chief Boatswain's Mate, her time in the US Coast Guard Reserve driving 41-foot and 44-foot search and rescue boats, various commodore pictures, and photos of her daughter. She pours the coffee. I sit quietly, waiting for the opportunity to unleash my sharp words to cut her way of seeing the world into one that matches my view, to make her feel something and make it hurt.

She speaks first.

She looks out the window and talks about Meg, how she doesn't visit often enough. She talks about her own divorce and how Meg's father maneuvered it in such a way that she didn't receive much money. The pain is still there. She talks about what it was like captaining a boat staffed by men.

"I always had to keep proving myself, Barbara, over and over again," she says, with growing anger. "Men didn't like it when I showed them up, and I was better than most of them." I could hear the years in her words, the voyages, the deep wounds, the fighting—the anger.

Now it's my turn. I have anger to express too.

"It's been a hard year for me, Jane," I say. I want sympathy. I want her to feel guilt.

"You know that time you both came to help me move into this house?" she asks.

I remembered. It was when I had first gotten the feeling she didn't like me.

"When you left, Jim, my boyfriend, told me, 'I like them. Barbara is really nice. But I do not like the way her husband treats her. He treats her like she's the help, not like she's his wife.'"

Jane leans forward. Her face is so close to mine that I can smell the coffee on her breath.

"You're not the help, Barbara," she hisses. "You're not help!"

I'm rattled by her words, her anger—an anger she has on my behalf. Is she telling me this to look good? What's her agenda? Has she sensed my eagerness to vent my anger at her? Can she be trusted, a woman with so much anger? Can I really trust her?

I leave her that day, still feeling hurt. Why did I feel hurt? I was still angry at her. At him. At myself, navigating between so many emotions, so many distorted rights and wrongs. Trying to find the balance within it all, mingled with the stress of finances, loyalties, being a single mother, and having an uncertain future. How blind have I been over the years? Who am I? Who have I been?

Who am I?

"Everything is connected."

Mike Leigh's words from decades earlier come into my head, as if to reassure me.

Secrets and lies.

An ocean of tears floods my cheeks again. Why? Because I'm in that in-between place again, where neither place has you. You can't judge. You can't say you're right, but you can't say you're wrong. The truth lies below many layers, under the surface, deep. It's impossible to make out the surface of truth or lies.

I think back to diving in Monterey, floating in between the surface and the bottom, finding that place of balance between the two. That is the place I must seek comfort, even on land, but it's so uncomfortable, like a throbbing jellyfish, always drifting, never taking hold of one place or another. Flotsam, the wreckage of a boat that floats endlessly, unwanted, never whole. Flotsam—the name of my Great-Uncle Don's boat. Maybe he's trying to speak to me too.

I have to drive to Ricci's house—our house—to deliver heavy textbooks for Lucy. I see Ricci's girlfriend's car in the garage. My garage. My house. It is time to face her. It is time to look at her straight in the eye and tell her how I feel about her. How dare a woman come into my family so fast, without warning, into my children's lives? Into my house—playing house. Wouldn't a real woman ask the hard questions before believing she can solve his and the children's problems? Such narcissism, I think. I have some sharp words for her and I will speak first. Maybe she can learn from all this too, and come to understand how it is for a mother. I wasn't just speaking for myself. I was speaking for the last two thousand years of mothers not being heard, and a message to those sisters not asking hard questions. We all should ask hard questions.

I knock and she answers the door. She is surprised to see me there.

"I'm leaving books for my daughter." I say. I look her straight in the eye. "It's taken me a full year to heal and have the energy to say what I want to say to you."

She is listening.

"It was a horrid thing you did. Absolutely horrid."

She softens.

"Would you like to come in and we can talk about it?"

"You're inviting me into my own house?" It was still my house. "No, thank you." I pause, my heart beating palpably. "If you had any idea how much you hurt my children, you'd be ashamed of yourself. And you teach woman empowerment too, don't you?"

She smiles, unrepentant. "I have not hurt them."

"Ricci and I hadn't even prepared them."

"Oh, children know." she says calmly, with her German accent.

I look at her in disgust.

"You show no respect. You deserve each other, and you deserve whatever you get."

The next week her house burns to the ground, victim to a blazing forest fire, one of the worst fires ever recorded in U.S. history.

My friend's house in the same area was untouched.

The following week a Tantra Mantra teacher, who had been this woman's guru, was shot dead in my hometown. He had given her her spiritual name.

Then Ricci loses his job.

I have had nothing to do with any of this.

Tonight I sit alone on my balcony, looking at the full moon rise above the hills.

"You are not alone," Captain Richard had said. "Know your power," Jenn had told me.

The stars are bright against a vast darkness. The universe is big. It's up to us to wonder and always ask the big questions. Humility and respect, I think, are good values.

I have had nothing to do with these perhaps karmic matters. Nothing. But ... what if?

November 2015

The fast one-eyed copepods have gone international! Our film has been selected for the Tasmanian eco Film Festival, that place on the opposite side of the planet where people live upside down and drive on the wrong side of the road. It's a place that can help you feel more put together.

Dr. Richard Kirby, from Plymouth, England, has joined us there, on a panel. He's an expert on plankton, but more than that, he has a missionary-like zeal to teach us the spirit of the sea, that which gives us life, oxygen, and plant plankton. And he loves the one-eyed copepods. Greenpeace Australia is there too, along with the Tasmanian Land Trust, Save the Rhino Trust Namibia, and MONA Art Gallery owner David Walsh, who many say has transformed Hobart into the artistic, foodie, edgy community it is today. Humility and kindness are apparent in the Tasmanians and they give me reason to believe there is hope for humanity.

The Hobart Sailing Race is imminent, and I had hoped we'd get some support from participants, the fancy sailors with their big boats, but nobody pays attention to us.

As sailors, we bear the greatest responsibility to convey this message. People like Sir Robin Knox-Johnston have derived their life, their name, their fame, and even earned a knighthood as a result of the ocean. They are, thankfully, not without exception, but those exceptions are few. The legendary Bernard Moitessier, for example, had once been way out in front on the first-ever around-the-world race where one had to sail alone, unassisted, nonstop, in 1968, almost assured of a win and the fame that comes with such an accomplishment. But rather than finish and revel in the commercialization of his achievement, he withdrew from the race (but not from the sail itself), permitting Knox-Johnston to win, putting, he said, his soul and his happiness first and foremost. He not only completed the circumnavigation but also circled the globe twice instead of just once, nonstop, in ten months, the longest sail on record. With the oceans acidifying and dying off at a frightening pace, it has never been more important for those of us who gain so much from the sea to give back at the highest level possible.

Billionaires, I know, spend small fortunes on carbon-fiber racing masterpieces. Were they to donate just a small portion of that to ocean renewal and protection via ocean foundations and science education, it would help ensure the future of their children and grandchildren. Currently, only five percent of all environmental foundation money goes to ocean work. And it's not enough. Not nearly enough.

The film festival enjoys a strong turnout. The message is grim yet inspiring in many instances, about the dangers posed by nuclear waste storage facilities, pollution, acidification of oceans, and activists climbing oil tankers in the Arctic to protest drilling. Filmmaker Ginger Maundy, from Africa, tells the audience that we have ten years left before wild rhinos become extinct. The value of their ivory tusks rises even higher as illegal poaching decimates their populations. Criminal poaching organizations stockpile ivory in anticipation of the impending extinction of these magnificent beasts, indifferent to the effects their loss will have on the world.

Kyia Clayton, a mother with Native American roots, organized the film festival. With fire in her eyes, she says to us, "This is my children's world. Why are people not getting angry?"

So many people are risking their own lives trying to make a difference. I think back to my own community in Marin. I would hear conversations about vacations, multiple homes, children's activities and fanciful parties, completely oblivious that people are risking their lives to solve a big problem we all face. What our children face. How can educated, wealthy people be so completely oblivious and apathetic? How can anyone be oblivious, rich or poor? How can parents be so short-term oriented? And how can others stand by and continue to pillage? This is our future.

I think about the homeless people on the streets and how, ironically, they are looked down upon, the lepers of our society, and yet they demand and take the least from the world. They do not rob it of its resources as the rich do, indifferent to the damage their plunder generates. The homeless personify humility, the pleasure to be had in a mere simple meal and a warm bed. We could learn from them.

I think about immigrant communities, those who seek their dreams and work together, as a community, sharing the simple things in life. We can learn from them.

I go diving in the Tasman Sea. I talk to the owner of a dive shop who shares how he has witnessed the water changing over the last twenty years. The fish have gone away, he says, the result of warming seas.

During the dive I look for fanciful sea dragons in beds of kelp that once stood twenty feet tall and now look mown down, like shag carpet. I find none.

"We used to find hundreds," David says sadly.

The weight of the world is getting heavier. Why are we oblivious to the work that lies ahead in order to secure our very survival?

I return home and stand before Clayton in *mabu* style, horse stance, in the grove of whispering redwoods, feeling the energy around me. He pushes me and I use my softness to yield, to turn toward him, and nearly knock him out.

"Oh, my gosh, I'm so sorry!" I gasp.

He laughs. "It's okay. That was good."

I'm a fighter. I see that now. I think about Deborah Sampson and Frank Thompson, the women from the Revolutionary and Civil Wars, who dressed as men in order to fight, and the courage and passion it took them to do such a thing.

I wonder if Bryna is watching, maybe from the top of the trees with the black crows. If so, she's no doubt up to something. I page through her book *Witches, Great Mysteries, Opposing Viewpoints*, where she wrote: "One thing all mysteries have in common is that there is no ready answer."

In *Frank Thompson: Her Civil War Story*, Bryna had written: "Things that people have done are more exciting than anything anyone could make up." My mother-in-law had said much the same thing, that real stories about real people are more interesting than anything a writer might make up.

If only I had a good story.

> *We are the giants of the sea, cried the Great Fishes. All creatures are afraid of us. But you, little Fishes, are helpless. You cannot defend yourselves.*

I think of that black and white photo I took of Bryna as she lay on the ground, her dark shadowy eyes looking at the camera, her fingers in the air playing the piano. She was speaking to me then. She is speaking to me now.

I feel the urge to visit the Simple Pleasures Cafe, to see the piano she used to play, the place where Ricci and I first met.

I need to page back to the beginning, to the start of my story.

The End

December 2015

This place, the Simple Pleasures Cafe, holds the memory of first glances, initially brief and then more enduring conversations, much of what lay at the start of a major chapter of my life. I felt the urge to return at least one last time, maybe to say goodbye, maybe to recall past times, perhaps simpler times, not with regret but with affection.

My son sips hot chocolate as I drink it all in. The place hasn't changed a bit in over twenty years. The same mirror reflects the dark wooden tables, yellow-tinged lampshades, and the worn countertop that bears sugar containers, spoons, and coffee mugs. The old wooden piano sits silently against the photo-filled wall, next to the sagging sofa and a scattering of bistro tables and chairs. There's comfort to be found in the familiar. It helps connect me to my memories. It cultivates the real.

"Well, I guess that day did bring me true love," I say to my son, with an affectionate smile. He is undoubtedly used to my uttering odd, out of context comments and so he doesn't ask, content to just nod. He looks so sweet. It is hard to reconcile this image with one of him as enraged, flinging fists, striking, punching, biting, kicking, as he has done so often without warning this past year. His chin is smeared with chocolate. I grab a paper napkin and wipe it off.

"Pure, unconditional love," I say. "I got you and your sister out of the deal."

I look over to the table where Ricci and I first met. I can still hear the music that had been playing, the chatter of conversations, some lighthearted, some serious, my shyness as I squeezed into a table to read *Brave New World*.

And it is a brave new world, I think. It's dystopian, one where fear dominates our actions, where we have become enslaved by consumerism manipulating our material desires and pleasures, all while we wreak havoc on our planet, ecological disasters too numerous to recount. And much of it began with the actions of a man who ironically labeled my father a federal criminal. Talk about projection.

Yet the crimes that Ronald Reagan committed against all of us isn't limited to our federal borders. The tsunami began beneath the surface and built up strength that none but a few detected, until now, as it threatens our world, the entire world. That's not a federal crime—that's a global crime, and one that continues to inflict damage long after he left.

It's time to clean house. Why shouldn't anyone who espouses Reagan's policies and plays a part in their continuation be tried for war crimes against humanity?

Who are we? What have we become? We dismiss our elders as useless burdens, the very persons who have accumulated wisdom and experience well beyond ours, and banish them to institutions where they languish, lonely, isolated, causing them to become useless because we deny them the very opportunity to be useful. We prefer to spend our waking hours staring at three-inch screens rather than interact with each other, to divert and avert rather than engage. We judge the merit of people by what they own instead of by what they do.

Schools perpetuate competition and standardized testing, turning us and our children into robots, into cogs, instead of individuals, with varying talents and abilities all with something unique to contribute. We do not cultivate inventors; we are, it has been said, cultivating a society of workers. "It's the way, though," a parent commented to me, shrugging when I challenged such a competitive way of being, having to compete for the few top spots, clawing past each other, instead of developing our varied talents.

I contemplate how women have been universally diminished in importance, the story that has been drilled into us that we come not from a place of equality but of secondary importance, allegedly from the rib of a man. What insecure, fearful man came up with that one, I wonder? We close ourselves up inside fancy manmade buildings to worship and give thanks, instead of by the glorious rivers and trees, truly sacred places that give testament to the power and greatness that lies beyond.

I never asked for this way of life, just like I never asked to be stuck inside a big house I could not maintain, something more than I would ever want to maintain, with no voice—no choice—in the matter. I was never given the option to decide whether I wanted to be part of the insatiable consumer appetite that is taking down this world. I just found myself in it. We all do. We're all mixed up in the darkness that surrounds us. But we still have light, if we look for it, if we choose to turn it on, to let it shine. We need to speak up, to speak loudly and clearly, make the necessary big bold move to navigate away from today in order to recreate our future.

"We need to change, don't we, my little prince?" Kyle nods again, lost in his own thoughts.

How do people survive being controlled with fear and domination, unless they just give up and die inside? I want to be free and now I'm closer to being free, because now I understand the guts it takes to become free, in the face of losing it all. I want my children to be free but I have to fight for it—we all do—otherwise too many people lay bricks and create false stories that imprison us when we fail to pay attention.

I have the spirits to thank, so many spirits. They have undoubtedly guided me into transition, into the beginnings of an entirely new way of life, a new way of being.

There is a loud burst of wind and light, and the doors of the cafe blast open wide. My dog Gizmo scampers into the cafe, alongside Carlos's dog Gem, barking in Paul Revere style.

Startled, I look around the cafe. My spirit guides are all here.

Mark O'Brien has emerged from the iron lung that imprisoned him on this earth and dances on the countertop, skinny legs and all. He flirts with me, asking me to join him for a dance. "No excuses," he warns, and laughs. The barista passes a poppy seed bagel through him to a customer. How is it she does not see him there?

I glance at the piano and see Bryna Stevens, who flexes her fingers and begins to play. Voices rise together to accompany her as I watch in astonishment and delight—Bob Marley, David Hess, Elvis Presley, Jimi Hendrix, Raul Ramirez, the poet and José's friend Sidão Tennucchi. There's a long-haired hippie with them whom I don't recognize at first. I look closer and my eyes widen. It's Ronald Reagan! And he's asking me to sign a Save the World petition!

"I did say one good thing during my presidency," he assures me with a grin. "'Live simply, love generously, care deeply, speak kindly, leave the rest to God!' See? I'm not all bad!"

Bryna begins to play David Hess's "Sand Castles," and Elvis croons it just as he once recorded it. I listen to soft music and words, like an ocean lullaby, about the still sky at night, of sand castles standing proud for each child, and the calling of the warm wind. A world is born.

Bryna winks at me as she plays. She's wearing a big purple ribbon in her hair. This is no doubt all her doing. She's been writing the story. No one puts Bryna in a box, to be forgotten!

Nancy Reagan sits at a table, fretting. She gives me an anxious look. "It's not my Ronnie's fault. They made him do it!" She's with her astrologer, Joan Quigley, and they are looking at celestial charts, eager to realign the stars and planets, to change our future readings.

"What does Joan say?" Galileo's voice booms from across the room. He's holding up a chocolate donut and peering through the hole, like a monocle, next to my grandfather and Dante, engineers, every one of them. They've been discussing the circle of life and celestial spheres.

Dante says, "If you eat lots of American chocolate donuts, you'll get a hole in your stomach; it's the true mortal link to heaven." Galileo disagrees, and they begin squabbling, in Italian, raising their fists in the air. Exasperated, my grandfather plucks the donut from Galileo's hand and eats it in one bite. I'm not surprised. He's always had a sweet tooth and likes to get straight to business.

My grandmother sits on the sofa, next to my Aunt Doris. Audrey Hepburn is with them. They keep time to the music by tapping their feet, and waving their fingers like conductors. They wave at me and giggle when they see me watching them. They point to the other side of the room and I turn my head to see.

There is a large round glass table, like a crystal ball, filled with images of people on Earth being kind and generous. It's reserved for the "The Do Gooders," the sign says. Mother Teresa sits with Glinda, the Good Witch of the South, and sips dandelion tea. Adjacent empty chairs with gold name plaques are saved for Dr. Sylvia Earle, Jane Goodall, Aung San Suu Kyi, Rigoberta Menchú Tum… and Anja, my mother-in-law!

I look across my table. Next to Kyle, who is blissfully unaware of anything but his hot chocolate, sits my Great-Uncle Bob as a young man, noble looking, a regal captain. He holds a great compass and scepter. My coffee has disappeared and in its place sits a highball. We raise our glasses in a toast. Madge, his beloved wife, holds his other hand. He looks happier than I've ever seen him.

Lightning flashes, illuminating the room brilliantly, and a spectrum of color bursts out of nowhere. A dancer emerges and moves gracefully, as light as a feather. It's Lua. Rob's daughter Amber plays a ukulele by her side. She has sea salt in her hair, and her face is sun-kissed.

I am in awe of all this.

Just beyond, in a shadowed corner, beneath a lamp, sits my Great-Uncle Don, in a large Victorian armchair. He draws me in as he boldly reads from a large scroll of Edgar Allen Poe's poem, "The Raven."

And my soul from out that shadow that lies floating on the floor;

Shall be lifted—nevermore!

I withdraw a bit, remembering the pain and sadness.

Conversation and music cease, as all the spirits stop and look. The mother goat has walked in, boldly, with fresh milk to share. She glances at Great-Uncle Don, and then me, and bellows loudly an all-knowing "Baah!" Everyone bursts out laughing.

Victoria Woodhull has a quill and paper. She's writing the *herstory* of humankind to set the record straight. A train of women triumphantly follows the mother goat—Betty Friedan, Anne Boleyn, Margaret Mead, Rachel Carson, Marianne North, Beryl Markham, Qiu Jin, Margaret Sanger, Deborah Sampson, Irena Sendler, George Elliot, Frank Thompson, Boudicca, Shajar al-Durr, Taj Al-Saltana, Susan B. Anthony, Hatshepsut, Mary Anning, Jane Addams, Laila of Shaiban-Bakr, Annie Jean Easley, Joan of Arc, Masako Hōjō, Queen Septimia Zenobia, Gráinne Ní Mháille, Catherine of Aragon, Phillis Wheatley, Diana, Princess of Wales, Clärenore Stinnes, Emmeline Pankhurst, Miria Sibylla Merian, Pocahontas, Trieu Thi Trinh, Alice Eastwood, Eleanor Roosevelt, Meena Keshwar Kamal, Queen Vishpala, Halide Edib Adivar, Harriet Beecher Stowe, Vibia Perpetua, Marie Souvestre, Cory Aquino, Huda Sha'arawi, Rosa Parks, Clara Barton, Amelia Earhart, Harriet Tubman, Dickey Chapelle, Mary Harris Jones, Mandukhai Khatun, Marie Curie, Sirimavo Bandaranaike, Frances Whipple Green McDougall, Margaret Kirchner, Ann Waldner, Blanche Osborn, followed by the wives of the most successful men in history. Following them, Hypathia's chariot arrives outside, with the millions of souls executed during such travesties as the Inquisition and numerous witch trials.

Fayaway? I thought she was just a character from Melville's imagination, but she smiles at me and says, "Gracias." She holds a colorful bird in the palm of her hand.

There's loud drumming—Cherokees, Hopi, Mayans, Ohlones, Lakotas, Polynesians, Dagaras, Aboriginals, and a line of Indigenous groups from around the world make their way in, bursting the roof off the cafe in a wave of energy, the guts of a volcanic eruption, rising up and out to the world in Big Bang style.

All turn to see Eve in the center, moving and writhing within a painfully bright light. She holds up a sign: "Do Not Believe Everything You Read!" The handle is made of fennel and wound with vine leaves. A live serpent sticks out its tongue and laughs.

The energy pulsates around and through me, and I hold on to my seat for dear life. Bryna continues to kick it up on the piano, jazz style. Musicians are jamming full swing, keeping up with her. It's a party, and they are all up to something!

I turn to my son and the picture fades. He's watching me, perplexed. I smile.

"I've got a big imagination. But… what if?" I reach for my highball to toast the thought and find a coffee mug in my hand. "It's beach time, buddy. Ready for sand castles at Ocean Beach?"

He nods enthusiastically. As I open the door, I hear a final key played on the piano, an F, I think.

For freedom.

With a broad smile, I walk outside into the brilliant sunlight and inhale deeply the ocean air.

2016

January 2016

"Hello? Captain Gillette?" It's late in the afternoon.

"Hello, Wonder Woman! What changes are you making in the world?"

I laugh.

"Hi, Captain. How are the islands?"

"I'm an island boy—you know it."

"I hope to get to those idyllic islands one day. "

"Ah, you need to change your language. It's all in the language. Intentions, intentions, intentions! You mean, you *will* get to the islands one day."

"Yes, Captain. I *will* get to the islands one day."

"Are you complete yet?" he says.

"I don't know," I confess. "I don't know."

I am preparing for my trip to New York City, to film José Neto as he recaptures his memories there. The crows are loud, squawking and scratching at the rooftop of my house. They have never done this before and I find it strange, like a warning, but of what I do not know. I continue my preparations, getting bunny food and leaving instructions for my housemate for my four-day absence in New York. I am catching the red-eye tonight.

First thing in the morning, after arriving in New York I get a call from home. A raccoon killed the children's rabbits during the night, mauling them to death. My housemate is burying them. I sigh. Each time I move forward with positive efforts, it seems, something negative happens. Alarms go off, cars get towed, or bunnies get killed.

I stay positive. Always positive. The housemate is burying them kindly. They had a long life and were free to run for most of it. I'll have to tell the children. The past years have been hard on them. They'll be fine, I tell myself. They'll be stronger for it.

There are more deaths. David Bowie died this morning, leaving a strange emptiness in the air. I watch his video, "Lazarus," a song from his final album, *Black Star*.

I know from the Bible that Lazarus is the only individual that Jesus personally refers to as having been dead and ultimately resurrected.

There's another mention of a resurrection, aside from Jesus's own, this one of a twelve-year-old girl, but Jesus described her as simply sleeping.

I read a blog post written by Jason Evangelho[***] on his interpretation of Bowie's video, about the message behind Bowie's video, the profound video he wanted to share with the world before he died. Evangelho wrote: "Do not waste any more time not expressing yourself. Say what you need to say, boldly and without reservation. Nurture your creativity and don't be shy about it. Stop constantly consuming and start creating before it's too late, and that dark, mysterious wardrobe into nothingness consumes you."

I feel a chill when I read those words. Or is it a vibration?

Bryna, on the other hand, must be thrilled to have a new member join her ensemble. I can see the handshaking and congratulating so vividly, though I'm sure Bryna's giving Bowie grief about his video, how he boxed himself up at the end.

"It was a wardrobe, a closet," Bowie says defiantly to Bryna. (And you know that comment opens a can of worms.)

Kimberly, a very supportive emerging filmmaker, and I meet José in Manhattan later the next day. It is mid-winter, with a cold bite and long shadows mix with a crisp light. Marquees around the city feature the same message: "RIP, David Bowie. We can be heroes, just for one day."

Neto takes us through the streets of New York, recounting memories dating back to when he was a young immigrant from Brazil, thirty years before, and had come with dreams of becoming a professional guitarist. We pass by the building where, in 1979, he auditioned for the legacy musician and activist Harry Belafonte, going on to travel with him for three decades, playing to support racial equality, both here in America and in South Africa.

He talks about the small jazz clubs, some of which are closed. We go by the old mom and pop music shops, but they have shut down too. He tells us of Flora Purim, often referred to as the queen of Brazilian jazz vocalists, and her husband, Airto Moirera, a drummer and

---

[***] See: https://medium.com/@killyourfm/david-bowie-s-lazarus-video-isn-t-just-a-goodbye-it-s-haunting-warning-67aef9c575c5

percussionist, and how they all traveled together to play with Neto's band, Fourth World, in London, New York, and Africa. "Burning Money" was one of their popular tunes, and a single one of their CDs sold for over four hundred dollars in Japan last year, I learn.

Kimberly trusts me with the project and joins me for a stroll with José through Central Park. We film him walking along the shadows of trees and forgotten ideals that musicians once carried. A flock of pigeons lands nearby, on the path, our only audience, and wind rustles through the sparse dry leaves of surrounding trees. I stop and watch, remembering the story I had recently heard about his daughter's funeral, when a flock of doves were released. We are where we should be. I am convinced of it.

We walk into an old record store that sells used vinyl LPs and CDs. Neto finds a bootleg CD of Steve Winwood and his own work. The shopkeeper sells it to him without flinching, despite it being illegal to distribute pirated recordings. We are momentarily silenced by the disrespect afforded artists.

I flip through stacks of albums, recalling my days working in a record store and the day I was ordered to toss my treasured musicians' LPs because they weren't big moneymakers. It was like book burning in the plaza, I think. There's another way. Of course there is another way. But it takes a dreamer and then it takes believers.

I'm finding redemption, pure redemption.

We head to Strawberry Fields in Central Park, to view the mosaic in John Lennon's memorial site that bears the name of one of his most famous songs, "Imagine." Handfuls of people stroll and linger there.

We walk south, to Times Square. I haven't been here in years and I'm shocked to see staggering display of billboards advertisements, money signs, and calls for Jesus. Shopping bags weigh down the arms of pedestrians, fuzzy cartoonish characters walk around wearing sandwich boards, offering candy to children. Shops attempt to lure with discounts and deals. People, dressed well, throng the sidewalks, eager for the next bargain, for more and more and more. It's overwhelming.

It feels wrong.

José points to a window. Ringo Star appears in a Sketcher's ad, hawking shoes that "offer comfort and bounce in every step," the fruits of a three-billion-dollar global leader in the high-performance and lifestyle footwear industry.

The End

What has happened to our heroes? In 1979, back when Carter made his famous speech on the crisis of confidence, warning us against following a material world, we didn't listen. Instead, we voted an actor who played Notre Dame's famous football hero, "The Gipper," into office, confusing perhaps the role with the man. As thanks, Americans were manipulated, dominated, and lied to.

I see the emotions play out in Neto's eyes as I snap photos and film him throughout the day. He's not saying it so much as feeling it, and it's expressed in his eyes. He looks like Dante, journeying through Inferno, in a state of wonder and sadness, but also like a teacher, showing us the work that lies ahead. A man I had first perceived as a disconcerting pirate, a convict, and a rebel is instead quiet, kind, and generous, someone who has stayed true to his music, without lusting after fame or money. Someone who has shared his spirit, without asking anything in return.

José Neto is an outlier, a rebel in today's world. Maybe I had him pegged all along.

As we walk the streets, I find myself humming Lennon's "Imagine," a song that comforts me. I find myself imagining a world where everyone coexists in peace, no countries to fight and die for, no killing, no fighting over possessions, and eliminating the greed that surrounds us. Could we become brothers and sisters, instead of competitive beings, and share the world without the need to compete against each other? I'm not the only dreamer. Lennon's values should speak to all of us. Imagine what the world would be like if we chose to embrace such ideals.

I blink. I am sitting face to face with living legend Mr. Harry Belafonte. An actor and singer, he has lived life taking a stand for justice, moving culture, fighting for racial equality, and risking prison and his own safety in order to serve humanity, to inspire people to be better.

José Neto sits to the side as I speak to his mentor and former employer, the very person who helped him immigrate to the United States thirty years ago to help fulfill his dream to professionally play the guitar. I am using my voice. Sharing my film idea. I lick my lips. I think of Blistex. *Why Blistex?* My old guitar teacher. Maybe this is a healing moment.

Mr. Belafonte's eyes pierce mine, as if looking into my soul. I like the way Mr. Belafonte does business. He wears a smile and gets people dancing in the face of opposition, fear, and domination. At eighty-eight years old, he still has that rebel fight in him, a boldness in his voice, and his dreams of class equality remain as strong as ever.

"Why do you want to make a film about Neto?" he asks.

I blink, and see the hawk, preparing to rise from the whispering redwood trees. It is time to soar, to take flight.

"Ronald Reagan."

His eyes pierce mine. "What does this have to do with Ronald Reagan?"

"Reagan fired my father and called him a federal criminal. I lost my guitar lessons because of Reagan."

"What did your father do?"

"Air traffic controller, back in 1981. Remember?"

He looks thoughtful. "Oh, yeah, I do remember."

"When I started researching and doing environmental work about the oceans, I discovered a dirty secret. Ronald Reagan and his accomplices, and his followers, were—are—the true federal criminals. Beyond federal, they're global criminals."

I had his attention.

"He took the solar panels off the White House and turned the dial up on fossil fuels. He got us on a bad track. Our oceans are acidifying because of his policies. My father stayed true to what he believed for over thirty-five years. He's a simple guy who never asked much for himself. He stood his ground against a powerful president, and risked it all. Not easy."

"And Neto?"

"Neto has done the same, staying true to his music. He's stood his ground without giving in or selling out. Again, not easy."

Mr. Belafonte nods as I continue.

"I believe the electric blast on José Neto's guitar will wake up the world to the living, like it did me."

Mr. Belafonte leans back in his seat. "What are we waiting for? Let's get filming."

He speaks to the camera.

Artists, musicians are our truth seekers. I'm not talking about the ones looking for fame or money. Those are the merchants. We need our artists. We need those who can weave a good story, and inspire people to be better than they think they can be....

March 2016

It's been a long haul, and I am preparing now for a new voyage.

I'm in Fremont. Fremont, Washington, part of Seattle, however, not the Fremont in California where I'd grown up, where I was when Reagan destroyed my life. Still, the feeling that I've come full circle is evident in more than just where I used to live versus where I am now. The power of music, a blue sea star, a chocolate donut, and magic have brought me to the place that many of its residents (and at least one of its signs) call "The Center of the Universe."

I'm staying here for a leadership conference, to provision myself with integrity and strength, to stand like a redwood tree against opposition, fear, and domination.

Nancy Reagan died today. It is the end of one thing and the beginning of another.

Last night I took a sumptuous lavender bath in a claw-foot tub, treating myself to a bit of luxury for the first time in a long time. I stroked my leg and listened to the drops of water fall, as I ran my fingers through my hair. I was gentle and kind. You have to start with yourself.

Outside, my country and the world have gone mad. People don't trust one another. Elderly are shipped away to decay in solitary silence, out of sight, children are ignored, and there's so much anger and hatred surfacing as we race endlessly. Armies build in China, Russia, and North Korea, as well as here, at home. ISIS has erupted, yet another terrorist group in a series of radicalists. We face the acidification of the world's oceans and melting polar icecaps, all of which threaten life on Earth. Politics and business interests drive fear and domination. It's full circle. Back to America, 1980, or Germany, 1939, Dante's Florence, or the Roman Empire.

It's time to stop. The stakes are higher now than ever before to get it right.

"Know your place in the universe," Dr. Sylvia Earle said. Know your place. Take your place.

Sheer white drapes hang from the window, filtering the morning light that enters my room in this old Victorian house. I've stayed the night awake, listening to creaks and groans, watching shadows move silently across rosy wallpaper and an oval mirror. I'm reminded of my grandmother, just before she died, when she expressed such delight in how the drapes swayed with the breeze one afternoon, as my grandfather sat by her bedside. He left to get her a glass of water as she lay, intent on finishing writing a letter. He returned to find the writing had stopped; the last loop of a letter trailed off. It was her time to go.

She once wrote a poem about dreams and reality, penning: *dreams are warm and softly lighted, the inner reflection of our soul, and what a day it'd be when dreams shake hands with reality.* Her grandmotherly hand, veins rippling, had held out a spoonful of quince marmalade to me once, pure sweet love.

I swallow all and let it all go. Sailors were fond of marmalade too. It kept them healthy at sea, keeping the dreaded scurvy at bay. We are all sailors who need to stay healthy.

We are all sailing through life. Aren't we?

Tomorrow is March 8th, my birthday. It's also International Women's Day. And tomorrow I submit my manuscript. What a day it will be.

I have a new dream. I have a new soul.

"Captain? Captain? It's me, Barbara. Do you read me?"

"Ahoy thar! I read you. And a happy birthday to you. A Pisces!"

"Thank you. You always remember. How are the islands?"

"Beautiful. A great voyage today. The universe has magic and life is a miracle. Have you been spinning yarns about the spirits?"

"Yes. Love, life, and politics."

"Are you complete?"

"Am I? I am. Yes, I AM." And I can feel the music of the universe speaking too.

"Ay. That's good, very good."

"Do you see the super moon, with the solar eclipse?"

"Ay, glorious. The harmonic convergence, world peace, and it's the Age of Aquarius."

"Oh captain, my captain. I hear the bells. We'll toast with a highball one morrow morn. Until then, I'm taking the helm of a big ship and we have to tack through a storm. I have no fear, no fear. And I feel it."

"Ay. That's good, very good. Keep watch with the moral compass. It will keep you safe on a true course and guide you well."
"Roger that. Fair winds, oh Captain, my Captain."

THE BEGINNING

MEMORIES

Uncle Bob and Grandpa, looking mischievous

PATCO Union Strike, 1981

Love you, Mom and Dad!
Dad's 78th birthday
Monterey, California, 2015

With Dr. Sylvia Earle, getting PADI certified

Brazilian guitarist, José Pires de Almeida Neto, the subject of "The Man Behind the White Guitar." Photo by João Gomes.

"The Man Behind the White Guitar"

The great Mr. Harry Belafonte, with José Neto, New York City, 2016
I like the way Mr. Belafonte does business. He wears a smile and gets people dancing in the face of opposition, fear, and domination. At 88 years old he still has that rebel fight and boldness in his voice, and dreams of class equality.

Tasmanian eco Film Festival! Dr. Richard Kirby, "the plankton pundit," with me, Carlos Grana (the guy who made it happen!), and Taylor Griffith

"Neptune," aka Kimball Livingston
at Jory Plum Studios, 2014

Captain Richard Gillette

Denis Delastrac
Filmmaker of *Sand Wars*; made me miss my pollywogs

Night showing of *Racing with Copepods*, Sausalito Community Boating Center, photo by Kimberly Blum

He's still alive! Malcolm Margolin, author of *The Ohlone Way*

Memories

Gianna Marino, artist, writer
Her mama would say, "Do it, and do it naked!"

Dante or Galileo? Kyle's doll that speaks from the universe.
It's all about love.

Youth counselor Nic Duro talking big about sailing and leadership

The author in Albania, 2003. The Enver Hoxha's regime created concrete bunkers, instilling fear and domination.

One more class to go, but I did the walk! Earned my M.A., Humanities, from Dominican University of California.
Thank you, Mom and Dad, and my angels too! They made it happen.

IN MEMORY OF
BRYNA STEVENS

Mother, Author, Musician and Mentor
R.I.P.

The Mother Speaks
La Finca, La Mancha, Spain
Photo by Kymm Falls

Barbara McVeigh is a writer, producer, filmmaker, activist, educator, mother, and sailor who learned the universe loves to laugh. She lives in northern California and calls on all musicians, mortals, mariners, angels, gods, and goddesses to join her for one mission: "Let's advocate respect for our natural world and ensure a healthy, happy future for all our children."

> "Don Quixote scared most people,
> because he dared to dream big."
> - Christina Bougas

In ancient times, when humanity was less physical than it is today, everything spoke and every human being was a prophet, able to hear and interpret the words of the gods sounding through all phenomena. Human beings were still heavenly beings and felt themselves woven into and part of a great symphonic stream.

The world, the cosmos, was music, and music was the world, the cosmos—every plant and tree and rock, the sunlight on the water, the shape of the clouds, the dew, the wind, the flame, all feeling and intention, every smile and tear and burst of laughter, the dance of the synapses and the tremors of the inner organs.

> "Everything sang. And in this singing the voices were
> those of the gods and the ancestors and the elemental
> beings who help sustain the Earth."
> - Rudolph Steiner

AFTERWARD

The film *Racing with Copepods* went international, accepted by the inaugural Tasmanian eco Film Festival, California Youth Forum, and the Wild & Scenic Film Festival, in addition to being shown in many classroom, library, and event screenings. Congressman Jared Huffman provided a video with a statement of support from Washington, D.C. We were humbled. The project also cultivated a new wave of seventeen parents who were inspired by my passion to create an even grander movement—Heirs to Our Oceans, a group of youth supported by the Sylvia Earle Alliance, who will travel the world and meet with global climate and ocean leaders to support decisions that matter in their lives.

Some of the dates related to personal events may not be rigidly accurate, although their spirit holds. And forgive me for any typos. We are human, after all! In writing, I had to recreate moments of my past, including the time when my brother and his wife came for the stereo—a very sensitive subject, as my brother says he had no idea at the time of the impact that event had on my life. We laugh at this now and I'm grateful I can take something that was negative and turn it into a positive. He is, after all, a good brother. That is our power, to find the good in all things negative. I have an AM/FM clock radio that he gave me thirty years ago that I keep in my kitchen and use to this day. My brother means the world to me, as do my sister and everyone else in my family.

This book was a journey, and continues to be one. It has also created big questions in my family as we sort through our lives and the truths we've lived by, only to discover they were constructed stories to provide meaning at the given time. We must all rewrite our own stories to ask the big question:

What has happened to us all these past thirty-five years?

My parents and I have grown very close and there have been many silver linings. For example, my son is now living in the countryside, with horses. And since this book became public, new information continues to emerge about how technology is devastating lives, addictive and potentially toxic, the same neurological addiction as heroin and other drugs. (Actual drug use among children has fallen as they transfer their addiction to mobile phones.)

Now is the time to ask big questions, before we are trapped again in a social technology-based system that is so luring, convenient, and financially attractive that we cannot get out. As I watch Apple, Google, and Oracle become leaders and take over our children's education, banking, libraries, and more, it is my fervent desire that we all start asking the questions before we are proverbially "hooked" and enslaved to a system that could hurt us in ways we cannot even fathom.

Power needs to be tamed—and that taming must come from activists, unions, and others to balance big business interests. Better yet, perhaps we can be driven by better motives—instead of money, let's think how we can reshape the American spirit with integrity, loyalty, and humility.

There is hope, as visionaries convert their dreams to reality, like Elan Musk builds his space-age endeavors and plans to colonize Mars. I am serious. This is a good thing. If all the billionaires get on board and blast themselves to outer space, the simpler, kinder folk can live in peace on Earth. This book is for you too, Mr. Musk. We need our captains on Earth, and to believe in magic.

Michael Reagan writes in his book *The Lessons My Father Taught Me* that Reagan always told him to face up to his mistakes. Today, Ronald Reagan's Presidential Museum in Simi Valley could serve the public well by showcasing the dark truths of his administration and open the venue to truths about big oil agendas and climate change realities, along with revealing the power of propaganda, storytelling, and manipulation. We cannot change the past. We have learned the hard way. But we have learned. We can change the future. It's not too late.

Ah, and as for my now ex-husband's girlfriend, the spiritual goddess, the high priestess—heck, she was powerful! She taught me my power as the Mother Goddess, the greatest goddess of all. Maybe feeling and understanding a mother's side of the story, she will understand the pain she brought to my family and be reminded that we must respect one another, especially our children, and not to ever belittle a mother. Remember sisterhood and give space and time to those who are healing. Ricci was right. Perhaps we do help each other rise to higher levels and they'll show the world the power of love and ecstasy through Tantra mantra, as her former guru taught. I like to believe in the best of people.

I would like to thank the professors at Dominican University of California—Dr. Chase Clow, Dr. Laura Stivers, Dr. Christian Dean, Marianne Rogoff, and Dr. Graham Guest of the graduate Humanities Department. This effort would not have happened without their incredible and unconventional trust and support through my studies. Thank you to Felecia Gaston, Kimball Livingston, Dr. Richard Kirby, Kyia Clayton, John Morrison, Harbormaster Pat Lopez, Joe Sciortino, Gianna Marino, the Schmidt Family Foundation, Behan Gifford, Nicole Renée, and Tom Wiley—and to Leonardo DiCaprio, and our Native American tribes, for showing us the conviction, hope, and spirit we need to establish for our future generations.

"Mom, maybe you should run for president," my son said to me one morning as I voiced frustration with our government leadership. He inspires me in ways he'll never know. All our children do.

The year 2020—the year of clear vision. Dream big.

Onward ho! It's a beautiful life. Let's live it. And live by it.

www.ingramcontent.com/pod-product-compliance
Lightning Source LLC
Chambersburg PA
CBHW071854290426
44110CB00013B/1140